May God Bless you!
+ Chip Brooks
2022

May God be glorified as you
run your race! 1 Cor 9:24-25

# Jesse Owens

**Recent Titles in Black History Lives**

W. E. B. Du Bois: A Life in American History
*Charisse Burden-Stelly and Gerald Horne*

Thurgood Marshall: A Life in American History
*Spencer R. Crew*

Barack Obama: A Life in American History
*F. Erik Brooks and MaCherie M. Placide*

Harriet Tubman: A Life in American History
*Kerry Walters*

Zora Neale Hurston: A Life in American History
*Stephanie Li*

Rosa Parks: A Life in American History
*Darryl Mace*

Jackie Robinson: A Life in American History
*Courtney Michelle Smith*

Booker T. Washington: A Life in American History
*Mark Christian*

# Jesse Owens

## A LIFE IN AMERICAN HISTORY

F. Erik Brooks and Kevin M. Jones

**Black History Lives**

An Imprint of ABC-CLIO, LLC

Santa Barbara, California • Denver, Colorado

**Library of Congress Cataloging-in-Publication Data**

Names: Brooks, F. Erik, author. | Jones, Kevin M. (College professor), author.
Title: Jesse Owens : a life in American history / F. Erik Brooks and Kevin M. Jones.
Description: First Edition. | Santa Barbara, California : ABC-CLIO, an imprint of ABC-CLIO, LLC, [2022] | Series: Black History Lives | Includes bibliographical references and index.
Identifiers: LCCN 2021017475 (print) | LCCN 2021017476 (ebook) | ISBN 9781440873829 (hardcover: acid-free paper) | ISBN 9781440873836 (eBook)
Subjects: LCSH: Owens, Jesse, 1913–1980. | African American track and field athletes—Biography. | Track and field athletes—United States—Biography. | Olympic Games (11th : 1936 : Berlin, Germany) | Olympics—Records. | Racism—Germany—History—20th century. | Ohio State University—Sports—History. | National Collegiate Athletic Association—History. | Sports—United States—History. | African Americans—Civil rights—History—20th century. | BISAC: BIOGRAPHY & AUTOBIOGRAPHY / Historical
Classification: LCC GV697.O9 B76 2021 (print) | LCC GV697.O9 (ebook) | DDC 796.42092 [B]—dc23
LC record available at https://lccn.loc.gov/2021017475
LC ebook record available at https://lccn.loc.gov/2021017476

ISBN: 978-1-4408-7382-9 (print)
       978-1-4408-7383-6 (ebook)

26 25 24 23 22    1 2 3 4 5

This book is also available as an eBook.

ABC-CLIO
An Imprint of ABC-CLIO, LLC

ABC-CLIO, LLC
147 Castilian Drive
Santa Barbara, California 93117
www.abc-clio.com

This book is printed on acid-free paper ∞

Manufactured in the United States of America

# Contents

# Series Foreword

The Black History Lives biography series explores and examines the lives of the most iconic figures in African American history, with supplementary material that highlights the subject's significance in our contemporary world. Volumes in this series offer far more than a simple retelling of a subject's life by providing readers with a greater understanding of the outside events and influences that shaped each subject's world, from familial relationships to political and cultural developments.

Each volume includes chronological chapters that detail events of the subject's life. The final chapter explores the cultural and historical significance of the individual and places their actions and beliefs within an overall historical context. Books in the series highlight important information about the individual through sidebars that connect readers to the larger context of social, political, intellectual, and pop culture in American history; a timeline listing significant events; key primary source excerpts; and a comprehensive bibliography for further research.

# Preface

In 1936, in Berlin, Germany, a blow was struck against white supremacy when Jesse Owens and 18 other African American athletes competed in the Summer Olympic Games. Owens won four gold medals over a two-day period, shattering the myth of Nazi Germany's faulty claim as a superior race. Because of Owens's lauded accomplishments, he was thrust into the limelight as a media darling. However, his status as an athletic celebrity and his Olympic achievements did not improve his economic status in the United States.

Owens was born in the segregated South in Oakville, Alabama. Feeling the sting of racism and discrimination, the Owens family moved to Cleveland, Ohio, to escape overt racial prejudice in search of better opportunities and a better life. In researching this book, my coauthor and I discovered many things about Jesse Owens. We discovered there is a hidden gem located in my birth state, the Jesse Owens Museum in Danville, Alabama. My daughter Savannah and I have traveled to museums all across the United States, and I have traveled to some museums in other countries; this small museum is comparable to them all.

Our sincerest thanks are extended to John Pinion, Nancy Todd Pinion, and Deborah Murner at the Jesse Owens Museum. We are also thankful for the assistance of Michelle Drobik at the Ohio State University Library. We must give a hearty thank you to Shelia Stuckey, Dantrea Hampton, Nkechi Amadife, Sharon McGee, and Bobby Walter at the Paul G. Blazer Library at Kentucky State University. Thanks must be also given to Karen Brown, and Roger Cleveland at Kentucky State University. Lastly, thanks must also be given to Marilyn Stepney and Teresa Tweedie at Central State University.

# 1

# Childhood in Oakville, Alabama

James Cleveland "J.C." Owens was born in Oakville, Alabama, on September 12, 1913. Oakville is located in the northern part of the state in Lawrence County, southwest of Huntsville. The area is now home to NASA's U.S. Space and Rocket Center and the FAME Recording Studios. But before becoming a famous tourist destination, the small town of Oakville was best known as the birthplace of J.C. Owens, who after his remarkable performance at the 1936 Summer Olympic Games became recognized around the world as "Jesse" Owens.

Oakville, Alabama, was a small rural town. According to the U.S. Census, the majority of its residents were white, and there were very few Blacks who owned land. The African American population only made up about 10 percent of the U.S. population. At the time of Owens's birth, the state of Alabama was concerned with its citizens having temperance and sobriety (Webb and Armbrester 2001, 158). Prohibition and the call to keep Alabama "bone dry" were not the only items on the state's agenda, Alabama's governor, Emmet O'Neal, advocated against "soft drinks" that contained cocaine, caffeine, and other habit-forming drugs in them (Webb and Armbrester 2001, 159).

Alabama was considered the "Heart of Dixie," being the location where the Constitution of the Confederate States was formulated and the state that housed the first Confederate capital. On January 11, 1861, Alabama seceded from the Union, and on February 4, delegates from six states met at Montgomery and formed the Confederate States of America, with

Montgomery as its capital city. The Confederate flag was designed and first flown in Alabama in 1861. Union troops were withdrawn from Alabama until 1876, when the state began its slow recovery from the Civil War. The condition of the newly freed slaves, however, did not change significantly after the end of the war. Jesse Owens's parents were the children of slaves. His grandfather was born in 1878, and at the age of 18, he married Mary Emma Fitzgerald, who was 21 years old. Blacks could not legally marry while enslaved; however, some 30 years after the Civil War, Jesse Owens's grandparents were legally married in 1896.

After the Civil War, Alabama's citizens were divided into four social subdivisions, which included the native whites, who were further divided into the former slaveholders and nonslaveholders; the Reconstructionist Northerners; and the former slaves. The former slaveholders were usually wealthy, and they were resentful for the most part because their way of life had been interrupted. They believed Black people should continue to be at the bottom of the class system, and they continued to distrust the Northern whites. Nonslaveholding whites were generally poor whites who could not afford slaves, and after the war, the poor and the ex-slaves found themselves in the same predicament: economically poor and poorly educated or uneducated.

There was not a comprehensive compulsory school set up for African Americans in Alabama. Education for Black people in Alabama was closely intertwined with slavery and Reconstruction. In response to Nat Turner's slave revolt and bloody massacre in Virginia in 1831, Alabama immediately adopted a slave code based on the State of Georgia's code, and the following year, it added teeth to the measure (Bond 1969, 9). The statute made it a crime to instruct any Negro, free or slave, to read and write; furthermore, a fine of $250 to $500 would be imposed on anyone found guilty of the offense (Anderson 1988, 2). Negroes were not allowed to gather together for any purpose, including religious worship services, unless there were five respectable slaveholders present or a preacher in charge held a license from an established white church.

The State of Alabama sought to solidify overt racial prejudice and limit opportunities for all Black people in the state through its statutes and laws. In 1856, the state legislature passed a statute titled "To Prohibit the Teaching of Slaves to Read and Write," and that law remained on the books until after the Civil War (Bond 1969, 12). The legislation imposed a penalty on persons who taught slaves how to read or write. The convicted offender could be fined no less than $100 or imprisoned in the county jail for no less than three months, or both (Bond 1969, 11). Many of these statutes were enacted because Southerners believed that it had been Northern propaganda that had motivated Turner's revolt. Among these laws was a state education code from 1895 that stated, "Black and white

---

### ALABAMA NATIVE AMERICANS

Jesse Owens was born in the state of Alabama. The state's name was derived from Native American words. The Choctaw words *alba amo* mean "clearing the thicket." The Alabama or Alibamu were a Native American people originally from Alabama. They were members of the Muscogee Creek Confederacy, which was located on the lands on the northern portion of the Alabama River. Other Native Americans that were original residents of Alabama included the Cherokees, Choctaws, Creeks, Chickasaws, Coushattas, and Yuchis. Many of the names of Alabama's counties and cities are derived from Native American languages. Alabama cities with Native American names include Tuscaloosa, Wetumpka, Eufaula, Letohatchee, Loachapoka, Opelika, Talladega, and Tuskegee. Alabama counties with Native American names include Autauga, Etowah, Choctaw, Cherokee, Conecuh, Coosa, and Tallapoosa.

---

children are not allowed to attend the same school. Penalty: Teachers who taught white and black pupils in the same school would not be compensated out of the public school fund" (Bond 1969). In 1872, an education statute "called for separate schools for white and black children with a penalty that shut off funding for schools that admitted both races." And in 1877, the state's constitution delineated that "schools shall be free to all children of the state, but separate schools shall be provided for white and black children."

Other statutes and laws would follow and be placed on the books, including statutes from the 1920s and 1930s that included a state race classification code that classified a "Negro" as "any person with at least one quarter Negro blood" and a state education code that required "schools to be racially segregated. Teachers who were guilty of receiving or teaching white and colored pupils in the same school would not be compensated." A miscegenation code stated that a "colored clergyman can marry Negroes only. The code also nullified interracial marriages if parties went to another jurisdiction where such marriages were legal." Starting around 1910, throughout the United States, local ordinances were enacted to segregate neighborhoods. Cities such as Baltimore, Maryland; Dallas, Texas; Louisville, Kentucky; Norfolk, Virginia; Oklahoma City, Oklahoma; Richmond, Virginia; Roanoke, Virginia; and St. Louis, Missouri, established ordinances that separated African American and white neighborhoods.

On April 6, 1917, the United States entered into World War I. It has been estimated that 370,000 African Americans enlisted in the military to defend the United States. More than half of them served in the French war zone, and more than 1,000 African Americans commanded troops. As a result of their courageous efforts, 107 African American soldiers are awarded the Croix de Guerre by the French government.

In 1919, the pamphlet *Thirty Years of Lynching in the United States: 1898–1918* was published by the National Association for the Advancement of Colored People (NAACP). This published account was utilized to appeal to lawmakers to end the social, political, and economic terrorism associated with lynching. Even with heroic military service, African Americans continued to experience terroristic actions such as lynching. Eighty-three African Americans were lynched in 1919, many of them soldiers returning home from World War I. At the same time, the Ku Klux Klan was growing and operating out of 27 states. These Klan chapters were located in southern, midwestern, and the northern states.

In Alabama, education was unequal. There were no trained teachers for Blacks in Alabama until after World War I. Blacks in Oakville, Alabama, who desired an education were taught by volunteer teachers with little to no training, just an inclination to teach. They did not have regularly scheduled hours of instruction. Many Blacks were barely literate and could not read and write because when it was time to harvest the crops, schools for Blacks were closed so sharecropping families could have all hands on deck to work the fields, especially during the fall months. In the spring and summer months, sharecroppers worked from sunrise until sunset. The Owens family was no different. Despite these impediments, Jesse Owens learned to read and write, though perhaps not very well.

Jesse Owens's parents, Henry Cleveland Owens and Emma Owens, were sharecroppers and theoretically free; however, they were bound by Jim Crow laws and the customary racism against Africans Americans in the South. Sharecropping was a way of life for most African Americans after the conclusion of the Civil War. Under a sharecropping agreement, the farmer and his family were provided with credit for seeds, tools, living quarters, and food in exchange for working the land. The farmers who worked the land would then receive an agreed portion of the value of the crop minus charges. This relationship often had an imbalance of power between the parties. The landowners, who were usually white, exploited the laborers, who were usually Black, by overcharging and undercutting them financially. These dishonest practices trapped African Americans in a perpetual cycle of debt. The profitability and life of sharecropping also largely depended on the weather and how well the crops grew. A drought or an unusually rainy season could adversely affect the profits of sharecroppers. Many African American sharecroppers, facing insurmountable and growing debts and increasingly poor treatment, looked for other opportunities and a better way of life in other areas of the country.

When Henry Owens married Emma Owens, he only had a mule that had been passed down from his father. Henry Owens was also bequeathed the small shanty on the land where his family sharecropped and the continued formal sharecropping agreement first solidified between his father and the landowner and farmer Albert C. Owens. Henry would later move his family to a shanty on Jim Clannon's place, where they sharecropped between 40 and 50 acres (McDaniel 2005). Three Black sharecropping families occupied the shabby tenements behind the landowner's main home structure. After a disagreement with Clannon over the year-end financial settling of the crops—and with the strong urging of his wife—Henry Owens finally moved his family out of Alabama in 1922.

During this time in Alabama and throughout the rest of the South, most African Americans had to pay deference to whites because the constant threat of being falsely accused of crimes or being lynched loomed close, particularly for Black men. Between 1882 and 1902, there were more than 100 incidents of lynching of African Americans each year in the United States. Therefore, deference and adherence to racist cultural norms were essential for survival in the South. Jesse Owens's father adhered to these norms by not looking white people in the eyes when speaking with them, walking on the opposite side of the road from white people if possible, and yielding the walkway to whites when it was not possible. Racial bigotry and segregation were the practices of the day in Oakville, Alabama. For a Black person, an unwarranted confrontation with a white person or being labeled "uppity" could be a matter of life and death through terroristic acts or vigilante justice by white people. In public, Henry Owens portrayed himself as stoic, timid, and divorced from any real outward emotions as a matter of survival and coping mechanism. He rarely talked in public and almost never raised his voice in public or private. In private, he had the same emotional highs and lows as any human being. He worried about the well-being of his children and the economic woes of being a sharecropper.

Jesse learned to portray himself as a smiling, happy-go-lucky, nonthreatening individual as a matter of survival. Though his demeanor was different from his father, his timidity was a method to portray himself as nonthreatening. Over time, it seemed this behavior became a natural fit for him. Throughout his life, most people described him as friendly, with a smile and a sunny disposition.

In total, Henry and Emma had 13 children; however, 3 of these children died during childbirth. When Jesse Owens was born, he was the tenth and youngest child in his family. Reportedly, Henry and Emma Owens had agreed to not have any more children, but they found themselves unexpectedly pregnant with Jesse, who was born on September 12, 1913. Jesse had six brothers and three sisters: Prentice, Johnson, Henry, Ernest, Quincy, Sylvester, Ida, Josephine, and Lillie. His siblings worked all day out in the cotton field while Jesse's parents tried to keep him healthy because

---

### END OF RECONSTRUCTION IN THE SOUTH

The 10-year period after the Civil War was called the Reconstruction. As early as 1863, President Lincoln offered a plan for reconstruction that would abolish slavery in individual state constitutions. The Civil War ended on April 9, 1865, and on December 18, 1865, Congress ratified the Thirteenth Amendment, formally abolishing slavery.

Southern states were required to take an oath of loyalty to the United States before being readmitted to the Union, but many continued their discriminatory practices once they were restored. Legislatures in southern states passed laws that restricted the civil rights of emancipated former slaves, often referred to as "black codes," to subject African Americans to many of the constrictions they experienced during slavery.

On March 3, 1865, Congress passed an act to establish the Bureau of Refugees, Freedmen and Abandoned Lands, often called the Freedmen's Bureau, to provide relief and assistance to the former slaves. In 1866, Congress passed the Civil Rights Act, which granted African Americans the right to make contracts, own and sell property, and receive equal treatment under the law.

---

he was a sickly child. Jesse suffered from upper respiratory ailments. These ailments were persistent because of being exposed to elements during the winter months and the lack of nutritious meals due to abject poverty. He often suffered colds, and, almost like clockwork, he suffered from pneumonia during most winters of his childhood. He was also prone to having polyp-like tumors on various parts of his body. Most often, they appeared on his chest and legs.

There was not sufficient health care provided for the poor in the early twentieth century, especially for the African American poor. Although the American Medical Association was formed in 1848, this organization was relatively weak and had not moved beyond the East Coast and Midwest. To compound this fact, medical education and training were also still poor and crude in quality at this time. There were a few Blacks practicing medicine during the 1800s, though they could not attend medical school because of segregation. Howard University became one of the earliest medical schools for African Americans in 1869. However, there was virtually no health care for poor people in Alabama, regardless of their race, during this time. For the poor, midwives delivered babies, and most poor people handled medical issues through home remedies and experimentation. This was the case with the Owens family and their health care.

On one occasion, when he was around five years old, Jesse had a cyst on his chest. He later recalled that the severity of the tumor had begun to press on his lungs. Emma sterilized a knife and performed surgery by lancing the cyst from young Jesse. His mother had previously removed another cyst from his leg (Owens 1970, 15).

Although he grew up in dire poverty in a rural isolated farm town in northern Alabama, Jesse Owens did not know how severely poor his family really was until he became older. The Owens home was merely a shanty consisting of three small rooms without indoor plumbing, running water, or electricity. One of the rooms functioned as a bedroom where all of the children piled up and slept on the floor. During the winter, a small potbellied stove kept this room and the entire house warm. There was only one bed in the entire house, and Emma and Henry slept there. The remaining room was a kitchen that contained a medium-sized table where the family gathered for meals. Breakfast consisted of molasses, cornbread, and available fruits, such as apples, peaches, and pears. The family's diet consisted of very little meat. They ate an assortment of beans, squash, onions, tomatoes, and corn. These dietary restrictions were because they were poor, and meals with meat as a main course were a luxury. Once a year, usually just before winter, the family would kill a hog, and this would serve as meat for meals during the winter months. From this hog slaughter, the Owens family enjoyed smoked ham and ribs.

Jesse recalled his childhood as mired in poverty but happy because he was unaware of the larger world. He was blissfully ignorant of their poverty-stricken status in Alabama. Jesse did not have sufficient clothing while growing up in Oakville. He wore hand-me-down clothes and recalled stuffing cardboard in his shoes to fill the holes in their soles. He mostly went barefoot as a child. This was a source of great embarrassment for him. Clothing would later become a mark of success for him. As an adult, Owens bought the best clothing money could buy and was always among the best dressed in any social or professional setting.

While living in Alabama, Jesse's family members were devout Christians and were affiliated with the Baptist denomination. The Owens family walked about nine miles each Sunday to attend church services. They regularly attended Oakville Missionary Baptist Church, where his father served as a deacon. The church also served as a school during the work week. Like many Africans Americans in the South during this period, they found solace in the church. It was one of very few places where African Americans could truly and publicly express their fears, hopes, and dreams. It was the place where they could outwardly long for a better life without fear of being reprimanded or chastised.

The Owens children were forced to memorize and recite various Bible verses as one of the pastimes in the household. The catalyst for this religious fervor was mainly their mother, Emma. Perhaps religion provided Jesse's mother with comfort and allowed her to make sense out of a world that seemed to hand African Americans more than their share of troubles.

In his work *The Avenue Clayton City*, professor and noted scholar C. Eric Lincoln describes the church as "a place that gave black people the license to break down—to scream and shout to moan and weep, to engage in the delirium of temporary relief from sadness, from fear, from hatred and frustration. . . . All in the name and presence of God" (Gaillard 1988). Eminent scholar, culture analyst, and cofounder of the National Association for the Advancement of Colored People (NAACP), W. E. B. Du Bois, in his seminal work *The Souls of Black Folk*, described the role of Black preachers as one to "facilitate a spiritual rebirth and reconciliation that would unite African Americans while helping them achieve self-assertion to face the racism of the time." Du Bois described the Black preacher as "a leader, a politician, and orator, a 'boss,' an intriguer, and an idealist" (Du Bois 2016 [1903], 190).

Evidently, hearing the rhythmic cadence of charismatic preaching must have influenced young Jesse. He would become a superb public speaker later in his life.

As far as social activities, Jesse and his brothers and friends from neighboring towns enjoyed swimming and fishing in a pond near the Oakville community. They also played games that became staples in American culture, such as hide-and-seek, tag, and other casual games that they created. The older children also played pickup baseball games on Sunday afternoons after church services. It was also not unusual for African Americans and poor whites to socialize and engage in activities such as hunting, fishing, baking, and cooking.

While balancing his time among school, work, and church, Jesse discovered the freedom of running through the cotton fields of Alabama. "I always loved running," he said about his youth in Oakville during an interview. "I wasn't very good at it, but I loved it because it was something you could do all by yourself, all under your own power. You could go in any direction, fast or slow as you wanted, fighting the wind if you felt like it, seeking out new sights just on the strength of your feet and the courage of your lungs" (Baker 1986, 11). While Jesse was thinking about his love of running and how it allowed him to transition and seek new sights, his parents were also thinking about new sights and transitioning from Alabama to Cleveland.

Emma Owens was usually more forward thinking than Henry Owens. Jesse Owens's lineage on his mother's side was affected by the institution of slavery operating in Alabama. Owens's maternal grandfather was Phillip Fitzgerald, the former slave of William Fitzgerald. Phillip Fitzgerald married Parthena Alexander, the former slave of William Alexander Jr. Like most slave marriages, these unions were not recognized by state or federal law (McDaniel 2005). Phillip and Parthena lived on separate plantations but became landowners. The former slaves owned a sizeable farm that would later become the Jesse Owens Memorial Park. There were four Fitzgerald brothers, but according to Marvin Fitzgerald, only Jesse's grandfather remained in the Oakville area.

It is uncertain how the land was acquired; however, most of the land was lost when a descendant mortgaged the land to a white cotton planter. Phillip Fitzgerald died between 1900 and 1910, and tax records show that his widow continued to prosper with real and personal property until 1925, when Parthena Fitzgerald's name leaves the tax rolls (McDaniel 2005). It is probable that her name left the tax rolls because she died. Another reasonable conclusion is that the family lost its property amid the economic devastation of the Great Depression. Perhaps Emma's progressive inclination was because of her brothers and the paternal side of her family; they had acquired land at time when it was extremely difficult for Blacks to own property and had managed to pass it down to family members. For the uneducated Black and also poor white land owners, there was a constant and looming threat of being tricked out of their ownership or being forced off their land.

The State of Alabama also used the convict leasing system and often leased prisoners to private railways, mines, and large plantations. While Alabama profited, prisoners earned no pay and faced inhumane, dangerous, and often deadly work conditions. It was common practice to round up unemployed Black men, prosecute them on trumped-up charges, and then sentence them to forced labor in the coal mines in northern Alabama. Use of this system began in Alabama in 1846 and was finally eliminated in 1928; it was the last state in the nation to do so. At the height of the convict leasing system, it is estimated about 10 percent of Alabama's total revenue was derived from convict leasing. With the effects of crippling poverty and the prospects of being wrongfully convicted of a crime and being forced into the convict leasing system, the Owens family faced the dilemma of looking for a better opportunity by leaving the rural South, like so many other Blacks were doing. If it were solely Henry Owens's decision, the family might have never moved. But the family would soon see the benefits of moving north.

# 2

## Family Life and Moving to Cleveland, Ohio

During the twentieth century, the majority of African Americans lived in southern states. However, in a mass exodus known as the Great Migration, many African Americans left these former Confederate states. There were more than six million African Americans who departed the South and journeyed to find better lives in northern cities and in the midwestern and western states from the 1900s to the 1970s. Motivated by the harsh realities of life for African Americans in the South, they headed for the promise of economic opportunity with the need for factory workers and other industrial opportunities. The northern, western, and midwestern states seemed to have less overt racism and discrimination than the southern states, and they faced a shortage of blue-collar workers. This shortage of laborers in the North combined with insect manifestations killing the agriculture industry by destroying crops in the South caused many African Americans in the South to seek refuge elsewhere. Also, northern factory jobs paid significantly more than sharecropping or other agricultural labor jobs in the rural South.

African Americans moving from the South to the North traveled by whatever means of transportation was available to them. Some traveled by train, boat, and bus. Others made the trip by horse and carriage. The most popular destinations included New York, Chicago, Philadelphia, and Detroit as well as Indianapolis, Denver, St. Louis, Pittsburgh, and Cleveland.

Southerners from the Carolinas and Virginia settled in Philadelphia, New York City, and Washington, DC. African Americans from Georgia, Alabama, and Mississippi migrated to Chicago, Detroit, Pittsburgh, and Cleveland. Those from Louisiana, Mississippi, and Arkansas moved north to Chicago. After arriving, many of these African Americans moved to smaller communities, away from the urban centers.

In their new states, African Americans were often met with discrimination in housing. White proper owners created restrictive covenants among themselves to not rent or sell to African Americans or, in some cases, other immigrants. The U.S. Supreme Court had first declared housing discrimination unconstitutional in 1917 and then declared these race-based pacts illegal in 1948. The Great Black Migration slowed during the 1930s due to the Great Depression, but during World War II, there was a need for laborers to produce products for the war.

As they escaped the racism and segregation laws of the South and relocated in new cities, African Americans hoped to build new lives and gain better economic, political, social, and educational opportunities. They created pockets of community in urban cities and continued to influence the culture of American society. When African American men reached their destinations, they found employment at foundries, factories, and meatpacking plants. In later years, they worked as automobile assembly line workers and steelworkers. Women usually found work as domestics, often employed as maids and cooks. These employment opportunities were in many ways only a little better than their past crop picking jobs, but they were much better than the scant job prospects and treatment of African Americans in the South. Lillie Owens, Jesse's sister, was among the African Americans who left Alabama for a better life in a northern city. After some relatives had relocated to Cleveland, Ohio, and told Lillie about the employment opportunities, she decided to take a chance and headed to Cleveland in 1922.

At its inception, the city of Cleveland was spelled "Cleaveland," after General Moses Cleaveland. On January 6, 1831, the *Cleveland Advertiser* discontinued use of the first letter *a*. It has been speculated that the letter was cut to save typesetting space on the newspaper's masthead, and this is why the city's name is spelled without the extra *a* in its current form. Cleveland became the Cuyahoga County seat in 1807. The population of Cleveland, Ohio, did not grow significantly until after the War of 1812. By 1820, only 606 people lived in the city of Cleveland, but with the advent of the railroads, Cleveland was poised for further development and a boom in its population. In the 1850s, railroads came to Cleveland, and the population increased from under 1,000 people to more than 40,000 people in a little over 40 years. John D. Rockefeller and his partners began the Standard Oil Company in Cleveland during the 1860s. At the same time, Samuel Mather began steel production and enhanced Cleveland's economic importance in the region and the United States. In 1880, a significant portion of Cleveland's men found work in the steel mills.

Initially, Lillie lived with extended family in her new city. In Cleveland, Lillie found gainful employment and met a man, fell in love, and got married. She was making more money than she ever had before in her lifetime. The sharecropping income of the South paled in comparison to the earning potential of industrial work in the North. Agriculture in Alabama, in particular the cotton crops, had been devastated by a boll weevil infestation. The crop infestation caused Alabama's economy to nosedive, and the exploitive sharecropping system hit Black farmers extremely hard.

Lillie sent letters back to her family that had remained in Oakville, Alabama. There were multiple purposes to her letters. She wanted to keep the family abreast of the events occurring in her life, and she lobbied the family to move to Cleveland. At the time, Cleveland had a reputation for being progressive. This reputation was not entirely true or deserved; however, it was much better than Oakville, Alabama. According to the U.S. Department of Commerce, in 1920, Cleveland's Black population was 34,451 or 4.3 percent of the total population of the city. This was a 307.8 percent growth in the Black population of the city of Cleveland between 1910 and 1920 (U.S. Department of Commerce 1910–1920). Lillie figured the best method to convince the family to move would be to convince her mother first and then her mother would convince her father to relocate. As the family grew weary from the travails of sharecropping, Emma and Henry passionately discussed and even argued about leaving Alabama and heading north.

Finally, after several heated conversations, Emma convinced Henry to relocate the family to Cleveland in search of a better life. Jesse noted that his father was so nervous that he could not stop shaking (Schaap 2007, 21). The family determined the best plan would consist of Henry and the older brothers moving first and finding gainful employment. The rest of the family would follow. They barely had enough money to get all their family members to Cleveland. Henry had difficulty adjusting to his new life. He was simply not comfortable with this newer fast-paced life of Cleveland. He also had difficulty in finding work because all he had ever done was be a sharecropper. He was a 45-year-old man without any high-level work skills or formal education. These factors contributed to Henry's difficulty in finding employment that paid a livable wage. Henry slipped into a somber fog because he could not support his family (Schaap 2007, 21).

The plan to leave the poor but familiar surroundings of Oakville, Alabama, for the potential economic gain in urban industrial Cleveland was a daunting task. In 1920, it has been estimated that 65,000 African Americans from Alabama participated in the Great Migration by moving to

---

**GREAT BLACK MIGRATION OR THE GREAT NORTHERN MIGRATION**

For most of the history of the United States, the majority of African Americans lived in southern states. This is one of the vestiges of the institution of slavery and slave labor in the United States. The Great Migration occurred in the decades after the American Civil War, when African Americans moved from the South to the northern and western states. At the turn of the century, about 9 in 10 African Americans lived in the South, predominantly in rural areas. At the time, the three states with the largest Black populations were Georgia, Mississippi, and Alabama.

This mass exodus of African Americans can be segmented into two periods of the Great Migration; 1910 to 1940 is considered the first wave, and the 1940s through the 1970s is considered the second wave. By 1970, New York, Illinois, and California had the most African Americans.

Several factors contributed to the Great Migration, namely a poor economic outlook and the lack of opportunities for African Americans. The Great Black Migration was the precursor to the American civil rights movement because after African Americans moved to cities in the northern states, it showed that racial tension and race issues were not just problems found in southern states.

---

northern cities. In 1922, a reluctant Henry Owens and his two oldest sons moved to Cleveland, and about a month later, the rest of the family relocated. Before leaving Oakville, Emma sold the majority of the family's belongings to help finance their trip.

When the entire family had settled in Cleveland, life was better, but they still experienced racial prejudices and discrimination. Eventually, Henry found work at a steel mill. Although it could be tough finding employment when African Americans relocated to northern states during the Great Migration, employment opportunities were more plentiful than in the South. With this move, Emma believed her youngest son would receive a better life and attend school on a full-time basis. The Owens family reached Cleveland at the same time that many other minorities and ethnic immigrants were moving to the city, and this contributed to heightened racial tensions and a rise in white prejudice. The influx of Blacks and other ethnic minorities to Cleveland neighborhoods stretched the bounds of the city's infrastructure and pushed the city government for more housing, restaurants, and services.

Whites in Cleveland resented the bulging Black and international immigrant populations. Witnessing the masses of new arrivals in the city tapped into the xenophobic fears of white Clevelanders, and as a result, the Ku Klux Klan was revived in the city during the early 1920s. As in other northern cities, the Ku Klux Klan burned crosses at masses rallies. Cross burnings in the front yards of the homes of African Americans and immigrants were a terroristic tactic the Klan used to strike fear and intimidation in the hearts of these residents of the city. Even with these intimidating tactics, the Owens' life in Cleveland was better than their life in Oakville.

Jobs were scarce all across the United States during the Great Depression. The fight for jobs and scarce financial resources also precipitated more racial violence. In some instances, white employers killed African American employees to create jobs for unemployed whites. In fact, the *Encyclopedia of the Great Depression*, elaborates on an instance in which white unionized workers along with railroad brotherhoods "intimidated, attacked and murdered African American firemen in order to take their jobs" (McElvaine 2004). During this period, there was also an upsurge in the lynching of African Americans in the United States.

The Owens family found a home on the east side of Cleveland. Because it was a low-income area riddled with poverty and the clash of cultures, this area was a tough neighborhood with a mix of African Americans and ethnic immigrants. On the east side, there were clusters of immigrants from European and Middle Eastern countries living in close quarters in the community. People of Polish, Italian, Hungarian, Romanian, Syrian, and Greek descent lived in the neighborhood or in close vicinity to home of the Owens family. Jesse engaged and played with all the children in the

---

### XENOPHOBIA

*Xenophobia* is the fear, dislike, or hatred of foreigners or people who are culturally different than oneself. It comes from the Greek words *xenos*, meaning "foreigner" or "stranger," and *phobos*, meaning "fear." Xenophobic behavior is based on existing racist, ethnic, religious, cultural, or national prejudice. *Xenophobia* and *racism* are often used interchangeably; however, there is a distinct difference between the two words. Racism usually entails distinction based on the color of one's skin color, hair type, or facial features. On the other hand, xenophobia infers behavior based on the idea that the other is foreign and originates from outside the community or nation.

Because differences in physical characteristics are often used to distinguish someone from the common community, it is often difficult to differentiate between racism and xenophobia as motivations for behavior. At the same time, expressions of xenophobia may occur against people of identical physical characteristics when such people arrive, return, or migrate to states or areas where the occupants consider them outsiders. Since 2016, there has been an uptick in xenophobic outbursts that were followed by an increase in acts of racist violence in the United States and in several other nations in the world.

neighborhood. The commonality of all of them being new to Cleveland and in a sense all dreamers seeking new lives in a new environment allowed for some comradery among the children of the east side. Although Emma Owens was more enthusiastic than her husband about the move to Cleveland, she also had a tougher time adjusting to the faster pace of life in the urban setting. She felt the vast differences between Oakville and Cleveland, and overcoming these differences was challenging for her. Emma became visibly more introverted. She often would not go shopping without being accompanied by someone else and often kept the curtains in the home drawn to ward off the fears of urban life, such as drug dealing, prostitution, and other peddling.

In their new neighborhood, young J.C. Owens raced other children on the sidewalks. Running came easily for Owens. He believed running was like freedom; you were in sole control of how fast or slow you ran. During this time in American culture, foot racing was a pure form of competition. It was a big event, and foot races were often held at carnivals and county fairs across the United States in the 1930s. Foot races often took place on the streets of Cleveland's east side. In addition to running, J.C. also held several part-time jobs, delivering groceries, unloading freight, and working at a shoe repair shop. Unloading freight helped his endurance and quick feet.

Education in Cleveland was different from the volunteer teachers and shabby schools in Oakville. Initially, Jesse was enrolled at Bolton Elementary School, three blocks from the Owens' family home. It was J.C. Owens's first experience learning and matriculating at a racially integrated school. It was at Bolton Elementary that "J.C." Owens was transformed to "Jesse" Owens. When a teacher asked him his name, he responded in his thick southern accent. The teacher misheard "J.C." as "Jesse." Too shy to correct her, or perhaps following the custom of the South of not correcting adults, especially white people, J.C. became "Jesse." Perhaps Jesse did not correct his teacher because he was eager to please her and make a good impression at his new school.

The administration at the elementary school assumed Jesse was illiterate because he was a Black boy from Alabama, so they assigned him to the first grade, even though he was at least three years older than the students in the first grade. Although far from an excellent education, the sporadic rudimentary education Jesse had received in Alabama had been better than the school administration's initial assessment, and as a result, Jesse was advanced to the second grade when he showed them he could read and write. Throughout his education experience, he would remain a little older than the other students enrolled in school with him.

After Bolton Elementary, Jesse advanced to Fairmount Junior High School. Fairmount was another integrated school that reflected the ethnic diversity and demographics of the neighborhood. Because many of the students at Fairmount were low on the socioeconomic spectrum and the majority were ethnic minorities and African Americans, the school's curriculum did not provide instruction in college preparatory courses. Instead, the school provided instruction in vocational courses to prepare the students for the manual labor employment that would be available to them once they graduated.

This follows the industrial model of education exposed by Booker T. Washington, a noted educator and founder of the Tuskegee Institute in Alabama. This model was used to guide Blacks to be trained for agricultural labor employment. The curriculum was not concentrated on a classical liberal education. Washington specifically stated,

> For 250 years, I believe the way of the redemption for the Negro being prepared through industrial development. Through all the years the Southern white man did business with the Negro in a way that no one else has done business with him. In most cases if a Southern white man wanted a house built, he consulted a Negro mechanic about the plan and about the actual building of the structure. If he wanted a suit of clothes made, he went to a Negro tailor and for shoes he went to a shoemaker of the same race. In a certain way every slave plantation in the South was an industrial school. On these plantations young colored men and women were constantly being trained not only as farmers but as carpenters, blacksmith, wheelwrights, brick masons, engineers, cooks, laundresses, sewing women and housekeepers. (Washington 1901)

Washington asked Blacks to temporarily accept racism and discrimination to uplift the race through hard work, patience, endurance, and thrift. He wanted to assure white southerners who objected to formal education for Blacks that they would not lose their labor force. Washington continued,

> I do not mean in any way to apologize for the curse of slavery, which was a curse to both races, but in what I say about industrial training in slavery, I am simply stating facts.

Much of the early education for Blacks centered on a rudimentary education, making sure they were literate enough to read the Bible, and preparation for vocational education. Washington learned the industrial model from his alma mater, Hampton Institute. He originally argued that Blacks should stay out of political matters, but he later recanted on this philosophy. A typical industrial model offered courses and training in carpentry, blacksmithing, printing, dairying, tin smithing, machinery, brick making, basketry, stock raising, mattress making, mechanical and architectural drawing, horticulture, saw milling, electrical and steam engineering, canning, brick masonry, canning, sewing, harness making, plastering, shoemaking, and tailoring (Washington 1901, 55).

From the Reconstruction era through the Great Depression, Black education, in particular Black higher education in the South, was essentially established as by consortiums of private liberal arts colleges. There were partnerships established between northern missionary societies, Black religious denominations, and white philanthropic organizations. Northern missionary organizations supported a classical liberal education for Blacks as a method of obtaining equality and a way of "civilizing" Blacks and training them for Black leadership. The classical liberal education consisted of courses in languages (French, German, and Latin), mathematics, science, history, philosophy astronomy, and English. They also offered a few industrial courses, such as agriculture, domestic science, and building trades. These courses were supplemented by racist undertones, as these white organizations believed they must provide Blacks with social values such as thrift, sobriety, and industriousness. The white philanthropic organizations had been involved in developing Black common schools and industrial normal schools. The Black religious denominations, especially the largest of the early Black denominations, the African Methodist Episcopal Church, paved the way for Black religious denominations to establish Black schools and eventually colleges. Each of these groups had their own take on what would be the role of Blacks in an integrated South. They also clashed on the value and the purpose of education, in particular Black higher education.

Eventually, these organizations pulled out of Black education, and Black colleges continued to grow under the veil of segregation. K–12 education in the United States was also segregated, and the responsibility of supervising Black education in was largely fulfilled by the Division of Negro Education, which was created in 1921 as a part of the State Department of Public Instruction. During the 1920s, racial segregation of public schools widened. In Cleveland, Black students were enrolled in 63 of the city's 142 public schools in 1924. The other 79 Cleveland public schools undoubtedly consisted of all white students. As the racial demographics changed in Cleveland, the racial composition of student enrollments and teachers in K–12 schools also changed. Over 100 African American teachers were employed in Cleveland schools, including at some white schools; however, as late as 1926, only one African American teacher taught above the elementary level (Miggins 2014, 129–130). There were several schools with all-Black student enrollments operating during the 1920s in central and southern Ohio.

Jesse's instruction at Fairmount did not prepare him for college, but there were three influential relationships that would be formed during his educational experience at Fairmount Junior High School. At Fairmount, Jesse would meet his future wife, Minnie Ruth Solomon; native Alabamian and future Ohio State and Olympian teammate Dave Albritton; and his track coach and lifelong mentor, Charles Riley.

Minnie Ruth Solomon was born on April 27, 1915, in Macon, Georgia. She and Jesse had a lot of similarities; both were from the Deep South and were accustomed to the poverty that most African Americans had experienced there, and they had both experienced the newness of relocating to an urban city in the North. In an interview, Jesse stated, "She was unusual because even though I knew her family was as poor as ours, nothing she said or did seemed touched by that. Or by prejudice. Or by anything the world said or did. It was as if she had something inside her that somehow made all that do not count" (Gentry 1989, 38).

For most of her life, Minnie went by her middle name, "Ruth." Jesse Owens met Ruth at Fairmont Junior High School when he was becoming a track star. He became fascinated with her because she was beautiful and wore fashionable clothing. Jesse began to pass Ruth notes in school and was soon regularly carrying her books home from school. He was 15, and Ruth was just 13. Their families were new to the Cleveland area. Ruth's family had moved from Georgia. They dated steadily throughout high school, and she was the first girl he had ever kissed. Ruth would be Jesse's greatest supporter for the rest of his life, even after his death.

According to an article in the *Lantern Oasis*, Owens stated, "I fell in love with her some the first time we ever talked and a little bit more every time after that until I thought I couldn't love her any more than I did. And when I felt that way, I asked her to marry me, even though we were only in the fourth grade, and she said she would."

---

### MINNIE RUTH SOLOMON OWENS

Minnie Ruth Solomon was born on April 27, 1915, in Macon, Georgia. Most of her life, she went by the name by her middle name, Ruth. Jesse Owens met Minnie Ruth at Fairmont Junior High School when he was a budding track star, and they dated steadily throughout high school. Ruth gave birth to the couple's first daughter in 1932. Jesse and Minnie Ruth were married on July 5, 1935. Minnie Ruth did not travel to Berlin, Germany, to see Jesse compete in the Olympic Games in 1936. The couple had three children, Gloria, born in 1932; Marlene, born in 1937; and Beverly, born in 1940.

Ruth Owens was board chairwoman and an active fundraiser for the Jesse Owens Foundation. This nonprofit organization was formed after her husband's death to give scholarships to students active in the community. After the death of Jesse, Ruth Owens saw one of her primary duties as protecting the legacy of her husband. She and Jesse Owens were married for nearly 48 years, until Jesse's death in 1980.

Minnie Ruth Solomon Owens died of heart failure at her home in Chicago, Illinois in June 27, 2001, at age 86.

In the same article, Ruth remembered Jesse was in her sister's class and made the first move. Ruth stated, "He was in my sister's class. He gave my sister a note to give to me. The short message scrawled on a note that said, 'I want to walk you home.'" Ruth was fiercely loyal to Jesse and protected him even after his death. She was the board chairwoman and an active fundraiser for the Jesse Owens Foundation, which was formed after her husband's death to give scholarships to average students active in the community.

Ruth spoke up for Jesse after his death, when it was revealed that for a period he had been under surveillance by the Federal Bureau of Investigation (FBI). Earlier than this, she had stood by him on those icy mornings in Cleveland when he was practicing his sprinting (McRae 2002, 85). Ruth gave birth to the couple's first baby daughter in 1932. Jesse and Minnie Ruth were married on July 5, 1935. They remained marital partners until Jesse Owens's death in 1980. The couple had three children: Gloria, born in 1932; Marlene, born in 1937; and Beverly, born in 1940. Ruth mainly saw her role in the marriage as a loving supporter who buttressed Owens's efforts and as the guiding force for their children while taking care of their home. She stated, "I would be getting the house ready for him and the kids together and putting in the foods he enjoyed eating" (Wallace 1986, 1). She also added that she "could not ask for a finer husband" (Wallace 1986, 1). Ruth described Jesse Owens as strict but loving. He was also the disciplinarian, and Ruth would often use the threat, "I will call your father and he will take care of it," when their daughters were exhibiting rebellious behavior. Like most loving parents, Jesse Owens wanted his children to have a better life than he did. Ruth noted, "Although Jesse was often out of town, his image was in the home at all times" (Wallace 1986, 6). His daughters recalled their father being a stickler, but he used a soft tone and was able to get his point across without yelling or screaming (Metz 2016). Ruth also made sure Jesse understood that though he traveled for work, he was the girls' father and her husband. She also made sure he did not get these two roles conflated.

Dave Albritton and Jesse quickly became friends. They had a lot in common, and they virtually had the same interests: namely, girls and sports. Albritton had grown up in Danville, Alabama, which was just down the road, less than 10 miles, from Oakville, Alabama. Their siblings were familiar with each other from social settings and sports after church, but Jesse and Dave were not acquainted until Fairmount Junior High School in Cleveland. The two would be teammates and roommates at Ohio State University, and both would compete in the 1936 Olympics in Berlin, Germany. Dave was a bit more quick-tempered than Owens and often ready to strike if provoked, while Owens took more of a pacifistic approach to incidents (Wallace 1986).

Another notable and influential relationship that began at Fairmount was with Charles Riley, a gym teacher at the school, where he noticed Jesse's talent for running. One day, Riley watched Owens run a 100-yard race in his neighborhood. Always searching for new athletic talents, Riley decided to use his stopwatch to time the foot race. Riley knew Owens was fast, but he could not believe how fast, especially for an eighth grader. Riley began training and conditioning regiments with Owens. Owens could only manage sporadic attendance because he needed to work during the evening hours; therefore, Riley held practice sessions in the morning before school. Owens called Riley "Coach," but he also frequently and fondly called him "Pop."

Riley was from Pennsylvania and had been a miner and a factory worker. He dropped out of high school but managed to go to Temple University and eventually became the physical education teacher at Fairmount. The job paid so little that Riley supplemented his income by taking a job as a playground attendant during the summer months. Riley had two sons of his own; however, one was born disabled, and the other had no interest in track and field. Riley told Owens to run as if he were running on hot coals and the track was on fire. He convinced Jesse's parents that he could be a great athlete. Riley picked Jesse up in his car and drove him around town.

---

### DAVE ALBRITTON

Dave Albritton was born in Danville, Alabama, in 1913. Danville is only a few miles from Jesse Owens's hometown of Oakville; however, Albritton and Owens were not friends in Alabama. Like Jesse's parents, the Albrittons relocated to Cleveland, Ohio, in search of a better life. Albritton and Owens's friendship began at East Technical High School. Then they both pursued a college education at Ohio State University and participated on the track-and-field team for the Buckeyes, coached by famed track coach Larry Snyder. As a sophomore at Ohio State University, Albritton won the National Collegiate Athletic Association (NCAA) championship in 1936.

In 1936, both Owens and Albritton were on the U.S. team for the Summer Olympics. At those Games, Albritton took home a silver medal in the high jump. As an amateur athlete, he won or tied seven national outdoor amateur championships from 1936 to 1950.

Albritton later entered the field of politics as a member of the Republican Party. In 1966, he was elected to the State of Ohio's House of Representatives, representing the Dayton, Ohio, area. Albritton was the first African American to head up a committee as a chair. He served six full terms as a state legislator.

In 1980, Dave Albritton was inducted into the USA Track and Field Hall of Fame. In 1994, he died in Dayton, Ohio, at age 82.

He often introduced Jesse to various track-and-field greats living in or near the area.

On one of these drives, Riley took Jesse to a horse racing track. At the track, Riley taught Jesse a valuable athletic lesson on staying focus. He asked Jesse to watch how the horses performed. He told Jesse to watch how the horses did not waste energy on unnecessary movements. Riley wanted to impress upon Jesse the need to concentrate on running his race and not his opponents. Certainly, he wanted Jesse to learn not to waste energy in attempting to intimidate his opponents. Riley told Jesse to focus ahead when running a race and not to look left or right—just run straight ahead. Riley believed that looking around while one ran was wasted energy. He told Jesse to observe the racehorses and notice how they did not look around but stayed focused ahead while running. This lesson at the track contributed to what would become Owens's running style and focus—effortless, and emotionless.

Under Riley's tutelage, Owens became stronger, faster, and more agile. Riley also became somewhat of a surrogate father figure for Jesse, often picking him up for dinner at his home on Sundays and offering mentoring sessions. Through this mentoring and observing, Owens picked up many of the social graces, social cues, and manners of those from a higher socioeconomic status. These observations of Riley's behavior and mannerisms translated to Jesse Owens being more polished in social settings as an adult. Spending time with Riley as a teenager allowed Owens to feel comfortable around white people and for white people to feel comfortable with him as he interacted with them. This easiness around all people seemed to carry over throughout the rest of his life. Riley did not just enrich Jesse's social graces and foster good behavior, he improved Jesse's budding amateur track career.

In 1928, Owens ran the 100-yard dash in 11 seconds. He also set two world records for his age group in the high jump and long jump. Riley continued to mentor and personally coach Owens even after he transitioned to East Technical High School in 1930. Coach Edgar Weil, the track-and-field coach at East Technical asked Riley to assist him in coaching the team. Of the 79 races Owens competed in while in high school, he won 75 of the races. For the most part, especially in the Deep South, African American high school athletes were not allowed to compete against white athletes; however, Jesse Owens competed against both white and Black athletes while in high school. A lot of Black athletes were restricted from competition in some sports during the nineteenth and early twentieth centuries; Black athletes had begun to dominate some sports, such as bicycling and horse racing, and as result, they were banned from interracial competitions. Also during the 1920s, several track-and-field associations were formed to regulate the sport. It was not until 1923 that women got the opportunity to compete in track and field, though they were subject to an abundance of sexist criticism and disrespect. The historically Black colleges Howard University and Hampton University began the annual intercollegiate track-and-field meet for Negro colleges in 1920 (Wiggins and Swanson 2016, 79). These schools became the preeminent track-and-field invitationals for Black high schools. Other Black universities became places to host and showcase Black high school athletic talent from the South as well as the North (Wiggins and Swanson 2016, 79).

In 1929, Jesse Owens's father was involved in a car accident. He was hit by a taxi, and his leg was shattered. As a result of this debilitating injury and chronic leg pain, Henry was unable to work and was unemployed for an extended period of time. The Owens family's misfortune was also heightened because of the Great Depression and the collapse of the American economy. The Great Depression was one of the most devastating economic events in American history. The Great Depression lasted over a 10-year period, from 1929 to 1939. Over a 5-year period, from 1929 to 1933, the national income fell dramatically.

The Great Depression was caused by the intersectionality of several events. The federal government had not done a good job of regulating the markets, and corporations pursued profits at all costs. There was also weak international trading and inequality of wealth. The inequality of wealth drove down the purchasing power of millions of Americans and slowed the economy to almost a screeching halt. The early 1920s had been outstanding economic times. People put their money in stocks and owned shares in companies. The prices of stocks plummeted in 1929. Americans' trust and confidence in banks and other financial and economic institutions quickly vanished. Many Americans of all races saw their life savings lost when banks closed. People also lost their jobs, and they had difficulty finding gainful employment; as a result, many people could not pay the mortgage loans on their homes, and these loans were foreclosed. African Americans were hit particularly hard by the Great Depression.

Prior to World War I, investing in the United States was mostly done by those of a high socioeconomic status. With the industrial effort, the federal government began issuing war bonds, which were made available to the wealthy but also allowed a small group of the middle class and other average citizens to participate in getting bonds. After the war, corporations looked for ways to decouple from their banking debts and began to issue stocks. This also caused an increase in the ability for the average citizen to participate in trading stocks. During this time, the concept of credit on the stock market meant that potential investors did not need money up front to buy stock in a company. Instead, they would borrow money to buy stock with the hope the stock price would rise, which would allow the investor to pay back the money borrowed and gain a profit.

By 1929, the stock market could not be controlled, and disaster loomed. One of the first signs that the market would crash came on October 24, 1929, better known as Black Thursday. The walls came tumbling down, and the stock market crashed the following Tuesday, October 29, 1929. In one year, most American banks failed during this time, and there was no insurance protection for savings. This meant that depositors lost all their personal savings. Home mortgage default rates grew as millions of Americans lost their homes due to the market crash. The Owens family was familiar with the depths of poverty the Great Depression brought because of their experiences in the rural South.

The Owens family had left the South, but many African Americans that remained there were trapped in an exploitive system of sharecropping, tenant farming, and other menial labor jobs. Cotton had remained the cash crop of many southern states since the 1800s, but cotton prices plunged to less than half its worth. African American farmers held very little social and political power and in most cases were pushed off the land. In the northern states, where many African Americans had participated in the Great Black Migration, African Americans also faced difficult times. African Americans who had left the South for better lives in the North were laid off in cost cutting measures. African Americans had lost jobs where they had gained traction and were able to climb the socioeconomic ladder, even if it was by blue-collar, low-end employment, such as finding work as garbage collectors or domestics. When the depression hit, even the competition for these jobs became stiff. To compound this matter, employers were pressured to outright dismiss African American workers and replaced them with white workers. As the United States saw a resurgence of blatant racial discrimination as a result of the economic depression, half a world away, Germany would also experience its own economic depression and see the rise and discrimination against Jews.

As the Great Depression began ravishing the United States in the late 1920s, on November 9, 1923, the National Socialist German Workers' Party, also called the Nazi Party, unsuccessfully attempted to overthrow the Bavarian government. At the onset of the economic depression, the Nazi Party was a small right-wing group on the political spectrum in Germany. The Nazi Party waited for the right opportunity and the schism in the country to deepen before taking full advantage of the fractious government a few years later. This coalition would become known as the Grand Coalition which included the Social Democratic Party, Catholic Centre Party, and People's Party. There was enormous growth of membership in the Nazi Party during the later 1920s, from 17,000 members to one million members over a four-year period (Cochrane 2000, 88). In the German parliamentary elections of 1924 and 1928, the Nazi Party received less than 3 percent of the vote in both elections (Cochrane 2000, 88).

The effects of the depression devastated the people of Germany. In particular, from 1930 to 1933, Germans experienced a great deal of national shame as the hardships of the depression affected the entire country. Millions of Germans found themselves unemployed. The high unemployment rate coupled with the humiliation of the country's defeat in World War I contributed to the nation's shame and the rise of Adolf Hitler and the Nazi Party. Hitler gained control of Germany through propaganda and well-crafted speeches to the people. He played on their economic misery, anxiety, and distrust of the national government. Hitler was a powerful and spellbinding orator who found a way to tap into the nation's collective anger and vulnerabilities and rally them to coalesce around a national agenda of making Germany grand again by restoring it as a world power.

Hitler and his circle of confidants were very successful in guiding the nation's anger to focus on the Jewish people living in Germany. His inflammatory political speeches fanned the flames of anti-Semitism and also denounced political groups such as the Social Democrats and Communists because they were in power and signed the armistice of November 1918 and the Treaty of Versailles. He also disliked these political groups because they had previously established the parliamentary republican form of governments in Germany. As a part of his political propagandist agenda, Hitler also promised to lift Germany out of its economic depression and restore Germany's cultural values, which had been diminished by previous governmental officials. Hitler personalized and custom-made his speeches to fit each group he was addressing. He promised to meet the needs of military veterans and soldiers. He promised farmers economic assistance. He promised workers that their pensions would remain stable and that there would be sustained buying power and economic growth. Between 1930 and 1932, there was a steady rise in the political power of the Nazi Party.

As the fissures in the German government continued to widen, the Nazi Party's opportunity came when the federal government made ill-advised political policies, engaged in misguided political maneuvering, and dissolved Germany's parliament within a two-year period. The most ominous political decision was on January 30, 1933, when President Paul von Hindenburg appointed Adolf Hitler as chancellor of Germany as a way to thwart growing Communist political power and a possible takeover of the country and thus prevent political chaos in the country. The German government hoped to exploit Hitler's grassroots popularity with the German masses to support resuming a conservative authoritarian form of government or possibly a monarchy.

Adolf Hitler did not win an election or the popularity of the vote to become chancellor, he made a questionable side deal with a small group of

---

### THE TREATY OF VERSAILLES

At the conclusion of World War I, England, France, and the United States conferenced in Paris, France, in June 1919. The purpose of this conference was to craft a treaty that would formally end World War I and prevent another devastating war. Out of the Paris Peace Conference, the Treaty of Versailles was produced. All provisions of the Treaty of Versailles were based on consent by Germany and the Allies of Article 231, the War Guilt Clause. Enforcement of the treaty began in January 1920.

Unfortunately, a few years later, the treaty would be used as the catalyst for World War II. The treaty outlined a reduction of Germany's land, and the redrawn boundaries granted land to Poland, Belgium, Lithuania, and Denmark. The Germans signed the treaty under protest. Hitler rose to power, and the treaty was abandoned. Conservative right-wing German political parties condemned the treaty as a betrayal, and terrorists assassinated several politicians whom they considered responsible for weakening Germany.

---

conservative German politicians who had given up on parliamentary rule. This deal may have even violated the German constitution, and within two years, Hitler and the Nazis had politically outsmarted and outmaneuvered Germany's conservative politicians and consolidated a radical dictatorship completely subservient to Hitler's personal propensities and political mandates.

As Hitler was rising to power in Germany in the 1930s, Jesse Owens was becoming an athletic star in the United States.

In 1932, Owens was 18 years old and had developed into a world-class sprinter and long jumper. There were whispers that Owens could qualify and make the American Olympic track-and-field team. Between 1930 and 1933, Owens was one of the most celebrated high school athletes in the state of Ohio. He became renowned for his celebrated achievements in several track-and-field events and began to garner national recognition in the media and from universities. He was accomplished at the 100 meters, 200 meters, broad jump, and hurdles. These would be the events he would excel in during the 1936 Olympics.

Over the course of three track-and-field seasons, Owens won nine events at the state meet and set seven state records. After crushing the competition in the broad jump during his sophomore year in 1933, he followed up in his junior year by winning four events. Owens bested his competition in the 220-yard dash, the 100-yard dash (9.9 seconds), the long jump (22 feet, 11.75 inches), and the 880-yard relay (1:30.8). He set or tied state records in the latter three events. He also led East Technical High School to the state of Ohio's track-and-field championship. Owens is the only Ohio athlete to ever set state records in four events in a single track-and-field meet.

In 1932, Jesse qualified for the regional Olympic track-and-field tryouts at Northwestern University, in Evanston, Illinois. The competition in Evanston was world class. Jesse was younger than most of the athletes competing at the trials, and it showed. He was only 18, and though he was strong, he was not yet physically mature enough to compete with the athletes at this event. Many of the athletes competing were over 20 years old and were both physically and mentally stronger than Owens. Twenty-three-year old Eddie Tolan, who would become a rival, friend, and, later, an Olympic teammate, also competed against Owens on this day.

Owens did not make the Olympic team, but he did learn from his defeat. Riley disclosed various flaws in the running techniques of many of Jesse's competitors. In turn, Jesse used this information to become a better competitor in future competitions. Owens was disappointed with his performance in Evanston. A month later he became a father with the birth of his daughter, Gloria Owens. Out-of-wedlock births were frowned upon at this time, so for a time, Jesse lied and claimed he got married just prior to Gloria's birth. As a new father, Owens continued to participate in athletics as a high school student athlete.

After Jesse Owens failed to make the team for the 1932 Olympic Games in Los Angeles, California, Coach Riley introduced him to Charlie Paddock, the 100-meter gold medal champion and world record holder from the 1920 Belgium Olympics. At the time, Paddock was known as the fastest man in the world. Paddock talked with Owens about what it took to become a champion. Jesse's athletic failure fueled his future goal of making the Olympics and probably motivated his stunning performance at the National Interscholastic Championship the following year. At the 1933 National Interscholastic Championship in Chicago, Illinois, Owens put on a spectacular show. He was stunning, winning the long jump, 220-yard dash, and 100-yard dash; Owens set and tied the world records in the latter two events. When he returned to Cleveland, the 19-year-old was honored with a celebratory parade fit for a triumphant king.

After Owens's spectacular high school performance, several universities competed to offer Owens a place on their track-and-field squads. Most of the schools in the Big Ten Conference and other universities in the midwestern states competed to get Jesse to sign with them. The University of Michigan recruited him aggressively. At this time in collegiate athletics, it was not uncommon for universities to offer money to athletes to choose their school or make side deals with the athletes' handlers to secure the athletes' services. Marquette University was also interested as well as Indiana University, but in the end, Ohio State University came up with the best offer. Dave Albritton stated that he and Jesse were examining various

---

> ## CLEVELAND, OHIO
>
> The city of Cleveland, Ohio was named after General Moses Cleaveland, an investor in the company that led the survey of its land within the Western Reserve. He had served under General George Washington for several years during the American Revolution and rose to the rank of brigadier general in the Connecticut militia. Cleveland was the first settlement founded in the Connecticut Western Reserve by the Connecticut Land Company. The town was located along the eastern bank of the Cuyahoga River.
>
> On January 6, 1831, the *Cleveland Advertiser* discontinued use of the first letter *a* from "Cleaveland." It has been speculated that the letter was cut to save typesetting space on the newspaper's masthead. "Cleveland" without the extra *a* was adopted and is still the current spelling.
>
> Cleveland emerged as an influential industrial mecca, but the Great Depression caused great economic hardship when the oil and steel industries went bust.

colleges, and on their way to Indiana University, they passed through Kokomo, Indiana, where an African American man had been lynched the previous day (Wallace 1986). This tragedy ended any chance of Indiana University landing the two track stars from Cleveland. Jesse also requested that his father receive employment when a vacant position opened, which would take almost two years. Jesse understood it had been difficult for his father to uproot himself and his family to move to Ohio. In a sense, his father had been cut off from all he had known.

Perhaps it was the lure of remaining a home state hero and loyalties to the state of Ohio that made Jesse Owens sign with the Ohio State University Buckeyes. Ironically, Owens was not recruited by any historically Black colleges or universities (HBCUs). At this time, Black colleges did not emphasize athletics. It was not until after Jesse Owens won his gold medals in 1936 and Joe Louis became the heavyweight boxing champion in 1937 that journalists and African American coaches began to pressure their administrations for more financial support for athletics to produce more athletes to be examples for the collective African American community. Black newspapers openly debated about where Owens would continue his collegiate athletic career. Many of these newspapers wanted Owens to attend an HBCU. Some of them hoped that if Owens did not choose an HBCU that he would at least choose a predominately white institution that had a history of treating African Americans fairly well. Most of the newspapers agreed that Owens would be an asset to his choice of school. Most likely, Jesse's decision to attend Ohio State University was not only tied to athletics but also the economic hardship his family had endured.

Owens enrolled at Ohio State University during the fall of 1933. The university apparently took into account that Jesse had failed to finish high school and agreed to ignore his lack of a diploma. The opportunity was too appealing to have the greatest high school track-and-field star wear the scarlet and gray to compete for the Buckeyes. The university was well aware that Jesse had exited East Technical High School before completing all the required courses for graduation. Even without a conferred and proper high school diploma, Jesse Owens was the first person from his family to attend college.

Dave Albritton found himself in the same situation as Owens, but he had to make up coursework to graduate before he could enroll at Ohio State University. Albritton would go on to graduate in 1938 with a degree in education. He worked for the War Department in the 1940s and became the head track coach at Dayton Dunbar High School and a state representative.

# 3

# Ohio State University and Big Ten Champion

Jesse Owens's Ohio State University and Big Ten championship dream started far before he knew Ohio State University or the Big Ten existed. It was customary for him and his family on the way to and from church to talk about their hopes and dreams and what they wanted to be when they became adults. Jesse's sisters would often talk about a life of marriage, what kind of man they desired to marry, and the possibilities of where they would live with their husbands. Jesse's brothers' dreams were draped in other desires. His brothers expressed desires to independently work without any remnants of the sharecropping way of life. Some of the brothers discussed the desire to own property and farmland outright and not have to pay a boss any money or divvy up the crops at harvest time. They had seen the mounting fees associated with sharecropping that the landowner levied upon their father at the end of each harvest season and of which only the landowner seemed to keep tally (Owens and Neimark 1970, 19).

Others wanted to be building managers and not engage in the back-breaking work their parents were forced to do as a matter of survival. Jesse's dreams differed from his brothers and sisters. His desire was to go to college and obtain a college degree. This desire to attend college grew out of his overhearing conversations of white people discussing the atmosphere of the university experience. Specifically, he heard the landowner's son discussing his college experiences. Though he did not fully understand the context of college experience, he only heard that sometimes people took a train ride to reach college, and this was enough to spark his desire.

Jesse's brothers' and sisters' dreams may have been more attainable because obtaining a college degree for African Americans during the 1920s and 1930s may have seemed like a pipe dream because of segregation policies, customs, and laws practiced in the United States. Jesse's family laughed at his dream of attending college. They could not conceive that anyone in their family would attend college let alone obtain a college degree. Owens's family thought of his dream as unrealistic because, at this time, many African Americans' attendance at grade school was sporadic at best, especially during the harvest season. Many did not attend school at all, and if an education was provided for African Americans, they usually only advanced to about the eighth grade. At least 1.7 million children under 16 years of age were employed in factories and fields in 1900, more than twice the number of 30 years before (Brinkley 2003, 490). Also, in 1900, three years before W. E. B. Du Bois published the essay "The Talented Tenth," only around 156 Blacks graduated from college. Then, over the next 50 years, the number of African Americans graduating from college increased. In 1910, only 510 African Americans graduated from college, and in 1920, 1,009 African Americans graduated from college. This increase steadily grew, and in 1950, 13,108 African Americans graduated from college (Smith and Horton 1995, 619).

Many African Americans were expected to be in the blue-collar labor force, working menial labor jobs not only in the South but the northern states as well. There was an expectation that every able-bodied African American would provide labor; education was not an expectation for African Americans. However, there were African American fraternities and sororities popularizing the idea of African Americans attending college by sponsoring meetings within Black churches and other Black organizations and entities.

Jesse and his siblings were expected to work. By the 1900s, women made up 17 percent of the industrial workforce, a fourfold increase since 1870, and 20 percent of women (well over five million) were wage earners (Brinkley 2003, 490). If Jesse's family had known about the historically Black colleges and universities (HBCUs) located in Alabama, maybe this desire would not have seemed so hilarious. Apparently, they were not familiar with Alabama State University, founded in 1867 as Lincoln Normal School of Marion; Alabama A&M University, founded in 1875 as the Colored Normal School at Huntsville; Miles College, founded in 1905 as Miles Memorial College; Talladega College, founded as the Swayne School in 1867; Tuskegee University, founded in 1881 as the Tuskegee Institute; or Gadsden State Community College, founded in 1925 as the Alabama School of Trade.

Even though Jesse's family's economic status may have excluded him from attending one of these HBCUs, they seemed to not even be aware of their existence, and perhaps this factored into why he did not choose to attend an HBCU when he made his college choice. Jesse's family being ignorant to the possibilities of higher education may not have merely been a matter of ignorance but a need for immediate financial stability. African Americans had to focus on daily provisions for their families. During the Great Depression, fewer than 15 percent of Americans pursued a college degree (Baker 1986, 33). The percentage of college attendance for African Americans during this period was far less. Owens went to East Technical High School, and due to financial hardship, some family members wanted Jesse to quit school and find full-time work. Owens's mother, Emma, ended this notion, and she and Coach Riley encouraged Jesse to develop his track talents. For African Americans, experiencing and reacting to racism was an expected part of life. Though the Owens family had moved from the unconcealed racism practiced in Alabama to Cleveland, Ohio, they still experienced widespread racism.

One of the more striking court trials that received both national and international attention and made the Owens family appreciative of the life they left behind was the case of the Scottsboro Boys. In 1931, a group of nine African American teenagers were stowed away and traveling in a railroad freight train. Though it was illegal, it was a common way of travel for poor people during the 1930s. The African American young men got into a dispute with a group of whites who also had "jumped the train" for a free ride. The boys were harassed and almost forced from the train, but they were able to overpower the white male group. Once overpowered and forced from the train, the white boys accused the Black boys of attacking them and reported them to the local authorities. Two white women who got off the train also accused the young men of rape. The penalty for an African American raping a white woman was death. This could come through the legal process or vigilante justice by a white mob. With an all-white jury and white judge, all but one boy was sentenced to death. There were multiple trials and mistrials for this case. In 1935, the U.S. Supreme Court ruling in *Norris v. Alabama* overturned the Scottsboro Boys' conviction. After their prison stays, all the African American teenagers involved in this incident lived troubled lives and dealt with the aftermath of the plethora of psychological traumas from the ordeal. Clarence Norris, one of the Scottsboro Boys, authored a book titled *The Last of the Scottsboro Boys: An Autobiography*; it provides a full account of the trial.

In 1932, an unethical secret clinical study began in Tuskegee, in Macon County, Alabama. The study was initially slated to last for just 6 months; however, it lasted for 40 years. Medical doctors under the authority of the U.S. government through the U.S. Public Health Service conducted the infamous "Tuskegee Syphilis Experiment." The official name of the study was the Tuskegee Study of Untreated Syphilis in the Negro Male. The study initially involved 600 men, with 399 men having the disease and 201 who did not have the disease. The researchers did not inform the men; they were simply told that they had bad blood. In this community, the term "bad blood" was used to describe myriad ailments. In exchange for participating in the study, the men were given free medical exams, free meals, and burial insurance. The men used as test subjects were allowed to die, despite the fact that a cure had been developed and available when penicillin was developed in 1947. This infamous study lasted from 1932 to 1972.

The accounts of the Scottsboro Boys trial and later the Tuskegee Syphilis Experiment may have helped relieve any doubts or regrets the Owens family may have had about leaving Alabama and the life they once knew. The *New York Times* and the *Washington Post* broke the Tuskegee story in 1972. In 1974, a $10 million out-of-court settlement was reached. As part of this settlement, the U.S. government established a program to give lifetime medical benefits and burial services to all living participants. In 1975, wives, widows and children were added to this settlement. In 1995, the program was expanded to include health as well as medical benefits. In 1997, President Bill Clinton apologized on behalf of the United States.

Though Ohio had a history of being a place where African Americans could carve out a life, there was still racism throughout the state. Not all of the state of Ohio was open and friendly to African Americans. Although many of the institutions of higher learning in the midwestern states, such as the University of Indiana, the University of Illinois, and Ohio State University, allowed African Americans to enter their institutions, they still practiced discrimination and did not allow African Americans to live in on-campus housing nor to use the campus dining facilities. Fred Patterson was considered the first Black man to attend Ohio State in 1889. He remained there until 1892, but he did not return to complete his degree. The reasons why Patterson did not graduate from the institution are unknown (Anderson and Oates 1998).

Sherman Hamlin Guss was the first African American to graduate from Ohio State University with a bachelor's degree in liberal arts in 1892. Even with the graduation of Guss, Ohio State University had a notoriously ruinous reputation for racially prejudicial attitudes and politics (Baker 1986, 33). In 1931, Herbert Miller, a professor of sociology, was fired for allowing Black and white students to dance together on a class field trip to Wilberforce University, an all-Black institution, in 1931 (Anderson 1988).

Prior to Owens's recruitment and application process at Ohio State University, the NAACP had filed a suit against the university for not permitting Doris Weaver, a light-skinned female coed, and Wilhelmina Styles, a brown-skinned coed to live in the on campus residence hall. Both students had enrolled in a mandatory course for their home economics major. This major required a one-quarter residency at the Grace Graham Walker House, an all-white women's dormitory. Admitting Styles and Weaver would have resulted in the integration of the residential hall, an act prohibited by the university's policy against racial intermingling. Implementation of this policy had an adverse impact by prohibiting Weaver and Styles from completing the requirements for their undergraduate degrees in home economics. Ruth Lindquist, the chair of Ohio State University's Department of Home Economics, stated, "The time is not ripe for colored and white students to be so intimately associated" (Steward 2014).

The university claimed the Black students presence in the dormitory might be offensive and even scare white female students. In response to the university's claim, Styles took an informal poll of her white classmates, only to discover that they welcomed her living in the residence hall; some even supported her matriculation. Nonetheless, when she presented the results to Ohio State's administration, Styles was refused for the reasons of "color and tradition." Weaver, on the other hand, was initially accepted into the Grace Graham Walker House. This is because Weaver was so light skinned that she was initially assumed to be white. Only a few days after her application had been submitted and accepted, her African American heritage was discovered. Thus, Weaver, like Styles, was also informed that she could not take the course due to the reasons of "color and tradition." But unlike Styles, Weaver, likely due to her lighter complexion, was given an opportunity to take her course in the basement of the Grace Graham Walker House and separate from the rest of her classmates.

The NAACP, though, made a fatal mistake in pursuing its case against Ohio State University. Rather than representing both Styles and Weaver for a robust case against the university, they chose to only represent Weaver, perceiving they may have a better chance of winning the case. Revealing the racism and color politics of the time, the NAACP felt that Weaver's nearly white skin might make it easier for her to win a case against Ohio State University than the darker-skinned Styles. Without the further aid of the NAACP, Styles was left with no other remedy but to substitute the Laboratory in Home Management course to obtain her degree, which she did in 1933.

But Weaver's case against Ohio State University did not help her to realize the goal of integrating the Grace Graham Walker House. Her attorneys relied heavily on Ohio statutory law and made several claims to Weaver's right to be allowed to enroll in her course alongside white female classmates in the home economics residence hall. They argued that the university's sole reason for refusing to allow Weaver to enroll in the Laboratory in Home Management course and subsequently live in the Grace Graham Walker house had been due to her race. The university never denied the allegation. Like Styles, Weaver was left with no remedy but to substitute the course and obtain her degree, which she did in 1934. Although both women struggled to be accepted as undergraduate students to obtain their degrees, Weaver attained a master of science in chemistry in June 1936, and Styles earned a master of arts in home economics in September of the same year. After completing their masters' degrees, which finally provided them with the instructional credentials they needed, both women taught in the Home Economics Department at Wilberforce University in Wilberforce, Ohio.

In February 1933, during what would have been Jesse Owens's freshman year, the Supreme Court of the State of Ohio ruled in favor of the university, but the incident merely confirmed what many Blacks already believed: Ohio State University was not an acceptable place for Jesse Owens and his kind (Pollard 1933, 309). Jesse Owens would have been fully aware of the developments of the case and the university's practices and policies when he decided to attend Ohio State because Weaver, one of the plaintiffs in the NAACP's suit, was from his hometown of Cleveland. Apparently, neither the discriminatory policy nor the pending lawsuit factored into Owens's decision to attend Ohio State University, and his choice of college was debated among all segments of society. This kind of attention for a Black high school athlete from predominately white colleges was unheard of at the time. Like the Black newspapers, many African Americans thought he should choose a historically Black college, in particular one of the HBCUs in his home state of Ohio, Wilberforce University or Central State University. However, some thought his athletic excellence should be displayed at a large and predominantly white institution to show African Americans were not inferior, athletically or intellectually.

Owens and Albritton had set their minds on attending the same college, and so they scouted colleges together. Indiana University appeared to be in the mix for Owens's athletic services, but on their way to the university, they passed through Kokomo, Indiana, where there was a buzz moving about the town because a man had been lynched the day before. This development aided in them ruling out Indiana University (Wallace 1986, 8). Albritton and Owens were close. Albritton stated, "We were synonymous. We lived, practiced, worked, and competed together" (Wallace 1986, 6). It appeared that Owens was all set to sign with the University of Michigan. It is important to note that schools did not award athletic scholarships as we currently do. They usually arranged for some kind of small employment and side benefits for scholar athletes through their alumni. Jesse stated that his signing was contingent on his father gaining employment. Members of the University of Michigan Detroit Alumni group were all set to secure the athletic services of Owens, but his father believed the salary was not high enough; the group subsequently withdrew their offer.

Perhaps Jesse chose Ohio State University because he was a new father and his girlfriend and new baby were in Columbus, Ohio, which was 145 miles away from Cleveland. Perhaps Owens made Ohio State his college choice because Riley approved of the coaching of Larry Snyder, the university's track-and-field coach. Perhaps the decision was made simply because the track-and-field program at Ohio State was a national juggernaut. Or maybe he signed because Ohio State agreed to provide his father with a job as a janitor.

Though Ohio State recruited African American athletes, racism was pervasive in its athletic department. William Bell was the first Black varsity football player in the 1930s. Bell suffered at the hands of both his teammates and opponents each game, when they used their metal cleats on his legs, leaving them bloody during each game.

Owens felt the sting of racism at Ohio State, where there were still vestiges of these policies. The university was slow to change. Owens seemed to go with the flow, never allowing these racist practices to bother him or outwardly showing any emotion or reaction to the racism at the university. Many African Americans referred to Ohio State as "a cracker town" (Schulte 1986, 8C).

In 1934, there were 15,000 students enrolled at Ohio State University, and of those, only about 100 were African American. Classes were large and impersonal, and this probably contributed to Jesse's and many other first-generation students' academic struggles as undergraduates. Jesse could not live on campus. There were very few places African Americans could live in Columbus at this time. Coach Snyder did not subscribe to or even like this practice of housing segregation. He and his fellow members of the Alpha Phi Alpha Fraternity, along with other African American students, rented rooms at a boarding house in Columbus while they were student athletes at Ohio State. Owens, Melvin Walker, and Dave Albritton lived in a rooming house. Albritton was Owens's closest friend on the team. They had attended East Technical High School together, and their families were both from Alabama. Albritton once noted, "We did everything together. We even dated two sisters and he married Ruth" (Wallace 1986, 6).

When the track-and-field team traveled through southern and other midwestern states for competitions, Owens and his fellow African American team members had to sometimes eat their meals on the bus while their white teammates and coaches were served inside the eating establishments because restaurants discriminated against African Americans. It is not understood whether Owens was truly bothered by this discrimination or chose to distance himself from his true feelings to protect himself from the hurt of being discriminated against; he rarely talked about the prejudice he experienced. At a track meet in Milwaukee, the team booked rooms at the Pfister Hotel because it allowed African Americans to stay there; however, it would not allow them to eat meals at the facility, so Owens and Albritton ate in their rooms. This was the same practice taking place in Columbus, Ohio. Charlie Beetham, a teammate of Owens who would later coach the cross-country team, noted that Owens and his roommates and other African American students were not allowed to eat at any of the restaurants outside of campus (*Lantern* 1986).

In the presidential election of 1932, African Americans were enamored with Franklin D. Roosevelt and switched their political support to vote for him. African Americans were largely drawn to Roosevelt because race relations had stalled under the previous two presidents. They also sympathized after discovering Roosevelt had polio and could not walk and that he had to overcome this adversity. They also thought this would help him be more sympathetic to their plight in society. A shrewd politician, Roosevelt knew he needed the support of southern Democrats to get his agenda passed, so he did not push for a federal anti-lynching law or attempt to ban the use of poll taxes to discriminate against African Americans in voting. Roosevelt also appointed African Americans to positions within his administration and increased the number of African Americans working in the federal government. He also used African Americans as special advisers, known as the Black Cabinet or the Black Brain Trust. Also, Roosevelt's wife was close friends with Mary McLeod Bethune, the founder of Bethune Cookman University, a historically Black college located in Daytona, Florida.

In March 1933, Franklin D. Roosevelt was inaugurated as the 32nd president of the United States. During his campaign, he had promised Americans a new deal and promised to get people back to work. He stated he would attack the Great Depression like he was fighting a war and demanded emergency powers from Congress. Through legislation, he tackled unemployment by providing public sector jobs through the Civil Works Administration (CWA) and its successor, the Works Progress Administration (WPA). Even with the jobs provided through these programs, unemployment remained high. Roosevelt's administration was revolutionary in its action. The level of expending by the federal government and the degree of federal involvement in business affairs were unprecedented.

In May 1933, the Federal Emergency Relief Administration provided funds for municipal governments to help provide relief programs for the unemployed. The biggest public enterprise was setting up the Tennessee Valley Authority (TVA). This put hydroelectric energy and other resources of a vast area that included seven states under public control. Under this project, dams, power plants, and power transmission lines were constructed using public services and funding. These were constructed to bring relief to impoverished areas, in particular to Alabama, Georgia, Tennessee, Kentucky, and South Carolina. This advancement helped provide power to farms and rural townships. Critics of the Roosevelt administration denounced these advancements as too much government intervention and called these actions communist.

In November 1933, the CWA provided jobs for men in projects such as road repair and parks improvement. White men were usually the first choice in filling these government jobs. Unemployment rates soared among African Americans during the Great Depression. According to Cheryl Lynn Greenberg, in her book *To Ask for an Equal Chance: African Americans in the Great Depression*, "unemployment rates in the South were double or even triple that of the white population and in northern cities, approximately 25 percent of white workers were unemployed in 1932. By the 1940s, African Americans would come to believe the New Deal's recovery programs would help them out of poverty along with poor whites while assisting African Americans to gain acceptance for political and civil rights" (Lawson 1997, 10). Roosevelt's New Deal programs provided some economic relief for African Americans, but they were still discriminated against when these programs were implemented, especially in southern states.

While the United States was dealing with domestic issues, Germany was being taking over by an authoritarian regime that would eventually lead to a world war, and Jesse Owens continued to dominate in collegiate track and field. Later, Owens would famously note that Roosevelt did not invite him to the White House after winning four gold medals.

While in college, Owens was employed as a gas station attendant, in the campus library, and as a freight elevator operator at the Ohio Statehouse. These were all common forms of employment for undergraduate students at the time but were most likely given to Owens because he was a star athlete. Owens worked the freight elevator located in the rear of the building, whereas many of the white students worked the elevator with passengers. Owens would have been one of 20 students in 1935 working as a page that summer. His salary would have been $21 a week. In 1935, $21 a week would be equivalent to about $385 dollars in 2019. There were also questionable and possibly illegal payments and benefits during some of his summer employment. Apparently, Owens was paid for work during a pay period when he was not even in the state of Ohio at the time. Also, Jesse's sister had received a job working for the governor's executive secretary, which may also be viewed as an extra benefit given to a student athlete.

Jesse held several jobs while he was a student athlete. He had become a father. The birth of his daughter, Gloria Shirley, facilitated another need for financial assistance. Shortly after Gloria's birth, Ruth's parents were

---

## ALPHA PHI ALPHA FRATERNITY, INC.

Alpha Phi Alpha was the first intercollegiate Greek-letter fraternity established for African American men. The fraternity was founded by seven college men at Cornell University in Ithaca, New York, on December 4, 1906. The seven fraternity founders—Henry Arthur Callis, Charles Henry Chapman, Eugene Kinckle Jones, George Biddle Kelley, Nathaniel Allison Murray, Robert Harold Ogle, and Vertner Woodson Tandy—are known as the "Jewels" of the fraternity. They recognized the need for a strong bond of brotherhood among African descendants in the United States. The fraternity initially began as a study and support group for minority students who faced racial prejudice, both educationally and socially, at Cornell University.

Between 1929 through 1932, three of the four fastest runners and top sprinters in the world were members of Alpha Phi Alpha. Jesse Owens was initiated into Alpha Phi Alpha in 1935 at the Kappa Chapter of the fraternity at Ohio State University. Owens became the winner of four gold medals at the 1936 Summer Olympics. Eddie Tolan was initiated into Alpha Phi Alpha in 1929 at the Epsilon Chapter at Michigan University. Ralph Metcalfe was initiated into Alpha Phi Alpha at the Alpha Xi Chapter at Marquette University.

Alpha Phi Alpha's core values rest on the principles of scholarship, fellowship, good character, and the uplifting of humanity. It is headquartered in Baltimore, Maryland.

---

furious with Jesse and refused to allow him to visit Ruth or the newborn. Ruth gained employment at a local beauty parlor in Cleveland and continued to live with her parents. Ruth's parents would later relent and allowed Jesse to see Ruth and Gloria. Monthly, Jesse sent money to Ruth and to his mother while he was a student at Ohio State. Ruth's parents were the primary caregivers for Jesse and Ruth's child.

At Ohio State, Owens and Coach Larry Snyder developed a close relationship, much like the relationship Owens had with Coach Riley in high school. Snyder began his tenure as Ohio States' track-and-field coach in 1934. He was a young man, only about 10 years older than Owens, and had been the captain of the Buckeyes track-and-field squad for two years before getting into coaching. The two coaches were similar because they quickly saw Owens's athletic talent and took a keen interest in his well-being, but the two were also starkly dissimilar in many ways. The first day, Snyder knew he had a special athlete. Owens was dressed impeccably and neatly in his Ohio State University uniform. Snyder gave Owens a once over, admiring his physique, specifically Owens's powerful legs. The two had an instant bond and partnership.

Coach Snyder knew Owens was a special talent but believed he had developed some bad track habits. In the sprints, Snyder believed Owens ran with weak arm motion and had a slow start because he needed to crouch in his starting stance more. In the long jump, Snyder believed Jesse should cycle his legs during his jump to gain more length on his jump. Snyder used unconventional methods of training the sprinters on the track squad. He played upbeat music over the loudspeakers at the stadium while the athletes ran to the rhythm of the music. He believed this helped his sprinters to find a running rhythm more quickly.

Owens continued to compete as a stellar athlete at Ohio State but slumped in his performances at times. He competed in a few junior varsity meets in 1934 and lost to Ralph Metcalfe, from Marquette University, on two occasions. In 1934, there were three African American members of the Ohio State University track-and-field squad: Owens, fellow underclassman high jumper Mel Walker, and sprinter Fred Thomas, who was an upperclassman. Owens was also struggling academically and was placed on academic probation because of his grades.

Coach Snyder used Owens as a public relations pitch man to promote Ohio States' track-and-field program. Snyder arranged for Owens to speak to local civic and social organizations in the Columbus area. Jesse's first speeches were unrefined and unsophisticated, but he soon became a smooth pitch man and Ohio State University's ambassador. Owens received $50 for each of the speech outings. Snyder knew that Owens's

---

### RALPH H. METCALFE

Ralph H. Metcalfe was known as one of the greatest track athletes in the world during the 1930s. While Jesse Owens received more notoriety than Metcalfe, many sports historians believe Ralph Metcalfe was, by far, a better athlete and sprinter than Owens. The height of Metcalfe's athletic feats occurred between the 1932 and 1936 Olympic Games. He won the sprints at the AAU and NCAA for three consecutive years between 1932 and 1934. Metcalfe also won the AAU 200 meters in 1935 and 1936 to give him a record five consecutive wins in this event. Metcalfe also earned a bronze medal in the 200 meters at the 1932 Olympic Games.

After his athletic career, Metcalfe moved into politics. He found success on the local and national political stages. He first served on the city council for many years, and then in 1970, Metcalfe was elected to the U.S. Congress from the 1st District in Illinois, a role he served in until his death in 1978. Metcalfe was also a cofounder of the Congressional Black Caucus in 1971.

Metcalfe was married twice. He married Gertrude Pemberton on June 9, 1937, in Dallas, Texas, and they later divorced. Metcalfe then married Madalynne Fay Young in 1947, and they had one son together. Metcalfe died an apparent heart attack at age 68 in Chicago, Illinois, on October 10, 1978.

great athletic ability and his public relations plan would put the university's track-and-field program on the map. This would serve as a training ground for much of Jesse's work later in life. In 1933, Owens was selected to the All-American track-and-field team. In 1935, he had outperformed many of his peers in several meets all across the country. While on a West Coast trip in California, Jesse competed in multiple events and placed first in each event. Within the span of two weeks, he had competed in 10 events and won all of them.

The most exceptional day of Jesse's collegiate athletic career occurred in 1935 at the Big Ten Conference track-and-field championship meet held at Ferry Field at the University of Michigan in Ann Arbor, Michigan. Owens had been playing around at the boarding house and fell and injured his back. Many thought he was too injured to compete at the track-and-field meet. Jesse went through therapeutic treatments, including stretching and hot baths. The team's athletic training staff gave him massages to loosen up his back, but nothing fully eliminated the pain. Snyder was visibly worried and wondered how well his team would do if Owens could not participate. In fact, Coach Snyder deliberated holding Owens out of the meet because he did not want him to jeopardize his athletic career due to the possibility of aggravating his injury. By this point, Snyder and Owens could tell what the other was thinking without speaking a word. Snyder knew Owens were in a great deal of pain. After conferring with Owens, and Owens reaffirming that he wanted to compete, Snyder relented and allowed Owens to compete in all of his usual events. Owens was in so much pain, he could not lift his sweatshirt over his head without assistance.

---

### Coach Lawrence "Larry" Snyder

Coach Lawrence "Larry" Snyder was born August 9, 1896, in Canton, Ohio. He was a track-and-field coach and a military veteran. Snyder had two tenures as the track-and-field coach at Ohio State University, from 1932 to 1942 and from 1946 to 1965. At Ohio State, Snyder developed some unorthodox training methods for his athletes. He had them run to music played on a phonograph. Snyder believed that training to music allowed athletes to get in a better rhythm. He also served as president of the track coaches association from 1940 to 1941. He was an assistant coach of the 1952 Olympic track-and-field team, and in 1960, he became head coach. In 1965, he retired from coaching.

Larry Snyder died on September 25, 1982. During his coaching career, his athletes set 14 world records and won 52 All-American honors and 8 Olympic gold medals.

At the championship meet, Owens set five world records and tied another at the Big Ten track-and-field championships. He jumped 26 feet, 8 1/4 inches. He ran the 220-yard dash in 20.3 seconds, and he won the 220 low hurdles in 22.6 seconds for a new record. He also equaled a world record in the 100-yard dash with a time of 9.4 seconds (Corrigan 2003, 13). After the meet, Owens was in excruciating pain, so much so that his fraternity brothers had to carry him up the stairs to his room.

Jesse was the first athlete to break that many records in one day. He had also broken the Ohio State University record for points amassed in a track season. He had overtaken the record that Snyder had accumulated as a collegiate athlete. Owens was also named the captain of the track-and-field team. He was the first African American to earn this honor in the Big Ten Athletic Conference in any sport. All the other Big Ten coaches were envious of Snyder and his star athlete.

Owens's athletic feats had become so legendary that he was even a media darling in college, before the 1936 Olympics. He was on the front page of most of the major news outlets, especially when Ohio State was the runner-up in the national track-and-field championship when Owens scored 40 of the team's 40.5 points at the meet. He became a fixture on the newsreels and became a source of pride for the Buckeye state. Thousands of people flocked to watch track meets when Owens competed. College track meets from the East Coast and West Coast became the popular places to be. When asked about his exploits at the meet in Ann Arbor in 1935, Owens told people he had run faster and laid claim to the notion that he could run 9.3 in the 100-yard dash. Owens continued to develop as a 5-feet, 11-inch and 164-pound collegiate track-and-field titan with long legs and a short torso. Over his collegiate career, Owens sometimes vacillated between being confident and being cocky. He often made very braggadocios statements to his coaches and teammates but controlled these statements with the media.

Owens had become somewhat of a celebrity even before his exploits at the 1936 Olympics. He began to meet Hollywood stars and members of the Black wealthy class. Because of his extensive travel for track meets, he met movie stars such as Lincoln Perry, better known as Stepin Fetchit; Bill "Bojangles" Robinson; and Will Rogers. He also met other members of the African American wealthy and African American elite. This kind of celebrity was unprecedented for an African American collegiate athlete, especially during the 1930s. He was covered by essentially all the African American newspapers and a number of white newspapers. His celebrity was at such a zenith that Owens was even covered by *Time Magazine*, and it rarely featured African Americans in its magazine.

Owens was a disciplined athlete with a phenomenal work ethic. The discipline displayed in track and field did not translate to his personal life.

While he was in a relationship with Ruth and away at college, Owens became romantically involved with Quincella Nickerson. Nickerson's father was a real estate and insurance executive. She came from a higher socioeconomic status than Owens. Her family was a part of the African American wealthy elite, and this must have appealed to Owens, having grown up in extreme poverty; it was difficult to fight off this temptation. It appears Owens became enamored with Quincella and her family's lifestyle, and from time to time the two were photographed in public. It was also reported that Owens had proposed to Nickerson (Schaap 2007, 45). When rumblings of Owens's philandering became public (Schaap 2007, 39–40), Owens downplayed the romance by stating Nickerson asked to see his fraternity pin and mistakenly kept it; when he went to retrieve his pin before he headed back east, she was a little upset (Schaap 2007, 47).

Ruth was white-hot with anger to see the father of her child and the man she thought she was in an exclusive relationship with another woman. She wrote a seething letter to Jesse, who was at a track meet in California. Ruth's letter had a few choice words for him. She threatened to sue him for not fulfilling his promise to marry her, but she would give him one final chance to clear all these stories up. Jesse tried to calm Ruth, but the issue continued to escalate. He knew he was wrong. He realized that he had embarrassed Ruth and broken her heart. The next morning, a writer from a Cleveland newspaper threatened to publish a photograph of Ruth and his baby in the newspaper (Schaap 2007, 39–40). Owens was distressed, and these developments affected him mentally and his athletic performance. At a track meet at the University of Nebraska, he finished third in the 100-yard dash behind Eulace Peacock and Ralph Metcalfe.

One of Jesse Owens's top rivals was Eulace Peacock. Peacock and Owens developed a rivalry in the year before Owens's historic Olympics in Berlin. In 1935, the year before Owens would win four gold medals, Peacock defeated Owens in 7 of their 10 head-to-head competitions. Because Peacock tore his hamstring muscle prior to the tryouts, he never made that Olympic team. Peacock and Owens had many similarities in their lives. Each was born in Alabama. Like Owens, Peacock was a son of sharecroppers who migrated north around the same time in search of better economic opportunity and a better life. While Owens's family moved to Ohio, Peacock's family moved to New Jersey.

Eulace Peacock was born in Dothan, Alabama, on August 27, 1914, and attended college in Philadelphia at Temple University. Peacock was an outstanding athlete. He became a gifted long jumper, pentathlete, and football player who went on to run track at Temple. In 1933, at Union High School, he set a New Jersey scholastic long jump record of 24 feet, 4 1/4 inches that stood until 1977. Owens's other rival was Ralph H. Metcalfe, who was known as one of the greatest track athletes in the world during the 1930s. While Jesse Owens received more notoriety than Metcalfe, Ralph Metcalfe was a better athlete and sprinter than Owens, according to many sports historians. The height of Metcalfe's athletic feats occurred between the 1932 and 1936 Olympic Games. He won the sprints at Amateur Athletic Union (AAU) and National Collegiate Athletic Association (NCAA) meets for three consecutive years between 1932 and 1934. Metcalfe also won the AAU 200 meters in 1935 and 1936 to give him a record of five consecutive wins in this event. After his athletic career, Metcalfe moved into politics. He found success on the local and national political stage. He first served on the city council for many years and then, in 1970, Metcalfe was elected to the U.S. Congress from the 1st District in Illinois, a role which he served until his death in 1978.

Peacock also beat Owens in the long jump at the meet in Nebraska. He performed poorly at this track-and-field meet, probably due to being overused at previous meets and the stress of Ruth's anger and the newspaper reporter's potential blackmail. He could not focus on running. He even botched two starts by jumping the starting gun, an infraction Owens rarely committed. After this mental anguish and athletic failure, Owens finally decided to settle down. He returned home from a meet, and Ruth did not meet him at the train station, which was uncustomary. After searching all the usual spots where Ruth spent time, he finally found her and declared, "We are getting married tonight!" (Schaap 2007, 50). Jesse and Ruth got a marriage license and petitioned the court to waive the five-day waiting period. They were married on July 5, 1935. After the wedding, Owens's slump continued over the next two weeks; he lost five straight times to Eulace Peacock in the 100-yard dash. Despite this apparent issue of infidelity while they were unmarried, Jesse and Ruth remained married until his death in 1980.

# 4

## Spiritual Life and Religion

Jesse Owens was described by many people as a deeply spiritual and Christian man. He indeed grew up in a deeply religious family who regularly attended church services. They were devout Baptists and members of the Oakville Missionary Baptist Church. Spirituality is the quality of being concerned with the human spirit or soul as opposed to material or physical things. Religion is viewed in the field of sociology as a set of beliefs and practices focused on the sacred or supernatural, through which life experiences of groups and individuals are given meaning and direction. Religion, particularly Christianity, has played an integral role in the history of African Americans in the United States, and it was important to the Owens family. They memorized and recited Bible verses as a family, and they walked about approximately nine miles to attend church. Though Jesse would maintain his spirituality and his belief in God throughout the rest of his life, he did not regularly attend church services.

With Jesse Owens, religion was an important part of his younger years. In some of his writings and public speeches, Owens noted that one of his favorite biblical scriptures was from Matthew 16:26: "What profit a man to gain the whole world and lose his soul" (Owens and Neimark 1978). In some sense, one could say that Jesse Owens gained the world and was in a continuous fight to maintain his soul throughout his entire life. It could be interpreted that Owens's myriad childhood illnesses and maladies helped him gained a spiritual relationship and a deeper understanding of God. This spiritual relationship was reinforced by frequently hearing his mother and father praying together and sometimes individually. This simple act of witnessing his parents pray also assisted in deepening his faith.

As a child, Owens began to consistently engage in prayer on his own. (Owens and Neimark 1978, 10). These prayers often centered on asking God to relieve his family from their deeply poverty-stricken status; however, his prayer did not consist of him praying that his family would become wealthy, rather for them to be able to have their basic needs met. Around the holidays, he prayed to have meat for holiday meals. In one instance, a young Jesse Owens prayed that his family would have some meat for a Christmas meal and a Christmas tree. When Jesse Owens and his siblings woke up on Christmas morning, they were disappointed because their parents could not provide the things he had so feverishly prayed for. In times past, Henry and Emma Owens had always managed to work a miracle and provide a modest Christmas holiday celebration and a gift or two on their children's birthdays, but not on this occasion. On another occasion, Jesse recalled hearing his father pray to God to heal young Jesse, who was battling through one of his serious illnesses and was hemorrhaging. He heard his father pleading to not let him die. Henry believed that Jesse's death would be so devastating that Emma would not be able to overcome the loss. Even with this crippling poverty, the Owens family's faith and their membership in their local church remained intact.

The term "Black Church" can be used to encompass both the historic Black denominations and the predominantly Black congregations housed in white denominations (Lincoln and Mamiya 1990, 411). The term is an uncomplicated way of discussing the pluralistic collection of religious institutions, including the seven independent Black denominations: the African Methodist Episcopal Church; the African Methodist Episcopal Zion Church; the Christian Methodist Episcopal Church; the National Baptist Convention of America, Incorporated; the National Baptist Convention, Unincorporated; the Progressive National Baptist Convention; and the Church of God in Christ. These denominations account for about 80 percent of all African American Christians.

In 1960, in an appearance on NBC's *Meet the Press*, Dr. Martin Luther King Jr. stated, "The most segregated hour in America is 11:00 am on Sunday mornings." Indeed, many of the United States' mainstream and traditional religious denominations have maintained segregated congregations for the most part. During the practice of the African slave trade in the United States, European slave traders rationalized that slavery was a "holy cause" because it introduced Africans, who they considered to be heathens, to Christianity. Many used the conversion of Africans to Christianity as a means to control the enslaved Africans' minds and behavior as one of the methods of gaining obedience and submitting to slavery. This psychological control of the minds of enslaved Africans accompanied physical segregation. Segregation was used to construct ideas of absolute racial difference and white superiority and Black inferiority. Locating Black and white bodies in different spaces was central to this process of control (Smith 2006, 50).

After the American Civil War, northern and southern churches were divided over the issue of slavery. The issue of slavery was so contentious in churches that many denominations separated over the issue. Many churches wanted to uphold the southern way of life, which meant preserving the institution of slavery and the oppression of Black people. Three major denominations, Baptist, Methodist, and Presbyterian, were not able to reconcile after the American Civil War because of lingering bitterness and resentment caused by opposing sides at the conclusion of the war. Specifically, many people in white southern churches continued to believe the notion that Black people were subservient to whites in the name of God, and their behaviors reflected these sentiments. For the most part, former Black slaves did not find any solace in the confines of the white church nor any sympathy within their white-dominated congregations. Former slaves appeared to migrate toward the Baptist and Methodist denominations because of the emergence of African American preachers, and the denominations appeared to incorporate some of their African practices into their worship and faith.

The African Methodist Episcopal Church and the African Methodist Episcopal Zion Church were organized by northern freedmen in 1787 and 1821, respectively (Lincoln and Mamiya 1990, 73). The African Methodist Episcopal Church grew out of the Free African Society, which was established by Richard Allen, Absalom Jones, and other free Black people in Philadelphia. Black churches were integral in helping build communities and develop leadership among the freed Black men in southern states. These churches were also foundational in building Black higher education. For colleges such as Morehouse, Howard, and Spelman, though operated by white organizations, their first facilities were Black churches, which were the training grounds for the training of Black ministers and missionaries (Lincoln and Mamiya 1990, 41–43).

Jesse Owens's family was affiliated with the Baptist denomination. Black Baptists were first governed by white Baptist churches and their national governing body. In 1845, northern Baptists and southern Baptists split over the issue of slavery. Southern Baptists supported slavery, and northern Baptists wanted to sever ties with the immoral practice. Two of the earliest all-Black Baptist associations began in Ohio with the formation of the Providence Association in 1834 and the Union Association in Ohio in 1836, and they assumed a strong anti-slavery position (Lincoln and Mamiya 1990, 41–43). The National Baptist Convention of America was founded in 1845 and became the most dominant Baptist governing body, but infighting persisted. In 1915, the National Baptist Convention presented nearly 3 million Black people in over 20,000 local Baptist churches (Lincoln and Mamiya 1990, 41–43). The convention was founded in 1895.

During the 1920s and 1930s, many African American preachers were preaching a conservative message focused on what was considered Christian behavior in the African American community. African American preachers of this era railed against the dangers of using alcohol, focusing on materialism, listening to jazz and blues music, maintaining morality, and sexual abstinence. They promoted wholesome forms of amusement, such as sober dancing and sensible amusement. Black clergy recognized there was a market for sermons on vinyl records. These Black clergy boomed as the Great Migration moved African Americans to their new urban cities in the North, but they missed the sermons of the South. The missed the call-and-response style of rural churches of the South that they had grown up with and were accustomed to. The call-and-response method of worship was steeped in the evangelical worship. The congregation engaged the preacher and responded back to the content of a sermon with shouts of "Amen," "Hallelujah," or "Preach, brother." These Black preachers wanted to make sure that as African Americans were leaving southern states, they were not leaving their faith in their new surroundings. At this time, most African Americans did not have radios, but many had phonographs because this machine did not need electricity to operate. They could play vinyl records on their phonographs. By the end of World War II, phonograph preachers waned because radios and electricity had become more common in the homes of many African Americans.

While conservative preaching may have dominated some of the early Black Church during the 1920s and 1930s, there were some sermons that addressed the conditions of African Americans in the United States. This would become a mainstay of Black preaching during the 1940s through 1960s, especially with the development of Black liberation theology. This theology relates religious faith to action by aiding and encouraging poor and oppressed people by becoming involved in politics and public policy. Those who subscribe to this theology believe God is concerned with the plight of poor people. This theology aspires to make the gospel relevant and to relate it to the struggles of African Americans. It nurtures self-respect and self-esteem in the African American community and displays that there is not a dichotomy between Christianity and being an African American; moreover, it shows a paradox of Christianity as this religion is practiced in the United States.

The Black Church also reflected the Great Migration of African Americans who left the South and relocated to the North. Black churches shift from rural to urban churches, with urban churches experiencing rapid growth. National Baptist Conventional became the more conservative wing of the African American Baptist, but they were not as conservative as the white Southern Baptists. Later, a more progressive wing of Black Baptists would form during the 1960s. The Progressive National Baptist Convention was founded in 1961 when some pastors challenged the president of the convention over voting procedures in the convention's meeting. The more progressive ministers, such as Martin Luther King Sr., Martin Luther King Jr., and Benjamin E. Mays, were committed to social change and social justice. After the split within the convention, both groups claimed to be the rightful governing body of Black Baptist churches. After which, Baptist denominations assumed loose-knit affiliations with autonomy. Even with their progressive stance on civil and human rights, women were largely left out of leadership of the Black Baptist Church, which directed them to lay positions within local churches.

There were two styles of preaching that were consistent during the days of the early Black Church. Some Black churches and preachers from the period after the Civil War up until World War I were exceptionally accommodating to white supremacy. In turn, they taught a submissive type of theology where their members were to be subordinate to white people and preserve their second-class status in society. White ministers, slave owners, and subordinate Black preachers wrongly taught slaves that it was in God's will for them to be enslaved. To justify this erroneous teaching, they used false interpretations of Genesis 9:20–27, which became known as the curse of Ham. The preachers' sermons were an extension of white racist ideology. The Black preacher under this structure was easily controlled, and if he did not adhere to the control of whites, he could be intimidated through terroristic threats or violence. More than likely, these are the kinds of conservative sermons the Owens family might have been exposed in rural Alabama. Being exposed to conservative messages may be a plausible explanation for why Jesse Owens rarely spoke about race relations for most part of his life and was not an active participate in the civil rights movement during the 1950s and 1960s.

Some of the early African American Christian denomination's preaching in the nineteenth and twentieth centuries centered on overcoming oppression and gaining equality for African Americans. Dr. Benjamin Mays, an admirer of a liberation gospel, preacher, president of Morehouse College, and mentor to Martin Luther King Jr., stated, "I never did accept what my eyes saw and what my ears heard. Everything around me said to me that I and my people were inferior. Negroes were constantly cringing and kowtowing in the presence of white people" (Gaillard 1996, 27).

During this time, the African American preacher most likely focused on liberation for Black people by using deep metaphors and telling stories of Jesus Christ, who liberated the oppressed and cared for people who were less fortunate. He used storytelling and a narrative approach to sermons

### CURSE OF HAM

False teachings about the curse of Ham have been used as divine justification for racism and the enslavement of African people. The belief is based on an Old Testament accounting of a curse Noah placed on one of his sons, which is referenced in Genesis 9:18–27. It is believed that Noah placed a curse on one of his sons that resulted in his skin becoming dark, and thus his descendants' skin was also dark.

Some biblical scholars believed African nations were largely Hamitic because Canaan's descendants were thought to have lived in what is modern-day Ethiopia. Ergo, dark-skinned people had their origins in Ham, and according to this logic, Black people were cursed to be slaves. This racist theory was quite prevalent through the eighteenth and nineteenth centuries and was even perpetuated after the abolishment of slavery. Although slavery was no longer the practice of the day, white ministers continued to preach about the lowly status of Blacks as being ordained by God and reinforced through speeches. White Christians used the curse of Ham during the fight against integration during the 1950s and 1960s, though modern biblical scholars have debunked it.

by invoking faith stories rooted in liberation stories and overcoming dire circumstances through God's Providence, such as Moses leading the children of Israel to the promised land, David defeating the giant named Goliath, and Joseph overcoming his brothers' devious plot to destroy him. Old Testament biblical stories such as these helped African Americans to anchor their core beliefs in Christianity and see possibilities and prospects of a better life. Moreover, these faith stories aided African American Christians in seeing the possibilities of an unfolding triumph that African Americans would gain full equality. These stories provided them with hope amid their extreme poverty and tragedy. This narrative and storytelling approach, as opposed to expository method of preaching, was mostly utilized because of the low literacy rates among African Americans at the time and the low number of Black preachers receiving formal seminary training.

It is unclear as to what type of preaching the Owens family would have been exposed to at their church in Oakville, Alabama. Being exposed to a more submissive type of theology would explain Jesse Owens's passivity on race issues during most of his public life. Being exposed to the progressive Black theology teachings would explain his optimistic life view and easy-going spirit. Through this lens of Owens's religion and spirituality, this submissive type of theology would explain how his faith informed his perspective and his calm reaction to the prejudice and injustices he faced in the United States. Specifically, a subservient and passive preaching at

## THE BLACK CHURCH

During the 1500s, the Portuguese landed on the shores of Africa and conquered kingdoms. They also carried Catholicism to West Africa and began to capture Africans and enslave them. It is likely that the slaves who arrived in Jamestown in 1619 had been baptized Catholic and had Christian names. For the next 200 years, the slave trade exported slaves from Angola, Ghana, Senegal, and other parts of West Africa to the southern states. The term the "Black Church" is the second iteration of the term that was developed from the "Negro Church," which sprang from noted scholar W. E. B. Du Bois's study of African American Protestant churches. While early African Americans did not think of themselves as a part of the Black Church, they did think of themselves as part of their denominational affiliations. African American Christians have never been monolithic and have been diverse since their inception, characterized by the highly decentralized nature of most African American Protestant churches.

The Black Church is widely understood to include the following seven major Black Protestant denominations: the National Baptist Convention, the National Baptist Convention of America, the Progressive National Convention, the African Methodist Episcopal Church, the African Methodist Episcopal Zion Church, the Christian Methodist Episcopal Church, and the Church of God in Christ. The Methodist and Baptist denominations both made efforts to convert enslaved Africans to Christianity.

Oakville Baptist Church would explain his nonchalant response to the ardent racism he experienced growing up in rural Alabama. This kind of passive theology would explain his conforming to the racial bigotry, on-campus policies of segregation, and double standard treatment toward African Americans he experienced as an undergraduate at Ohio State University. It would also explain his somewhat indifferent response to his treatment in finding it difficult to maintain steady employment despite being an Olympic and American hero. If passive preaching was taking place, this may have been where Owens learned deference and adopted his easygoing smile to appear nonthreatening to whites as a mode of survival (Wiggins 2006, 113). This would also explain the imagined spectrum of Blackness and the "good" and "bad" Negro (Bass 2005, 20). Whites tended to measure African American athletes and African Americans in general, labeling them "good" Negroes by how obedient, pliable, and agreeable they were with white people. By the same measure, those African Americans who were confident, unafraid, and unabatingly bold enough to think independently and who did not have accommodating views on the issue of race in the United States were called "bad" Negroes.

Around 1919, the term "New Negro" was created by young Black radicals as a method of distinguishing themselves from Black leadership that had been too accommodating to whites (Rhoden 2006, 110). This spectrum of the concept of "good" and "bad" Negroes dates back to slavery and white preachers and accommodating Black preachers spreading a false narrative of white supremacy. Successful and assertive African Americans were also deemed "uppity" and as "getting out of their place" in the social order of segregation (Martin 1998, 5). On this spectrum, Jesse Owens was somewhere in the middle but closer on the accommodating end. During several instances of his life, various white people called on Owens to quell issues dealing with race and to protect the privilege of whiteness. No matter the theology Jesse Owens experienced from the pulpit of Oakwood Missionary Baptist Church, it is certain that he experienced a style of preaching known to build to crescendo at the close of a sermon to make the congregation not only hear the sermon but feel it as well. This raised conclusion to a sermon dates back to slavery and is a mixture of cathartic and powerful celebratory shouting. It is a blend of voice inflection, rhythmic cadences, and vivid and vibrant storytelling, which are valuable tools in Black preaching. This is evident by Owens's use of this expressive muscular oratory style of the Black preacher during his public speaking engagements.

By many accounts, when Owens found himself in extremely difficult periods in his life, he returned to his faith and spirituality to help cope with these difficulties. Though there were periods of inconsistencies in adhering to the more dogmatic elements of Christianity, throughout his life, Owens used spirituality and his religious roots as his chosen method to overcome adversity and tragedy. In 1978, Owens and Paul Neimark coauthored a book titled *Jesse: A Spiritual Autobiography*, in which Owens recounts his life through the lens and language of his faith. In this work, Owens discusses prayer and recounts his personal prayers. He also discusses the prayers of others in his family. In this work, Owens describes how he would lean and depend on his faith to face hardships: "I was brought up with a belief in God and the teachings of Jesus, His word, to have His spirit to believe to know that if we struggled to the utmost and climbed the highest mountains within ourselves that above the final summit he will be there" (Owens and Neimark 1978, 55).

One stressful instance in particular that Owens recalls in his book was when his cleaning business went bankrupt. He states that God brought particular biblical scriptures to his mind. These scriptures were constantly on his mind and provided comfort and confidence to be content, no matter the outcome of the bankruptcy. According to his spiritual autobiography, the scripture was a passage from Ecclesiastes 1:2 (Owens and Neimark 1978, 86). This passage from Ecclesiastes reads,

The words of the Preacher, the son of David, king in Jerusalem. Vanity of vanities, saith the Preacher, vanity of vanities; all is vanity. What profit hath a man of all his labor which he taketh under the sun? One generation passeth away, and another generation cometh: but the earth abideth forever. The sun also ariseth, and the sun goeth down, and hasteth to his place where he arose.

This biblical scripture also rang out in Owens's mind because it was the scripture he often heard his father recite when he was faced with trouble. Owens seemed to interpret this scripture as an overemphasis on materialism and trivial aspects of life that mean so little or the overvaluing of material possessions.

For Owens, religion and spirituality were important to him, and indeed his Olympic victories that were to come later in his life would create another "black messiah," as Frederick Douglass was before Owens and the Reverend Dr. Martin Luther King Jr. would become after Owens (Ross 2004, 162). As professor and scholar Dr. Cornel West notes in his book *Race Matters*, "Religion is a major constructive channel of black rage in America. . . . Hence the centrality of religion and music those most spiritual of human activities in black life" (West 1994, 143).

During Owens's time at Ohio State University, Coach Charles Riley would shape Owens's spirituality and behavior. During a collegiate track meet, one of Jesse's teammates used profanity in the presence of Coach Riley. Riley quickly verbally reprimanded the athlete. Riley could often be found in his office reading his Bible, and Owens took notice. And though Jesse exhibited a deep faith throughout his life, he was spiritually adrift during his years as a student athlete. His spirituality was on display again when he competed in Berlin. He recalled praying during his performances at the Olympic Games (Owens and Neimark 1978, 86–87).

During the summer of 1935, Owens's faith would be tested. He worked at a gas station in Cleveland. There were accusations that Ohio's legislature was paying Owens to do nothing when he was working as a page. Records showed Owens had been paid for work in Ohio when he was away from Columbus competing in a track meet in California. The Amateur Athletic Union (AAU) held a hearing in Cleveland to determine the status of Owens's eligibility as an amateur athlete. If it was determined that Owens was ineligible, it would end his collegiate track career and his chances of competing in the Olympics. It would be three weeks before the organization's final decision was announced in Jesse's favor. Owens was relieved. He had prevailed, and his faith had prevailed.

After his phenomenal performance at the Olympics and his inability to find gainful employment upon his return to the United States, Owens was reflective and again turned to religion and spirituality. While staying in a luxurious hotel in New York City, he haphazardly flipped through a Bible and landed on Old Testament passages from Ecclesiastes 1:2–11:

> The words of the Preacher, the son of David, king in Jerusalem. Vanity of vanities, saith the Preacher, vanity of vanities; all is vanity. What profit hath a man of all his labor which he taketh under the sun? One generation passes away, and another generation cometh: but the earth abides forever. The sun also arises, and the sun goes down, and haste to his place where he arose. The wind goes toward the south and turn about unto the north; it whirls about continually, and the wind returned again according to his circuits. All the rivers run into the sea; yet the sea is not full; unto the place from whence the rivers come, thither they return again. All things are full of labor; man cannot utter it: the eye is not satisfied with seeing, nor the ear filled with hearing. The thing that hath been, it is that which shall be; and that which is done is that which shall be done: and there is no new thing under the sun. Is there anything whereof it may be said, See, this is new? It has been already of old time, which was before us. There is no remembrance of former things; neither shall there be any remembrance of things that are to come with those that shall come after.

Evidently these passages resonated with Owens. They discuss the concepts of vanity and the utter emptiness and frustrations of life. The passage also discusses that there is no memory of former things. Perhaps these passages appealed to his sensibilities and help sooth his frustrations.

Clearly, Owens was frustrated with his status as a national hero and second-class citizen in the United States, and perhaps he wondered whether his achievements at the Olympics was all for nothing, as it did not improve his lot in life. Jesse Owens's religion and spiritual grounding were integral throughout most of his life, remaining through his time at Ohio State University, the Olympic Games, and beyond. As Owens emerged as a sought-out speaker by mostly conservative audiences, the topic of Christianity was one of the recurring themes in his speeches.

# 5

## Race, Politics, and Adolf Hitler

Since the arrival of the first 20 Africans to the shores of the Virginia Colony on the land that would become the United States in 1619, the dilemma of race has been a contentious matter for the country and has produced a paradox for African Americans in the United States. This paradox forced many African Americans to be in a perpetual state of attempting to prove their intellectual prowess and self-worth. W. E. B. Du Bois described this concept as a "two-ness" or double-consciousness. Du Bois specifically described it as follows:

> It is a peculiar sensation, this double-consciousness, this sense of always looking at one's self through the eyes of others, of measuring one's soul by the tape of a world that looks on in amused contempt and pity. One ever feels his two-ness, an American, a Negro; two souls, two thoughts, two unreconciled strivings; two warring ideals in one dark body, whose dogged strength alone keeps it from being torn asunder. The history of the American Negro is the history of this strife—this longing to attain self-conscious manhood, to merge his double self into a better and truer self. In this merging he wishes neither of the older selves to be lost. He does not wish to Africanize America, for America has too much to teach the world and Africa. He wouldn't bleach his Negro blood in a flood of white Americanism, for he knows that Negro blood has a message for the world. He simply wishes to make it possible for a man to be both a Negro and an American without being cursed and spit upon by his fellows, without having the doors of opportunity closed roughly in his face. (Du Bois 2016 [1903] 2–3)

Jesse Owens was constantly faced with this two-ness, and this would come to the fore as he made the Olympic track-and-field team and competed with the backdrop of racism, ethnic cleansing, and Nazi Germany.

Racism is a concept that is difficult to define with a measure of exactness. African Americans have dealt with racism, stereotypes, and myths, especially in regard to their intellectual and athletic abilities in the world of sports. White supremacy and the ideas associated with this mindset have been used to justify racism in the United States. Although white supremacy and racism are not strictly American phenomena, in the United States, white supremacist thought has been justified and used in politics to guide public policy since the beginnings of the country.

Stereotypes of race issues have been prevalent in American sports. They served as the backdrop to American collegiate sports as Owens entered college and would be a constant of the 1936 Olympic Games. The contemporary world is filled with stereotypical images of African American athletes. It has been erroneously thought that Black athletes are born with natural athletic ability. There have been sportscasters that have described a Black athlete as "a natural," as if to intimate that the athlete is free from thinking and this athletic ability or talent has been rendered from some cosmic force or by nature, while white athletes are generally described as "crafty," "cagey," and "smart." American sports and African American athleticism have also become a part of collective sport folklore; the physical feats of Black athletes have become metaphors for what African Americans might do to level the playing fields in other aspects of society. This was especially on display at the 1936 Summer Olympics when Jesse Owens, the other African American athletes, and the collective African American community supported and celebrated every Olympic event in which an African American athlete competed.

Initially, Jesse was hesitant about participating in the Olympic Games. There were calls for athletes to protest the games because of the treatment of Jews in Germany and African Americans in the United States. However, many African American newspapers opposed a boycott of the 1936 Olympics. Black journalists often underscored the hypocrisy of pro-boycotters who did not first address the problem of discrimination against Black athletes in the United States. An alternative to the Olympic Games was being planned for Barcelona, Spain, but it was canceled with the outbreak of the Spanish Civil War of 1936.

African American athletes were viewed as heroes to the Black community. Through sports, Jesse and all African American athletes could display their abilities and the possibility of achievement if provided with an equal playing field.

Some African Americans resented the portrayal of African American athletes as the reigning symbol of success and even genius in the African

## THE BLACK EAGLES AND THE BLACK AUXILIARY

In the 1936 Olympic Games in Nazi Germany, 359 U.S. Olympic athletes competed in 21 sports. Among these athletes, 18 were African Americans. The Nazi press referred to these athletes as the "Black Auxiliary." Reporters of the *Pittsburgh Courier*, an influential African American newspaper, dubbed the 18 athletes the "Black Eagles." The Black Eagles consisted of 16 men and 2 women.

While Jesse Owens got most of the headlines after his performances in Berlin, the other African American athletes held their own as well. In all, the United State won 24 gold medals, with the 18 African Americans winning 14 medals; 8 of those were gold medals. The entire U.S. Olympic squad came in second in the medal counts; the Black Eagles won more medals than all other countries except Germany, which won 33 medals.

Other African American athletes from the 1936 Olympics included Dave Albritton, John Brooks, Jack Wilson, Art Oliver, Howard King, Ralph Metcalfe, Mack Robinson, James Howell King, Clark Atkinson, Cornelius Johnson, James LuValle, Frederick "Fritz" Pollard, Jackie Wilson, Willis Johnson, John Terry, Archie Williams, John Woodruff, Tidye Pickett, and Louise Stokes.

American community. There were varying opinions about the importance of sport during the mid-1930s at Historically Black Colleges and Universities (HBCUs). There were some college administrators who were resistant to sports at their universities as a part of the higher educational experience. Segments of the African American community thought sports would foster better race relations and viewed athletics as a universal language that would assist in destroying prejudice and discrimination. Other segments of the African American community believed that participating in sports would assist in helping African Americans assimilate into mainstream society; however, assimilation was impossible for African Americans because of the simple outward marker of having darker skin. Jesse assimilated by being accommodating and not pushing back on the issues of race and equality, even though he first called for the United States to boycott the games if Jews were being discriminated against in Germany.

In the early to mid-1900s, some predominately white colleges in the Midwest and on the West Coast began to allow Black athletes to enroll in their colleges. However, once these athletes were admitted, they were not permitted to utilize on-campus housing or other facilities on campus. In fact, Owens was not permitted to live on campus, so he lived off campus. At the time Owens was enrolled at Ohio State, there was only one male residence hall, and he was prohibited from living there because of his race. The policy of segregated residences on Ohio State University's campus was challenge by two African American women, as it was required for the completion of their home economics major. The African American members of the track team lived in a boarding house and had to cook their own meals because no restaurants along the university's main street would serve African Americans.

Owens's teammates at Ohio State recalled that Owens did not outwardly show his frustration with segregation. Charlie Beetham stated, "He may have had problems, but you would never know it. He was just cheerful jolly and had a big smile on his face all the time" (Wallace 1986, 7). Mel Walker, who later founded a vocational school and then worked as a personnel manager for Kraft Foods, noted that Owens was a very giving person: "He would reach his pocket and give you his last nickel" (Wallace 1986, 7). In a specific memory of Owens's generosity, Walker recalled that before the 1936 season he wanted to look his best for a West Coast track-and-field meet. Walker had ordered a new fashionable three-piece gray plaid suit from a Columbus-area clothier that cost $22.50. Though Walker worked in a state office building, as most athletes did during this time, he did not have enough money to pay for the suit. He only had $15.00 to put toward the purchase. By chance, a day before the track team was to leave for the meet in California, Walker ran into Owens in downtown Columbus. When Walker told Owens that he did not have enough money to purchase his suit, Owens gave him the $7.00 needed to make up the difference to get the suit. Walker also noted that Owens did a remarkable job of balancing his hectic life. He also observed how Owens balanced practice, competition, school, work, and a wife and child in Cleveland as an undergraduate student. It is unknown whether Walker really knew the difficulty Owens was having in his studies at Ohio State.

When the Ohio State track-and-field team traveled, especially in southern states, African American athletes were often refused service and would have to eat on the team bus and stay in boarding houses because they were not allowed to stay in whites-only hotels. Segregation ruled the day and could be found in all aspects of life in the United States. During this period, newspapers often focused on Black athleticism more than the achievements of African Americans in politics, science, religion, or the arts. Even when articles featured African Americans, they were described with words that had a tinge of racism. While competing at Ohio State, Jesse Owens was described as the "Ebony Antelope" by some newspapers (McDougall 2011, 39).

W. E. B. Du Bois saw sports as a social activity rather than an essential or significant activity for African Americans. Jesse Owens may have been a bit naïve to believe that white people would readily accept African Americans after his feats at the Berlin Olympics. He also believed his accomplishments would help the entire race because individuals of the same race are inexplicably tied together. This sentiment has been called *linked fate theory*. It is mostly used to explain the voting patterns of African Americans who tend to vote for African American political candidates. Linked fate theory is the sentiment among African Americans that individual African Americans' prospects are ultimately tied to the success of the race. In more practical terms, the theory supports the notion that African Americans prioritize the well-being of the group over their individual interests because "we are in this thing together" and "if one African American does well then we all do well."

African American athletes have symbolically carried the weight of the race's eternal burden of proof; their performances were among the most visible evidence that as a community they were good enough, smart enough, strong enough, brave enough—indeed human enough—to share in the fruits of this nation with full citizenship and humanity (Rhoden 2006, 3). Jesse Owens carried this burden of the African American athlete and the entire race with dignity, nobility, grace, and style. The African American community considered Jesse Owens as a hero, and they regarded his phenomenal performance as linked to the entire community. They believed his achievements would show those in the United States that African Americans were equal and deserved equal treatment under the law. Though Jesse Owens was an exceptional athlete, he was not an exemplary student. He struggled with his studies in college; in fact, he was a few high school credits short from graduation when he was admitted to Ohio State University.

Owens and other African American athletes began to ascend to national prominence in sports, and with this rise, a debate emerged about the physical abilities of Black athletes that gave them an advantage over white athletes. Dr. William Montague Cobb, an African American medical doctor, examined Owens and some other athletes to determine whether African Americans were athletically superior to white people (Schaap 2007, 56). Cobb had top-notch medical credentials and studied Owens for two days, putting him through a battery of examinations. He took x-rays and measured Owens's thigh and calf muscles. At the conclusion of these examinations, Dr. Cobb stated that race did not contribute to Owens's exceptional athletic ability. This great athletic ability could be attributed to training, motivation, and determination rather than any of the myths that had been proposed by another community of scholars.

Looming in the distance was a concerted effort to prove white supremacy and Black inferiority through scientific methods. There have been public disputes over whether there is truly a difference between white people and Black people. There have been many legitimate attempts to show that there are differences, and there have been attempts through an erroneous pseudoscience called *eugenics* to show the inferiority of Black people and some poor whites. Eugenics grew out of racism and the mission to scientifically prove the inferiority of Blacks and the superiority of educated whites of a higher socioeconomic class. These early beginnings point to a historical movement that involved leading public intellectuals, university professors, and public officials who showed tremendous angst and a great deal of fear because of miscegenation. Eugenics would be used as an underpinning philosophy in the rise of Nazi Germany and was a backdrop of the 1936 Olympics.

Although eugenics was debunked and dismissed by the scientific community at large, there was a close social and ideological alliance between eugenic scientists from the United States and Nazi Germany. Stefan Kuhl showed that Nazi eugenic enthusiasts, who were also dubbed "racial anthropologists," were adamant about proving that whites were superior to all other races. Some of the leading racial anthropologists were Madison Grant, Lothrop Stoddard, and Clarence G. Campbell. These men were leading eugenicists who blindly believed in white supremacy, and they were also anti-Semites who admired the sterilization laws that were being used in the United States (Jackson 2005, 21). They supported eugenic racism in Nazi Germany and supported ethnic and religious discrimination against minorities.

The National Association for the Advancement of Colored People (NAACP) began to rebut these erroneous notions of eugenics and the use of racial interpretations on intelligence assessments. The NAACP's official magazine, *The Crisis*, and publications by other African American interest groups printed a number of works to contradict and combat the idea of

---

### EUGENICS

Eugenics was a racist pseudoscience created to demean, discredit, and undermine all people deemed as "unfit." This pseudoscience offered to improve a human population by controlled breeding to increase the occurrence of desirable heritable characteristics. It was developed for the most part by Francis Galton, who was the cousin of Charles Darwin, the father of the theory of evolution. Eugenics was used as a method of improving the human race. It fell into disfavor only after the perversion of its doctrines by Nazi Germany.

At the turn of the last century, Chancellor Adolf Hitler of Germany studied American eugenics laws. He tried to legitimize his anti-Semitism by using language from eugenics, a racists and pseudoscientific academic discipline. Hitler was able to recruit more followers among reasonable Germans by claiming that science was on his side. The intellectual outlines of the eugenics that Hitler adopted were formulated in the United States.

Black inferior intelligence, the validity of the findings, and the methodology used for the evaluations that supposedly showed an intellectual inferiority in African Americans. In the spirit of its organization's mission of challenging white supremacy and racism, the NAACP also called for a boycott of the 1936 Summer Olympic Games in Berlin because of the hostility and hatred displayed toward Jews in Nazi Germany. Meanwhile, in Germany, there was a steady drumbeat of eventual war as Adolf Hitler positioned the Nazi Party for power.

It was the Great Depression and the fear of communism that brought Adolf Hitler and his Nationalist Socialist Party to power in Germany. In 1929, the party only had about 120,000 members, and one year later, it was the second-largest party in the Reichstag with 107 seats (Cochrane 2000, 88–89). By 1932, the National Socialist Party had 800,000 members and a private army called the Sturmabteilung. Political instability brought about elections and won more seats than the Communist Party. On January 30, 1933, Adolf Hitler became chancellor of Germany. On that night, he put on a torchlight parade, and under the order of Hitler and his henchmen, the secret state police, also called the Gestapo, was formed; they also added to the army.

Under his constitutional powers, Hitler began to break all oppositional political parties and media outlets (Cochrane 2000, 88). A month later, on February 27, 1933, a disgruntled or demented loner set ablaze and burned down the Reichstag (Cochrane 2000, 88). This was the opening Hitler needed to assume more power through an emergency decree that abolished civil rights granted by the German constitution. In March 1933, Hitler ordered another round of elections to gain more power and to give the appearance of a democratic election so he could claim the legitimacy of being democratically elected (Cochrane 2000, 92–93). A few weeks later, Hitler's enabling acts ended democracy in Germany, making it a totalitarian state and with Hitler as its dictator. Germany still had a president under its constitution, Marshal Paul von Hindenburg. When he died in 1934, Hitler merged the office of the president and chancellor and called it the *führer*, which means leader.

During this time, all non-Nazi political parties were outlawed. Members of other parties were hunted down and beaten, put in prison, or killed. Some escaped or went underground. While it is widely known that Hitler used concentration camps to hold and kill masses of Jewish people, the first concentration camps were not originally set up for them. Initially, these camps were set up for his political enemies and were then expanded as he began to fulfill his anti-Semitic and bigoted policies against Jews. All officers and men were forced to take an oath to Hitler. During the early days of the Nazis taking control, Hitler's close circle did not trust each other and often produced rivals who, for the most part, were consumed with the quest for power instead of formulating domestic policy.

In 1935, the Protection of German Blood law was announced. It outlawed relations between Aryans and non-Aryans, which included Jews, Gypsies, and other ethnic and racial minorities. After the Olympics, the persecution of Jews and Nazi expansion continued. In 1938, Hitler flexed his muscle and took control of the Austrian chancellor, Kurt von Schuschnigg, and forced him to put a Nazi in control of the Austrian police. In March 1938, Hitler brought Austria under German control. Hitler sought out Austrian Jews, liberals, socialists, and communists. Those who were intellectuals were forced to become street cleaners and to clean the streets with their bare hands. Those who the Nazis considered undesirables were murdered or sent to concentration camps. After capturing Austria, the Nazis sought to conquer the nation of Czechoslovakia.

Jews were denied citizenship in Germany, and in 1938, the intensity of the persecution against Jews increased. Jewish passports were stamped with a "J" to distinguish them from Aryans. Jews were stripped of their property and murdered. Jews in medical professions were no longer able to offer their services to Aryans. November 9, 1938, Kristallnacht, the "Night of the Broken Glass," marked the campaign of systematic violence against Jews started by Joseph Goebbels. On this night, 91 Jews were killed, and 200,000 were sent to concentration camps (Cochrane 2000, 88–89). Synagogues were burned down, and Jewish shops were destroyed. Afterward, there was a concerted effort to drive Jews out of Germany (Cochrane 2000, 88–89).

As the 1936 Olympics approached, many African Americans continued in the struggle of building a Black nation within a nation. The United States continued to practice segregation, keeping African Americans and whites separate in all aspects of life. Along with this struggle, Blacks battled against negative stereotypes, racial tropes, racial discrimination, and outright second-class citizenship. Black athletes and sports heroes became symbolic figures in the struggle. Jack Johnson, who was the heavyweight boxing champion during the 1900s, faced the color line at the height of the Jim Crow era in American sports and became the symbolic image of the big, brash, Black brute who conjured up fear in white Americans of what could happen if African Americans experienced full citizenship. Later, heavyweight boxing champion Muhammad Ali and National Football League (NFL) quarterback Colin Kaepernick would awaken some of the same fears in the United States.

During this time, many people played into the dehumanizing ethos and the stereotype of Black athletes' great athletic and physicality, and believed this was a sign of their lack of intelligence. Others believed great athletic ability and physicality should not serve as an indication of intellectual limitations. Black athletic success is complicated in the African American community and has been made one of the most prominent symbols of success. The brashness of Jack Johnson's confident and sometimes cocky attitude drove many African American athletes to put on a passive public persona to make white Americans feel comfortable with their success. In public spaces, many of these heroes appeared accommodating to whites. Smiling and appearing to be easygoing and nonconfrontational was the mask that many African Americans athletes wore to advance their sports careers. They became passive sports heroes who were for the most part silent and did not publicly address discrimination and segregation.

While there were small steps made toward integration of American sports during the nineteenth century, there was a failure to integrate African Americans into other aspects of society, in particular the ballot box and the right to vote. During the 1930s, the role of Black athletics at Black colleges was the dominant topic at the Colored Intercollegiate Athletic Association (CIAA). Some people resented the portrayal of Black athletes as the reigning symbol of success and genius in the African American community, and there were indeed African American athletes who showed that one can indeed be exceptional athletically and intellectually.

In 1937, President Arthur Howe of the Hampton Institute stated at the CIAA national conference that training students for professional sports is not a matter for education because it is temporary. He believed that athletics averted educational institutions from their missions and would not provide long-term educational training for students. Howe and others celebrated and appreciated the pride that athletics provided the African American community, but they did not believe it would advance the race and that it confirmed the racial tropes held by many racists, such as African Americans being crude and vulgar and lacking moral character. Advocates of the use of athletics to advance the race argued that athletic achievements helped with integration and provided a solution to

---

### JACK JOHNSON

Jack Johnson, "the Galveston Giant," was born in Galveston, Texas, in 1878 and became the first African American world heavyweight boxing champion in 1908. Johnson held the heavyweight boxing crown from 1908 to 1915 and boxed until age 50.

Johnson was rich, flamboyant, brash, and braggadocios. He earned considerable sums outside of the ring by endorsing various products and patenting medicines. He also sported tailored suits and participated in car racing. He flaunted his wealth by purchasing jewelry and furs for his wives.

In total, Jack Johnson's professional record included 73 wins (40 of them being knockouts), 13 losses, 10 draws, and 5 no contests. Johnson died in an automobile accident in Raleigh, North Carolina, in 1946.

inequality. In 1949, Paul Robeson noted at a gathering at the Paris Peace Conference that "it is unthinkable that American Negroes would go to war on behalf of those who have oppressed us for generations . . . against a country which in one generation has raised our people to full human dignity of mankind" (Clarke 1978, 223–241).

In 1915, Robeson won an academic scholarship to Rutgers University. Despite blatant violence and racism from his teammates at Rutgers, he won 15 varsity letters in football, track and field, baseball, and basketball. He was a two-time All-American in football. Robeson dispelled the image of the superior Black athlete who lacked intelligence and other racial tropes about Blacks that played a part in the resurgence of fallacious eugenic notions. He became a member of Phi Beta Kappa, the most recognized honor society, during his junior year; belonged to the Cap & Skull Honor Society, and graduated as valedictorian. Robeson would later become an opera singer, actor, activist, and African American advocate, and he had a successful stage career. He was a Renaissance man and a symbol of Black excellence. Upon graduating head of his class at Rutgers, he did not pursue a professional sports career. Instead, he enrolled at law school at Columbia University and graduated with his law degree in 1923. Robeson certainly was not a one-dimensional, passive African American athlete who was unconcerned with political and social issues.

Jesse Owens and many of his teammates at Ohio State University seemed to be unaware of or turned a blind eye toward the segregation they faced. Charlie Beetham, who was white, a teammate who would later go back to Ohio State to coach the cross-country team, had rarely been touched by discrimination. The first time he met discrimination and segregation policies face to face was when he was in Milwaukee for a track meet. Beetham recalled that Black people were allowed to stay in the hotel but not allowed to eat meals in the hotel's dining room, so they had to eat in their rooms. This policy was also used by many of the restaurants and diners off campus in Columbus. Beetham recalled that when they were student athletes, one could purchase a "T-bone steak, potato, salad, three vegetables and dessert for 45 cents at a local restaurant not far from where Owens and his roommates lived" but Black student athletes still could not eat in those restaurants (Wallace 1986, 7).

While Hitler was building his evil empire, Owens and his teammates concentrated on track and field. During this time, the track-and-field facilities were not optimal, but they allowed the Buckeye athletes to condition and remain in shape. The temperature dipped below zero during the winter months of the indoor season. At this time, track surfaces were still made of dirt, and the people in athletics sprayed the track with water to keep the dust down as the track-and-field team practiced. During the winter months, they had to be careful not to use too much water or the track surface would turn into an iced oval. Because Ohio State University did not have an indoor facility, the team would have to travel to other universities to compete during the indoor season. On some of these trips, Owens and his other African American teammates had to stay at the local YMCA instead of checking into hotels with their white teammates. Beetham noted this was widely accepted. "No one really thought about it. That was just accepted" (Wallace 1986, 7). Beetham claimed he never heard anyone say a negative thing about Jesse Owens throughout his entire college career.

Jesse Owens was shaped in this tradition of passive African American sports heroes. He may have appeared to be neutral on race issues or perhaps muzzled by the mores of the time, but this seems to have been a consistent pattern throughout Owens's life. In 1968, Owens was criticized by many African Americans for seeming to represent the white interests to quell a potential Olympic boycott of the games and subsequent protest of Tommie Smith, John Carlos, and Lee Evans at the 1968 Summer Olympic Games in Mexico City. Indeed, when Owens participated in the 1936 Olympic Games, he only spoke about the athletic events. He did not make any commentary about politics, civil rights, or race. Ruth Owens stated she never feared for her husband's safety while he was in Berlin, Germany, but she feared for him in the southern states. When Owens served as a surrogate and campaigned in Mississippi for a Republican presidential candidate, Ruth asked him not to make a public endorsement or speak at political campaign rallies.

There were ample warnings and indications of the intentions of Adolf Hitler and Nazi Germany. In some of his published writings, Adolf Hitler proclaimed in no uncertain terms his beliefs that Jews and African Americans should not be allowed to participate in the Olympics. There were several obvious indications there was a wave of anti-Semitism and a racist undercurrent taking hold in Germany. Hitler ordered the removal of the "Jews Not Wanted" signs that hung at tourist attractions around the host city of Berlin and displayed the Nazis' hatred for Jewish people, and the official state newspapers ceased printing anti-Semitic headlines or news stories while the games were taking place. During the Olympics Games, the Olympic flag was prominently displayed in Berlin as well as the Nazi flag. The Nazi government attempted to project an air of tolerance, but it was only a cover to hide their nefarious practices.

In 1935, the German government introduced the Nuremburg Laws. These laws prohibited Jewish people from gaining German citizenship. They also prohibited Jews and non-Jews from getting legally married and stripped away their political rights. All these discriminatory practices were hidden from the world prior to Nazi Germany becoming the host country for the Olympic Games of 1936.

The German Olympic Committee also barred German Jewish athletes from participating in the games. To deflect shame of a claim they were barring Jewish athletes, the Nazis solicited one female athlete to train for the games. Helene Mayer, who had one parent who was Jewish, was the only German Jewish athlete to participate in the 1936 Olympic Games. Many other Jewish athletes from other countries chose to boycott the Olympics. As a multinational boycott of the Olympic Games loomed, Hitler backed off his stance. He realized the world was watching, and therefore he must at the very least put up a façade of racial tolerance. Meanwhile, some countries seemed to acquiesce to Hitler's racist views, as many countries did not allow Jewish athletes to participate in the events or be on their teams.

There were wide-ranging conversations in the United States and Canada about whether there should be a boycott of the Olympic Games. Owens stated that if the Nazi government was discriminating against minorities in Germany, the United States should not compete in the 1936 Olympics. During this time, the United States and Germany had strong economic ties. The NAACP convinced Jesse Owens to make a public statement about a potential boycott of the games. Owens knew that if he boycotted the Olympics, he may miss the chance of a lifetime. He would miss an opportunity at generational wealth and fame. He stated, "If there is discrimination against minorities in Germany, then we must withdraw from the Olympics" (Schaap 2007, 98).

---

### THE 1936 OLYMPIC BOYCOTT

As Hitler's campaign to commit genocide against Jews developed, some Jewish people in the United States began to protest German goods and put forth broad-scale arguments to boycott the Berlin Olympics. Some top Jewish American athletes opted to not compete in the 1936 Summer Olympics. The controversy was highlighted in 1935 when Avery Brundage, the president of the American Olympic Committee (AOC), alleged that the boycott was a Jewish-communist conspiracy devised to prevent the United States from participating in the Olympics.

Ernst Lee Jahncke, of the International Olympic Committee (IOC), was an ardent opponent of sending a team to the Olympics in Berlin. In July 1936, after taking a strong public stand against the Berlin Games, Jahncke was kicked out of the IOC and replaced by Avery Brundage. President Franklin D. Roosevelt did not get entangled in the boycott issue, despite warnings from top American diplomats about Nazi propaganda.

Black journalists often underscored the hypocrisy of pro-boycotters who did not first address the problem of discrimination against Black athletes in the United States. Boycotts efforts also sprang up in Great Britain, France, Sweden, Czechoslovakia, and the Netherlands.

A pedestrian in New York City reads a notice announcing a public meeting, scheduled for December 3, 1935, to urge Americans to boycott the 1936 Berlin Olympics. The racist and xenophobic policies of German chancellor Adolf Hitler and the Nazi Party led many countries to call for a boycott of the games, arguing that participation would amount to an endorsement of Hitler's regime. (United States Holocaust Memorial Museum, National Archives)

Larry Snyder was determined that Owens would travel and participate in the Olympics and was criticized for attempting to change Owens's thinking about a possible boycott. He also noted that Owens had participated in states that sanctioned segregation, so what was the difference? When the two men met, Owens initially would not back away from his decision, but his coach from Ohio State University convinced him to back down. Snyder was progressive in his thinking, but he selfishly wanted Owens to participate in the Olympics, no matter what discrimination was taking place.

The African American media pleaded in the pages of their newspapers and called for Owens to not compete. Walter White, the head of the NAACP, made a sustained effort to convince all the African American Olympic athletes, but in particular Jesse Owens, to not participate in the Games. White sent Owens a personal telegram in an attempt to convince him. He knew that if he could convince the most elite track-and-field star in the United States to boycott, the others might follow suit. When Owens received the letter, he read and contemplated the contents. He wanted to talk with Snyder about the letter to get some advice, but in something like a divine intervention, Owens stopped. His decision was made. He would participate in the Olympics.

Calls for a boycott of the Games brewed beyond the African American community. Prominent politicians and members from other communities called for a boycott as well. Many of these individuals not only supported the boycott because of the treatment of Jews but also because the Nazis were anti-Christian. One of the largest backers of a boycott was Jeremiah Mahoney, who had sat on the New York Supreme Court from 1932 to 1938. Mahoney had run for governor of New York but was defeated by Fiorello La Guardia. During the 1930s, Mahoney had also served as president of the AAU. When Avery Brundage ascended to the presidency of the AAU, he ruled with an iron fist and became the most powerful man in amateur sports.

Avery Brundage was the president of the American Olympic Committee (AOC) and an admirer of Nazi Germany. Brundage could be arrogant, condescending, and boisterous, and these behaviors were on display time and time again when debating whether the U.S. Olympic team would participate in the 1936 Olympic Games.

To suppress some of the criticism of the United States' participation in the Games, Brundage took a trip and toured Germany to ensure that critics knew there were not any anti-Semitic sentiments evident or discrimination taking place in Germany. After the visit to Germany in 1934, Brundage provided a glowing report stating that, in his estimation, Jewish

---

### AVERY BRUNDAGE

Avery Brundage was born in 1887. He was a former amateur athlete who competed in the 1912 Summer Olympic Games. He was also the fifth president of the International Olympic Committee (IOC), serving from 1952 to 1972, and the only American to hold this position. Brundage is remembered as an overzealous advocate of amateurism and for his involvement with the 1936, 1968, and 1972 Summer Olympic Games. Many of the African American athletes from the 1968 Olympic track-and-field team nicknamed him "Slavery Avery."

Hitler invited Brundage to tour Berlin, Germany, prior to the 1936 Games. When Brundage returned to the United States, he reported there was no evidence of discrimination against Jews, and he stated that Jewish athletes would be allowed to compete and African American athletes would be safe.

Avery Brundage died in 1975.

athletes were being treated fairly and recommending the Olympic Games remain in Germany. Calls for a boycott grew louder. Brundage argued that politics had no place in sports, and he continued to head off any potential boycott of the 1936 Summer Olympics. He even went so far as to put language in the AOC's official marketing literature that American athletes should not get involved in altercations between Jews and Nazis.

Brundage believed the boycotts were backed by communists and Jews. Mahoney took a strong public stand and pushed attempts to boycott the 1936 Olympics. He pointed out that Germany had violated Olympic policies that prohibited discrimination based on race or religion. In Mahoney's view, the United States' participation in the Games would send the wrong message by endorsing Hitler's Reich. President Franklin D. Roosevelt did not get involved; he stayed neutral on whether the United States should boycott, even though there were ample indications from high-level American diplomats that the Nazi government was using the Olympic Games as a propaganda tool. Once it was decided the United States would participate, Jesse Owens and the other American athletes seemed to turn a blind eye to the treatment of Jews in Germany. The American public also seemed disengaged with the happenings of Hitler and the wicked and demented developments in Germany.

There was a temporary Olympic boycott effort that emerged in Great Britain, France, Sweden, Czechoslovakia, and the Netherlands. Communists and socialists from Germany who had been exiled from the country also voiced their opposition and supported of the boycott. Alternatives to the games were also proposed. However, once the AAU of the United States voted to participate in the Games in December 1935, other countries followed suit. Forty-nine teams from around the world competed in the Berlin Games, more than in any previous Olympics.

# 6

# 1936 Berlin Olympics Games

The modern era of the Olympiads have been described as full of pageantry and competition. For host countries, the Olympic Games are an opportunity to raise the profile of the host country. The Olympics can be a key method to expand a country's global footprint and gain loftier international acceptance or change perceptions and create new narratives about a country. Being a host country can be essential in gaining benefits, such as investments in infrastructure projects and economic boosts, due to an influx of tourism dollars during the competitions.

Initially, Hitler did not want to host the Olympics. He believed it was a showcase for Blacks and Jews. Hitler's propaganda minister, Joseph Goebbels, convinced him that hosting the Olympics Games would be an opportunity to showcase the superiority of the Nordic Superman and promote the idea that the use of sports would harden the German spirit and instill unity among German youth. After agreeing to host the Olympics, Hitler publicly noted that the athletes of Nazi Germany would run faster and jump higher than the rest of the field, proving their superiority. Domination at the 1936 Olympic Games became a national goal for the Nazi government. Beyond being an opportunity to show Germany's domination, hosting the 1936 Olympics was an opportunity to distribute propaganda and promote its notion of superiority and gain greater world influence.

In the United States, the attitudes toward Germany and the Olympics were mixed. It was known that Nazi Germany was mistreating and oppressing

Jews, and there were calls for the U.S. Olympic team to boycott the 1936 Games. The focus of many citizens in the United States were on day-to-day living as they struggled to recover from the economic woes of the Great Depression. Many of these individuals viewed the Olympics as a diversion from harsh domestic affairs, such as the country's economic collapse. They used the 1936 Olympics as a rallying cry for unity in the nation. Many cheered U.S. Olympic athletes of all races competing in the games but failed to see the sad irony of the mistreatment and oppression of African American athletes on their home soil. African Americans were locked into second-class citizenship in the United States, and Nazi Germany increased its efforts to further oppress Jews in Germany.

Months before the Berlin Games, Germany hosted the 1936 Winter Olympic Games in Bavaria. Bavaria was very anti-Semitic that openly displayed anti-Jewish signs. Upon seeing these signs, the International Olympic Committee (IOC) told Hitler that if these signs were not removed, the country would lose its host status for the Summer Olympic Games. The signs were removed, but the critics later realized that the Germans were only paying lip service and did not have any intention of quelling anti-Semitism or changing their policies toward Jews. The Nazi government wanted to use the 1936 Summer Olympic Games as a propaganda tool, and they decided to create a film about the Olympic Games. They did not want to use still photos in their propaganda; they wanted to unfold the story and create cinematic drama as they showed the world their superiority.

German filmmaker Leni Riefenstahl was chosen to tell this story on film. Riefenstahl was a former actor who had turned her attention to being behind the camera. Riefenstahl and her movie crew shot copious amounts of film at the Olympic Games. She produced a two-part movie titled *Olympia* that was released almost two years after the games were completed.

---

### LENI RIEFENSTAHL

Helene Bertha Amalie "Leni" Riefenstahl was a German film director who was responsible for filming the 1936 Olympics in Berlin, Germany. Riefenstahl was born in 1902 and grew up in Germany. She became the leading German filmmaker during the 1930s. She was tapped by the Adolf Hitler and the Nazi Party to produce propaganda films and became known as Adolf Hitler's favorite filmmaker. Her documentary of the 1936 Summer Olympic Games is titled *Olympia*, and it became a renowned and famous film. This film, along with other propaganda films, ruined Riefenstahl's career as a film director. Ultimately, *Olympia* has also been judged as propaganda.

Leni Riefenstahl died in Poecking, Germany, on September 8, 2003, a few weeks before she turned 101.

*Olympia* was innovative to German moviegoers because most German cinemas of the time were shot indoors.

This film was created outside, and she was able to focus on the athletes' bodies and do close-up shots. She and her camera crew invented a camera that could film underwater, and this innovation gave her the ability to film the swimming and diving events. She and her crew also dug a trench to capture the long jumpers as they soared above and landed in the sand pit. If she missed events, she had the athletes recreate the events so she could capture it on film. Much like modern-day sports films, she had narrators describe the sporting events on the film.

Riefenstahl saw her filmmaking more as art rather than propaganda. She hoped to show the preparation and beauty of the athletes. A narrator was employed to do voice-overs, and music accompanied the footage. She was also the first to use slow motion in the footage of sporting events. The Germans distributed shorter versions of the film to various countries.

Riefenstahl received critical acclaim for *Olympia*. Goebbels had planned for the movie to be strictly a propaganda film and did not want Riefenstahl to show any of the African American athletes film. Riefenstahl defied Goebbels and used footage of some of the African American athletes. In fact, she seemed enamored with Jesse Owens. She often got close shots of Owens, and his long jump competition became the centerpiece of part one of the Olympiad movie.

On August 1, 1936, approximately 90,000 fans filled the stadium in Berlin, Germany, to witness Owens and his fellow athletes crush the myth of white superiority (PBS 2012). The closing ceremony for the Games occurred on August 16, 1936 (PBS 2012). With plenty of pomp and circumstance, Hitler made his way to his spectator box suite that was perched above the

---

### JOSEPH GOEBBELS

Paul Joseph Goebbels was a German Nazi politician and the Reich minister of propaganda of Nazi Germany from 1933 to 1945. Goebbels was born October 29, 1897, in Rheydt, Germany, and he became one of Adolf Hitler's closest and most devoted confidants. He was responsible for crafting the political messaging for the Nazi Party and Adolf Hitler.

In 1928, Hitler assigned Goebbels to the position of national director of propaganda for the Nazis. Goebbels began to build the myth and fabricated folklore around Adolf Hitler, with the aim of getting Germans to assimilate and blindly follow Nazi ideals. It permeated all forms of media in Germany. Following Adolf Hitler's suicide, Goebbels served as chancellor of Germany for a single day before he and his wife poisoned their six children and then took their own lives.

Berlin's Olympia Stadium, built for the 1936 Summer Olympics in Berlin, Germany. (Vasilii Maslak/Dreamstime.com)

stadium. He was able to gaze down on the competitions as if he were a godlike being approving or disapproving of every move or maneuver of the athletes. The opening ceremony was akin to a church ceremony. The music of Germany's great composers Ludwig van Beethoven and George Frideric Handel was featured. Choirs and bands performed to provide a pious display of religious pageantry to display the superiority of white supremacy to the world.

During the opening ceremony, as teams from various countries paraded by Hitler's box suite, they had to make a political choice. They could dip their country's flag in deference to Hitler and present the Nazi salute, Olympic salute, or simply no salute or acknowledgment of the German leader at all. This choice was made more complicated by the similarities in the Nazi salute and the Olympic salute. The Olympic salute was the right arm extended parallel to the ground by the athlete's side. The Nazi salute was the right arm extended just above the parallel status of the Olympic salute and just below the athlete's shoulder. Depending on the angle in which fans were situated in the stadium, they could easily get these salutes confused.

When the French athletes entered the stadium, they presented the Olympic salute, and the German crowd misidentified it as the Nazi salute and gave a thunderous applause. The Italian athletes entered the stadium and gave the Nazi salute to the approval of the fans and were greeted with a return salute from Hitler and the fans. The athletes from Great Britain and Japan did not present a salute but did dip their flags when they passed

The opening ceremonies of the Berlin Olympics, held on August 8, 1936. (The Illustrated London News Picture Library)

Hitler's suite. Athletes from the United States did not salute or dip the flag. The athletes simply took off their hats and placed them over their hearts as they paraded in front of the box suite. Like the Americans, Canadian athletes removed their hats and did not salute Hitler or dip their flag in deference.

After the opening ceremony, Hitler gave a short salutation to the crowd to officially open the games. Then pigeons were released in the stadium, and their flight signaled the games were about to begin. A German distance runner carrying the Olympic torch entered the stadium, and the crowd stood and gave the Nazi salute. As choirs sang "Hallelujah," accompanied by musicians, the athlete ran around the track carrying the Olympic torch to ignite the Olympic flame that would burn for the duration of the games. The Nazis originated the torch run from ancient Greece to the site of the Olympic Games.

There were only eight African American athletes on the 1936 Olympic track-and-field team (Draper, Thrasher, and Underwood 2020). Eulace Peacock, an African American athlete, did not qualify for the team. Peacock was one of the most dominant track athletes in the United States during 1935. Unfortunately, he was injured early in the 1936 track-and-field season and did not sufficiently recover from his injury and did not qualify for the team. Owens was slated to compete in three events, the 100-meter dash, the 200-meter dash, and the long jump, but after a controversy about Jewish runners competing in the 4 × 100 meter relay, he ended up competing in four events. There were 310 athletes from the United States that competed in the 1936 Olympic Games. This was second only to the host country, Germany, which had 348 athletes at the Games.

The actual competitions kicked off on August 2, 1936. Jesse Owens watched several qualifying heats of the 100-meter dash to gauge the styles and competitiveness of any potential opponents he may face in the finals. Several runners had great starts, so Owens knew he needed a great start to win the race. He was a notoriously slow starter. Owens concentrated on practicing his starts in an attempt to get the rhythm of the German official who would call the start of the races. The heats were first. The fastest two runners in each of the 12 heats advanced to the quarterfinal round.

Sweden's Lennart Strandberg, Japan's Takayoshi Yoshioka, and Germany's Manfred Kersch were projected favorites in the sprints. The three were in heat 1 and placed first with a time of 10.7 seconds, second with a time of 10.8 seconds, and third with a time of 10.8 seconds, respectively. The Japanese sensation Yoshioka had competed in the previous Olympics in 1932. He was the first Japanese runner to make it to a finals competition and had held the world record in 1935 with a time of 10.3 seconds. Four other

## EULACE PEACOCK

One of Jesse Owens's top rivals was Eulace Peacock. Eulace Peacock and Jesse Owens developed a rivalry in 1935, the year before Owens's historic Olympics in Berlin in which he won four gold medals. That year, Peacock defeated Owens in 7 of their 10 head-to-head competitions. Because Peacock tore his hamstring muscle prior to the tryouts, he never made the 1936 Olympic team.

Peacock and Owens had many similarities in their lives. Both were born in Alabama, and like Owens, Peacock was a son of sharecroppers who had migrated north in search of better economic opportunity and a better life. While Owens's family moved to Ohio, Peacock's family moved to New Jersey.

Eulace Peacock was born in Dothan, Alabama, on August 27, 1914, and he attended college at Temple University in Philadelphia. Peacock was an outstanding athlete. He became a gifted long jumper, pentathlete, and football player and went on to run track at Temple.

Peacock and Owens would eventually go into business together when they opened the Owens and Peacock Company, a meatpacking company, during the 1960s.

In his final years, Peacock suffered from Alzheimer's disease. He died in New York on December 13, 1996, at the age of 82.

athletes had this time; however, he was the only person of Asian descent who had accomplished it.

Ralph Metcalfe, age 26, was Owens's teammate and a fellow African American athlete. He was placed in heat 7 and won it with a time of 10.8 seconds. In his qualifying heat for the 100-meter dash, Jesse Owens was placed in heat 12. His most formidable opponent was Kichizo Sasaki of Japan. The 22-year-old Owens ran a blistering 10.3 seconds, and Sasaki placed second with a time of 11.0 seconds. Owens began neck and neck with Sasaki, but the "Buckeye Bullet" pulled away at about 50 meters into the race. With his upright running style on full display, Owens eased up as he crossed the finish line. His time tied the world record, and he advanced to the quarterfinals. The Japanese runner finished fourth in the heat and was eliminated from the competition.

In the quarterfinals, the fastest three runners in each of the four heats advanced to the semifinal round. Owens was in heat 2 in the quarterfinals. Again, Owens bested his world record qualifying time by posting a time 10.2 seconds. Owens flew past Paul Hanni of Switzerland and Jozsef Sir of Hungary to qualify for the finals. His teammate Metcalfe was placed in heat

Jesse Owens (left) with Ralph Metcalfe at the Olympic tryouts at Randall's Island Stadium in New York on July 11, 1936. (Library of Congress)

3 and edged out Alan Pennington from Great Britain and Wil van Beveren from the Netherlands. Metcalfe's time was 10.5 seconds in his heat. The fastest three runners in each of the two heats in the semifinals advanced to the final round. Both Owens and Metcalfe qualified for the 100-meter finals and the opportunity to compete for the gold medal.

On August 3, 1936, the finals for the 100-meter race took place. In the finals, Owens was placed in the inside lane. His stiffest competition would come from Erik Borkmeyer, a German sprinter, and Ralph Metcalfe, Owens's U.S. teammate. The runners were set, and Owens led the entire race. Metcalfe lagged behind at the beginning of the race but quickly advanced, catching the other sprinters and finishing second behind Owens. Owens won the gold medal and equaled a world record. Metcalfe won the silver medal, and Tinus Osendarp from the Netherlands won the bronze medal. Owens's time was 10.3 seconds, Metcalfe's time was 10.4 seconds, and Osendarp's time was 10.5 seconds. As he stood on the top spot of the podium, Owens was dressed in a blue sweat suit trimmed in white with the letters U.S.A. in red prominently emblazoned on the front of his crew sweatshirt. A laurel wreath was placed on the heads of each placed finisher, and they were given a small tree that could be planted after the Olympic Games. Owens would receive four of these trees. As the American national anthem was being played and the American flag raised, both Owens and Metcalfe saluted. The German crowd all gave the Nazi salute as "The Star-Spangled Banner" cascaded through the stadium. Owens gave a short speech after the race. Dressed in his U.S.A. tracksuit, he said, "I am glad to have won the 100 meters here in the Olympic Games Berlin. In a very beautiful place and a very beautiful setting. The competition was grand. We are very glad to come out on top. Thank you very kindly."

The world watched to see whether Hitler would shake hands with Owens. It was common practice for the leader of the host country to shake hands and greet the winners of events. Hitler refused to shake Jesse Owens's hand to congratulate him on his gold medal victory. He publicly greeted the German and Finland winners in earlier events, but Hitler did not want to be photographed shaking hands with a Black person. A photograph of Hitler with an African American athlete would shatter the myth of white racial superiority and acknowledge that those theories that underpinned the Nazi philosophy were not valid. Olympic officials told Hitler that he would have to greet and acknowledge all winners or none at all. Hitler made the choice to not formally meet with any athletes. He did still meet with some of the white athletes in a private spot under the stadium. Later in life, Owens stated the two exchanged a friendly wave but later contradicted this statement and denied that Hitler had acknowledged him.

When Owens returned to the United States after the Olympic Games, President Franklin D. Roosevelt did not meet with Owens to congratulate him or send him a congratulatory communication. It had been a tradition for U.S. presidents to meet and greet Olympic winners after the Games were completed. In fact, it took 40 years before Owens received the appropriate recognition from a U.S. president, when Gerald Ford awarded Owens with the nation's highest civilian award, the Presidential Medal of Freedom, in 1976. The African American community and press was furious over this humiliating rebuff. The headline in several American newspapers read, "Hitler Ignores Negro World Record Breaker." The *Cleveland Post* read, "Hitler Snubs Jesse." The *Baltimore Afro-American* headline read, "Adolf Snubs U.S. Lads." The African American community saw the snub of Jesse Owens as a snub to the entire race. Owens would continue prove through his grace and athletic success on the track that African Americans were not inferior.

The long jump was Owens's second event, and it took place on August 4, 1936, the day after his 100-yard dash victory. There was high drama on this day as Owens almost failed to qualify for the long jump finals. German athlete Luz Long, a European record holder, was Owens's toughest competition in this event. Long was a walking advertisement for the Aryan nation: he was tall with blond hair and blue eyes—the model for Hitler's propaganda. Long won the German long jump championship six times, in 1933, 1934, 1936, 1937, 1938, and 1939. His European long jump record stood until 1956.

---

### THE PRESIDENTIAL MEDAL OF FREEDOM FOR JESSE OWENS

The Presidential Medal of Freedom is the highest award given to civilians. This honor is awarded to individuals who have made "an especially meritorious contribution to the security or national interests of the United States, world peace, cultural or other significant public or private endeavors." Recipients of this honor and award are selected by the president of the United States, with the assistance of the Distinguished Civilian Service Awards Board. Although the majority of honorees are U.S. citizens, people from other countries are also eligible.

On July 6, 1945, President Harry S. Truman signed Executive Order 9586, establishing the Medal of Freedom to recognize notable service by civilians during World War II. President John F. Kennedy reestablished the award as the Presidential Medal of Freedom and expanded its scope to include cultural achievements.

Jesse Owens received the Presidential Medal of Freedom from President Gerald Ford at the White House after the 1976 Olympics. A celebration was held on the White House lawn for the greatest American Olympian to receive this highest honor.

This long jump competition set up a battle of the races: Long against Owens. As the competition commenced, Owens seemed a bit nervous and was uncharacteristically sloppy in his approach to the board. He fouled on his first and second attempts. Owens struggled making this jump because he scratched by beginning his leap just past the board on his first qualifying jump. If Owens scratched again, he would be disqualified. In this long jump competition, athletes would have to make a jump of at least 23 feet, 5 1/2 inches. This distance should not have been a problem for Owens because he had jumped this distance in high school. Long suggested that Owens move his launch point a foot back and leap from behind the board so that he would be assured that he would not scratch again. Owens took the advice and jumped a comfortable 25 feet, qualifying for the finals. This set up the showdown that many fans had hoped for, and many billed it as the battle between the white race and the Black race.

In the final round of the long jump, Owens and Long put on a phenomenal show of athletic abilities. Jump after jump, each competitor got better and better. Owens heeded Long's advice and changed his launch point, which easily qualified him for the long jump finals. An appreciative Owens could be seen shaking hands with Long and telling him thank you. It appeared as if Owens controlled gravity as he came down from his jumps when he decided to or when he knew victory was at hand. Owens jumped 26 feet to capture his second gold medal. In the finals, Lutz Long could not match Owens's jumps. Owens held the long jump record for decades.

After the competition, Long and Jesse Owens walked arm in arm around the stadium to cheering fans. This was a defiant act, as Long did not hold the same worldview as Hitler and the rest of the Nazi

---

### NAOTO TAJIMA

Tajima Naoto was born in Iwakuni, Japan, on August 15, 1912. Tajima was a Japanese athlete who competed at the 1932 Summer Olympic Games in Los Angeles, California, and at the 1936 Summer Olympics in Berlin, Germany. Shortly before competing in the 1936 Olympics, he graduated from Kyoto Imperial University with a degree in economics.

In 1932, Tajima finished sixth in the long jump event. In 1936, he finished third in the long jump and won the bronze medal. He was bested by Jesse Owens, who won a gold medal, and Germany's Luz Long, who won a silver medal in the long jump. Tajima is often seen in the famous photo of Owens and Long on the medal podium. Tajima was a member of the Japanese Olympic Committee and coached Japan's track-and-field team at the 1956 and 1964 Summer Olympics.

Naoto Tajima died on December 4, 1990.

government. Long seemed to embrace all humanity. He viewed Owens as a fellow human being and competitor and treated him with dignity and respect. Long and Owens walking arm in arm around the stadium showcased the sportsmanship and competitive spirit that the Olympics Games represents. There is a famous photograph of the two relaxing and conversing on the infield of the track while waiting for the medal ceremony to begin. Over the years, Owens remembered Long's kindness and sportsmanship. Long later learned that the Nazi government was extremely angry with his show of friendliness toward Owens. Reportedly, he was reprimanded and told to never hug a Black person. In July 1943, Long died fighting with the German army in San Pietro Clarenza, Catania, Italy, during World War II.

On August 5, 1936, the third day of Olympic competition, Owens looked to win another gold medal in the 200-meter dash. At this time, the German fans understood they were witnessing history in the making. As the athletes prepared for the event, the German crowd began to chant Jesse Owens's name in unison. Owens was assigned to the third lane from the inside of the track. When the starter pistol sounded, he blazed through the curve of the track, and as he came around and headed into the straightaway, with his upright running style, Owens had a commanding lead on all his competitors. The winning time was 20.7 seconds and a new world record. Mack Robinson, Owens's teammate, finished second for the silver medal with a time of 21.1 seconds. Owens had won his third gold medal. In reflecting on the 200-meter race of the 1936 Olympics, Robinson stated, "Jesse got the coaching, I didn't. I saw his television program about his return to Berlin. He said that he and the coaches had studied the styles of every runner. That was true. They studied me, too. It's not too bad to be second best in the world at what you're doing, no matter what it is. It means that only one other person in the world was better than you. That makes you better than an awful lot of people" (Litsky 2000, C30).

After Owens won his third medal, he was arguably the best and most famous athlete in the world. He stopped and signed autographs for adoring German fans. Hitler and Goebbels were furious that they had been shown up and their lie shattered. They believed the white race should be ashamed that African Americans were defeating them in these sporting events. In another interview at the Games, Owens expressed his gratitude for the opportunity to compete at the Olympic Games, but it all appeared to be superficial speak. He had been taught by his Jim Crow and de jure segregation experiences while growing up in the South and de facto segregation experiences of the North to not express his inner thoughts and emotions or deep feelings with most people, especially white people. These superficial comments after competitions were perfect for the media reports in the United States.

Jesse Owens at the start of his record-breaking 200 meter race at the 1936 Olympic Games in Berlin. Owens won four gold medals in track and field at the summer games. (Library of Congress)

### MATTHEW MACKENZIE "MACK" ROBINSON

Matthew Mackenzie "Mack" Robinson was born in Cairo, Georgia, on July 18, 1914. He was the older brother of Jackie Robinson, who broke Major League Baseball's color barrier when he joined the Brooklyn Dodgers in 1947. Mack was a great athlete in his own right, although he never reached the iconic heights of his brother. He did win the silver medal in the 1936 Olympic Games in Berlin, Germany. Robinson came in second to Jesse Owens, who won four gold medals at those Olympics.

After returning from the Olympics, Robinson felt underappreciated, and his feats on the world stage were forgotten. Robinson felt his notoriety never came because it was eclipsed by his brother's accomplishments. He also believed the City of Pasadena failed to celebrate his accomplishment as a son of their city.

Robinson was selected to carry the Olympic flag in the opening ceremony of the 1984 Olympic Games in Los Angeles, California. In 1997, the City of Pasadena honored both Robinsons with memorial statues in Centennial Plaza, which is located just a stone's throw from City Hall.

Mack Robinson died in 2000 in Pasadena, California.

## ADIDAS AND ADOLF DASSLER

Adolf "Adi" Dassler was a German cobbler, inventor, and entrepreneur who founded the German sportswear company Adidas in Bavaria, Germany. In 1919, Adolf and his brother, Rudolph, founded Geda. Originally, they worked together on creating a sneaker that featured two stripes on the side. They began sewing and making shoes in their parents' laundry room, and by 1924, they had registered a trademark of the name "Gebrüder Dassler Schuh-fabrik." After the business began to grow, they sought new facilities.

Dassler wanted his handcrafted shoes to be worn by as many athletes as possible in Berlin at the Olympic Games. In 1936, Adidas got a big boost when some German athletes and Jesse Owens wore the handcrafted shoes made by the brothers during the Summer Olympic Games.

Adi Dassler died on September 6, 1978, shortly before his 78th birthday.

Controversy clouded Owens's quest for a fourth medal at the games. Originally, Owens was not on the 4 × 100 relay team. The circumstances surrounding why Owens and silver medal–winner Ralph Metcalfe were added to the relay team remain unclear. Some of the U.S. Olympic officials simply wanted to improve their chances of winning another gold medal, so they added Owens and Metcalfe. Some believed that the track team's assistant coach, Dean Cromwell, wanted to make sure the runners from his school received accolades. Cromwell coached at the University of Southern California (USC), and Foy Draper and Frank Wykoff had gone to school at USC. Draper had lost to Sam Stoller at the time trials the prior week. Others believed that the Germans and Dutch were posting some astonishingly faster times, and Owens and Metcalfe were the two fastest athletes at the 100-yard dash.

Marty Glickman and Sam Stoller believed they were removed because of prejudice. Others believed that Brundage and U.S. Olympic officials did not want Glickman and Stoller to compete in the Games because they were Jewish and thus were replaced by Owens and Metcalfe.

Glickman thought that coaches Lawson Robertson and Cromwell and Olympic official Avery Brundage were anti-Semitic and did not want to face German officials who did not want to have two American Jewish athletes on the victory stand. In fact, Stoller and Glickman were the only two Jewish competitors on the track team. The relay team with Stoller and Glickman on it had been practicing in the Olympic Village for two weeks prior to the event. Metcalfe and Owens did not even touch a baton nor practice on the relay team prior to the event. The substitution did not come until just moments before the race was to begin, and no official reason was given for the switch. However, it is believed the Germans pressured the U.S. Olympic officials to make the change.

---

### MARTY GLICKMAN AND SAM STOLLER

In 1936, Marty Glickman and Sam Stoller, the only Jewish athletes on the U.S. track-and-field team, were replaced on the 400-meter relay squad at the last minute by Jesse Owens and Ralph Metcalfe. Based on practice sessions prior to the Olympic Games, Glickman and Stoller were to run the first and second legs of the relay ahead of Foy Draper and Frank Wykoff.

Jesse Owens protested and argued that he and Metcalfe already had medals; therefore, Stoller and Glickman should run their legs of the relay team. However, Glickman and Stoller never got the chance to run. In his official report, Avery Brundage denied any involvement in removing Glickman and Stoller from the team because they were Jewish.

---

All the sprinters were summoned to a meeting and told that there was a credible rumor being spread that Germany was hiding its best runners but were going to use them in the 400 relay to upset the U.S. relay team. There were some reports that Owens did not want to substitute; however, some Jewish runners have suggested that Owens had told a few reporters that he would not mind a shot at another gold medal and would compete on the relay team if asked. If the latter is true, it might have made it easier for the coaches to remove Glickman and Stoller from the relay team. It was reported that Owens told the coach he had won three gold medals. The coach then put his finger in Owens's face and told him, "You will do as you are told!" So, Owens relented. Metcalfe did not utter a word. Glickman attempted to plead with the coaches to let them compete. Years later, Glickman was still angry about being removed from the team.

After the substitution was complete, the new relay consisted of Jesse Owens, Ralph Metcalfe, Foy Draper, and Frank Wykoff. The addition of Metcalfe and Owens bolstered the United States' chances of obtaining a gold medal substantially. Owens ran the first leg of the race and took off like a cannon, quickly overtaking the Italian relay runner and making up the staggered start of the relay. As he handed the baton to Metcalfe for the second leg, a substantial lead was already forming. Metcalfe blew past a Canadian runner and handed off to Draper, who ran virtually alone and unchallenged. Draper handed the baton to the last leg of the relay team, Wykoff, who sprinted to the finish line all by himself, approximately 15 yards ahead of the competition. With a time of 59.8 seconds, this relay team helped Owens win his fourth gold medal of the Games. The German track-and-field team placed fourth but moved to third when another team was disqualified after a lane violation. African Americans dominated the 1936 Olympic Games, winning the following events: the 100-meter dash, the 200-meter dash, the 400-meter dash, the 800-meter dash, the long jump, and the high jump.

In 1936, the Amateur Athletic Union (AAU) was financially in the red and almost bankrupt. The organization decided it would send the U.S. Olympic team on a barnstorming exhibition tour to compete against local athletes to raise money for the cash-strapped organization. After his Olympic feats, the organization knew Owens would have a large financial draw. The promoters promised more money to the AAU if Owens appeared at events. They were counting on him to participate in these exhibitions. Owens was torn. He wanted to help make the organization financially solvent, but he was experiencing his own financial woes. He even considered turning pro, meaning he could accept money for taking part in athletic and commercial events, but then he would be ineligible to return as a student athlete at Ohio State University.

On top of his financial woes and a need for financial assistance, Jesse missed his family and wanted to return to the United States. Feeling the pressure of the AAU, Owens toured with his teammates to a few countries. He was exhausted and did not fare well on the exhibition tour. Owens met with Coach Snyder and officials from the National Collegiate Athletic Association (NCAA), and they could tell that Owens was exhausted and homesick. Many of the other athletes were also so tired that they under-performed in their competitions. On top of being tired, they were financially destitute and did not have any money to even enjoy entertainment or souvenirs. After a few stops on the tour, Owens decided to return to the United States. He did not have enough money to purchase a ticket, so he asked Larry Snyder to give him some money to get home. Snyder reached into his pocket and gave Owens whatever money he had. Owens thanked him and then purchased a ticket, boarded a ship, and headed back to the United States. He then sent a telegram to the AAU. The telegram read, "Sick and underweight. Cannot compete in Stockholm. Family waiting for me. Going home. Jesse Owens." Owens quit the tour because he was home-sick and missed his wife and his child and simply wanted to go home. Furious at Owens's decision to cut his tour short, the AAU suspended him and banned him from competitions.

Owens's banishment appears to have been an act of revenge by the organization. This AAU banishment affected Owens in many ways and cut off his means to pursue financial independence as an amateur. The organization's decision meant Owens could not compete as an amateur, and it also ruined his opportunity to return to Ohio State University to pursue his undergraduate degree. He would never perform as an amateur athlete again. At the time, Owens did not care, but as time went on, he realized that this action closed opportunities for him. He also believed the same thing was happening to all Black people around the world.

The AAU's brass sought to punish Owens after he quit the tour. Meanwhile, during this personal turmoil, Jesse was also receiving word of potential lucrative financial deals back in the United States. There was word circulating that the AAU would suspend Owens and strip him of his amateur status. The truth of the matter was that Owens had not accepted money to run track. He merely mentioned he was considering turning pro when he left the barnstorming tour, and under the rigid amateur rules of the time, this statement was enough to rob the world's greatest track-and-field athlete of his amateur status. This move also highlighted the growing tension between the two dominant amateur athletic organizations, the AAU and the NCAA, and their fight for power in controlling collegiate athletes.

When Owens returned to the United States, reporters swarmed him and asked numerous questions about his plans for the future. There were ticker tape parades in multiple cities held in honor of the new American Olympic hero. Jesse still faced segregation and discrimination in the United States. In one instance, several hotels in New York City refused to allow Owens and his wife to check into a hotel. Finally, one hotel agreed to allow them to stay overnight, provided they used the service entrance and not the main entrance. In some interviews, Owens stated that he did not know what he was going to do. In other interviews, he stated he wanted to return to Ohio State and complete his undergraduate degree. In the end, he would be ruled ineligible, stripped of his amateur status, and forced to turn pro. He could now pursue lucrative financial opportunities, but things would not turn out as he had planned.

# 7

## Opportunities after the Olympic Games

When Jesse Owens returned to the United States after quitting the post–1936 Summer Olympic tour, he was swarmed by news reporters hoping to catch a glimpse of the great athlete and get great quotes from the Olympic champion and winner of four Olympic gold medals. He was both a hero and a second-class citizen in the United States. Video from one of these interviews seemed to be staged. The questions seemed prepackaged and rehearsed. The reporter asked, "What was your biggest thrill in Germany?" Owens stated, "My biggest thrill was winning the hundred-yard dash and the American flag went up and they were playing the Star-Spangled Banner. We stood up there and saluted." The reporter then asked, "How did you like the German meals?" Owens responded, "The German meals were fine; it just took a little too long to get them!" The reporter then asked, "Jesse what are your immediate plans?" Owens was somewhat stiff in his response, perhaps pointing to his uncertainty about his future, "My immediate plan at this present time is to return to Ohio State University and finish my last year in college. This has been my ambition for the last four years and I want to go back and finish it. I have another year in college, and I want to get my degree in June." He was also asked about his suspension. Owens replied to this question by stating, "My suspension I really don't know what it is all about. I have been on the boat for four days and I really don't know what it is all about."

It appears most people were pushing for Jesse to turn pro. Ohio State University showed a little interest in Owens returning to school. They knew he was a poor student, but they also knew he would remain a great marketing tool and a cash cow for the Athletic Department and the university. One professor remarked that Owens was more interested in a track-and-field career than a formal education. The professor also alluded to Owens not being intrinsically motivated to complete the requirements for a degree.

In a somewhat ill-advised move, Jesse Owens decided to run professionally, with the hope that he would cash in on some offers he was allegedly receiving and be able to take care of his family. In the end, the university did not interfere with Jesse turning pro, but the Athletic Department's administration was bothered that its track-and-field team would no longer have the services of the "Buckeye Bullet." Owens had a real desire to return to Ohio State University, but he did not want to miss out on a chance to earn good money and become financially secure.

Within months of returning to the United States, Owens could not find steady employment. He worked a variety of jobs, and he also earned money participating in various stunts and exhibitions. Owens became employed as a supervisor at a playground. He would also lend his name to a chain of cleaners. In the 1940s, he worked at the Office of Civilian Defense in Philadelphia. He also worked as the director of Minority Relations at Ford Motor Company in Detroit, Michigan, and later as a sales executive at a Chicago-area sporting goods company. He was also the secretary of the Illinois Athletic Commission and a goodwill ambassador of sport under the Eisenhower administration. He also headed up his own public relations firm in Chicago.

When Owens returned to the United States, he received a hero's welcome befitting an international Olympic champion and hero. There were ticker tape parades in his honor in New York and Cleveland. But despite his being a source of pride for the nation, a celebrity, and Olympic hero, he and his wife struggled to find a hotel room in New York City because many hotels operated under segregation policies. The city's finest hotels discriminated against African Americans, and Owens realized that despite four Olympic gold medals, it was tough being an African American in the United States; racism was an unyielding practice in the country. At a lavish reception honoring him as an Olympic hero at the Waldorf Astoria, Jesse and Ruth had to ride the freight elevator instead of the elevator designated for the hotel's white guests. In an interview later in his life, Owens revealed his frustration with the hypocrisy and double standards practiced in the United States: "When I came back to my country[, the United States], even after all the stories about Hitler, I was not allowed to ride in the front of the bus," he noted. "I was asked to go through the back door. I could not even live where I wanted. Hitler may not have invited me to shake hands with him, but neither did the President of the United States." Ed Temple, the famed track coach at the historically black college Tennessee State University who had coached 23 Olympians, described Jesse Owens as "fantastic and an example to society and a national hero on the track and off the track" (Stokes 1986).

Owens believed he would be an advertising pitchman and even had some promises and prospects of employment opportunities. Unlike the millions of dollars modern-day Olympic champions receive after great Olympic performances, at the time of Owens' return from Germany, there were not many, if any, African American advertising pitchmen who had endorsement deals and certainly not lucrative advertising deals. He realized some of the people with whom he had had discussions about possible deals had made empty promises, and without an undergraduate degree in hand, it would be difficult for him to find employment. The job as a playground supervisor paid $30 per week, which was modest pay and certainly not befitting of an Olympic champion and hero. This meager amount was not enough to take care of his family or pay tuition to reenter Ohio State University if he wanted to return to the university.

To make more money, Jesse accepted a job working with the Negro Baseball League as a featured entertainment attraction for fans. Before baseball games, Owens would race a horse in a 100-yard dash. For this debasing event, he would earn a nickel out of every dollar that fans paid to see this spectacle. Owens frequently traveled the United States to race dogs, motorcycles, and horses. He usually won the races against horses because he would make a deal with the person who fired the starting gun and instruct them to fire the gun close to the horse's head. The shot usually startled his opponent and gave Owens a head start. Jesse wrote in his autobiography that the experience was "degrading" and "humiliating," but he saw it as a means to an end. He also hoped he would earn enough money to return to Ohio State University to complete his degree.

With all of the notoriety from the Olympic Games, Owens received offers of employment and endorsement opportunities when he returned to the states. A lot of these propositions were not real offers. He was showered with gifts and admiration from all corners of the United States. There

---

### BOOKS WRITTEN BY JESSE OWENS

There have been several books written about Jesse Owens, but there have only been a few authored or coauthored by him. These books are coauthored with Paul Neimark: *Blackthink: My Life as a Black Man and a White Man*; *I Have Changed: A Shockingly Personal Statement in a Tragically Impersonal Time*; *Jesse: The Man Who Outran Hitler*; and *Jesse: A Spiritual Autobiography*.

was widespread talk of several financial deals for Owens. On some occasions, he was handed paper bags with stacks of money in them. There were purportedly offers totaling approximately $100,000 (McRae 2002, 164–165). These offers also were not true. One such offer was allegedly from the California Orchestra for $25,000 to appear on stage with the musical group (McRae 2002, 164–165). As with many of the alleged offers, this offer turned out to be untrue.

There was another alleged offer of $40,000 for Owens to make personal appearances on radio shows (McRae 2002, 164–165). These false offers were many, and the real offers were few. A few of the leading African American newspapers publicly reported these supposed offers as bona fide without any verification. Many promoters and entertainers attempted to introduce Owens to the entertainment industry to earn money. If anything, he would have become a sideshow if he had pursued this line of employment. Several promoters wanted Owens to race against Eddie Tolan, the gold medal winner from the 1932 Olympic Games, for a payday of $50,000 or more. This arrangement did not work out either. Ironically, if Owens had chosen to get paid under the table, he most likely would not have lost his amateur status.

Both major political parties called on Jesse Owens to assist with their political campaign efforts. The Democratic Party probably had the inside track because Owens had history with the political party; it had given him employment while in Columbus, Ohio. In truth, Owens really did not have any strong political interests or allegiance to either political party. He was not even politically active or a member of any African American political interest group. He was not a member of the Congress of Racial Equality (CORE) or the National Association for the Advancement of Colored People (NAACP). During the 1940s, he did join the Urban League.

The national Democratic and Republican Parties both vied for Owens's endorsement. The state parties also sought his affiliation. In an effort to secure the allegiance of Owens, the governor of Ohio, Martin L. Davey, gathered a group of Clevelanders to buy Owens a home in the city. But this home offer had strings attached. The party expected Owens to support the Democratic Party and be beholden to the political party. This offer would later be pulled when Owens began working with the Republican Party and stumping for its candidate.

Both political parties also began to court Owens and seek his endorsement in the 1936 presidential elections between Democrat Franklin D. Roosevelt and Republican Alfred M. Landon. Both parties knew that an endorsement from an African American of Owens's status could sway the African American community and possibly a close election. The 1936 presidential election would be the first that the African American vote would have weight in the outcome. It is remarkable that both political parties sought Owens's endorsement because neither political party had sought the endorsement of African Americans nor paid much attention to Black voting, with the exception of Democrats curtailing the right to vote in the southern states. African Americans grew to like Roosevelt and his New Deal because it provided some economic relief to African Americans. After being given between $10,000 and $15,000, Owens stumped for the Republic Party and its presidential candidate, Alfred Landon (Gentry 1990, 126). African American newspapers condemned Owens's actions and believed he was destroying his reputations, especially with African Americans who had held him up as a hero and a symbol of Black pride.

There were rumors that Owens would sign a movie deal. Again, this was a phony deal that never materialized. Owens did win a prestigious award in 1936. He was named the Associated Press Athlete of the Year, beating out Joe DiMaggio, Max Schmeling, Dizzy Dean, and Joe Louis, among others. He traveled with a 12-piece band, but this could not replace the hole left by having his first love, track and field, taken from him. Owens could have also become the track-and-field coach at a historically Black college in Ohio. Wilberforce University made an offer to Owens for an annual salary of $2,800 to become its track-and-field coach (Schaap 2007, 231). However, this deal was contingent on Owens completing his degree at Ohio State University.

Owens got paid for a few public appearances, and the money from these appearances kept him financially afloat for at least a year. Some of these appearances may have been considered gimmicky, at best, or degrading, at worst. At one of these events in Havana, Cuba, Owens raced a horse. Initially, Jesse was not supposed to race the horse. He was supposed to race the fastest runner of the island, Conrado Rodrigues, but the AAU threatened to pull his amateur status if he raced Owens, causing Rodrigues to back out of the race. This may have also been retaliation against Owens for

---

### WILBERFORCE UNIVERSITY

Wilberforce University is the nation's oldest private historically Black university that was owned and operated by African Americans. As a historically black college, Wilberforce has a strong history of and commitment to the education of Black Americans. Wilberforce University's beginnings can be documented to its founding in 1856 by the Methodist Episcopal Church at Tawawa Springs, near Xenia, Ohio. Wilberforce University was named for the great eighteenth-century abolitionist William Wilberforce, who was white. Central State University, a public historically black college and university was formed out of an academic department of Wilberforce University.

his leaving the post-Olympic tour. Not wanting to lose out on the opportunity for a payday, Owens agreed to race a horse instead. Owens was given a head start, and he beat the horse and its jockey, earning $2,000 (Burlingame 2013, 59).

Some were angry that Owens had to race a horse to get money. At the time, Owens shrugged it off. In an interview later in his life, Owens stated, "People say it was degrading for an Olympic champion to run against a horse. . . . But what was I supposed to do? I had four gold medals, but you can't eat four gold medals." Owens was embarrassed to make money this way, but without gainful employment and a steady paycheck, he really needed money to support his wife and three daughters. For the entirety of Owens's life, he continued to bounce from job to job, trying new business ventures and changing employment every three to four years.

Economic opportunities continued to remain dry for Owens. From 1938 until 1941, Owens struggled financially and personally. Owens and his partners opened up a chain of dry cleaning businesses. It was dubbed in its advertisement as "Speedy 7 Hours Service by the World's Fastest Man" (McRae 2002, 213). Owens did not have the business acumen to operate a business, and his partners swindled him out of unspecified amounts of money. The cleaners soon went belly-up. In 1938, a lien was placed on his home for failing to pay taxes. This would not be his last entanglement with the Internal Revenue Service (IRS). In 1939, Owens filed for bankruptcy in federal court in Cleveland, Ohio. He would later barnstorm with the Indianapolis Clowns to make money. Again, Owens was used as a sideshow attraction. After baseball games, he raced a horse in a 60-yard dash. Between 1936 and 1940, Owens periodically proclaimed he would return and complete his degree at Ohio State. By 1940, he was determined to go back to college. Things would be more difficult than ever because he had three children, Marlene, Beverly, and Gloria, all under 10 years old.

Owens returned to school as a student in 1940. Coach Snyder hired him as an assistant track-and-field coach. Officially, Owens was listed as an assistant trainer in the Athletic Department. In this instance, Owens was not able to balance work and school as he had in the past. During his first term back in school, Henry Owens, Jesse's father, suffered a heart attack and died, and this grief added more difficulty to Jesse's life. At this time, there were many demands on Owens. He was working a full-time job, working with the track-and-field team, and going to school. It is unclear whether Jesse Owens's heart simply was not up for the challenges of these life events or whether he had become overwhelmed by the events of his life.

Then the Republican Party came calling again with a request that Owens campaign for Republican candidate Wendell Willkie during the 1940 presidential election. They wanted Owens to serve as a surrogate on the campaign trail. Up to this point in his life, Owens had not been an overly political person, although he stumped for Republican presidential nominee Alf Landon in the 1936 presidential race. For that political campaigning, Owens had received $10,000. Owens turned down the offer to campaign for Willkie and the Republican Party. World heavyweight boxing champion and fellow Alabama birth native Joe Louis stepped in and served as an alternative surrogate in Jesse's place. Joe Louis was not an eloquent speaker nor as charismatic as Owens. Louis was also not as comfortable around people, and this showed on the campaign trail. Willkie was soundly defeated by Democrat Franklin D. Roosevelt.

Jesse Owens was expelled from Ohio State University for poor grades, but he was readmitted after being reviewed by the administration as a special case. The faculty seemed to not care about Owens's status as an Olympic sports hero and held him to rigorous standards, just like any other student. Owens withdrew from the university in 1941. He then tried his hand at various types of employment, but none seemed to truly capture his attention and excite him like track and field did. He ran a dry cleaning business, was a gas pump attendant, worked with Ford Motor Company, coached basketball and baseball teams, worked at the Parks Department for the City of Cleveland, was employed at the State of Illinois, served as a greeter at sporting events, raced horses for money, and eventually went bankrupt. Most of these jobs were not the kind Owens had expected or had hoped for with his celebrity status. He also organized and managed a

---

### FRANKLIN D. ROOSEVELT

Franklin D. Roosevelt was in his second term as governor of New York when he was elected as the nation's 32nd president in 1932. He served as president of the United States from 1933 to 1945, which is the longest term served as president. With the country mired in the depths of the Great Depression, Americans elected Roosevelt in part because they believed he could handle this financial crisis better than President Herbert Hoover. Under Roosevelt's leadership, and with the urging of his wife, Eleanor Roosevelt, the Democratic Party included the first specific African American plank in the party platform at the 1936 convention. Ironically, this was the same year President Roosevelt failed to invite Jesse Owens to the White House after his four gold medal performance at the Olympics in Berlin, Germany.

Roosevelt was reelected as president in 1936, 1940, and 1944, and he led the United States from isolationism to victory over Nazi Germany in World War II. President Roosevelt is the only American president to be elected four times. Roosevelt died in office in April 1945.

Black basketball team named the Olympians. He continued to bounce around from job to job, not really finding employment that he truly loved.

On December 7, 1941, Japan attacked Pearl Harbor in Hawaii, and Adolf Hitler officially declared war on the United States a few days afterward. The United States' entry into the war improved the Allied forces. In 1943, the Allies invaded Sicily and removed Mussolini from power and kept advancing their forces. By 1944, the Germans were reeling from several defeats, and their resources were dwindling. There were several attempts to kill Hitler, but none was successful. Angered by these attempts, Hitler killed anyone he suspected of not being loyal to him. Most of Hitler's final days were spent in hiding as he attempted to develop strategies to change the course of the war. He soon realized there was no way his forces could win. In one of his last acts, Hitler married Eva Braun, his longtime girlfriend, on April 29, 1945. A day after the marriage, Hitler poisoned his dog, and he and Eva Braun committed suicide. Three days after these events, Germany surrendered, and this was the beginning of the end of fighting in World War II. Japan would later submit to an unconditional surrender aboard the USS *Missouri* in 1945.

From 1943 to 1945, Owens worked in personnel for the Ford Motor Company in Detroit, Michigan. In 1948, President Harry S. Truman desegregated the military in the United States with the signing of Executive Order 9981, and Owens did not speak for or against this presidential action. In 1949, Owens and his family moved to Chicago, Illinois. In Chicago, he worked with youths and became a director of the Southside Boys & Girls Club in 1951. When World War II began, Owens became the director of the National Fitness program in the Office of Civilian Defense. He traveled the country organizing exercise programs, conducting clinics, and providing lectures about health and fitness, mainly to African Americans. This public sector job provided Owens with the job security he had been seeking for quite some time, but he soon left this job to pursue an opportunity to work with Ford Motor Company in Detroit. This was a good opportunity because Ford Motor Company was building machines that assisted the military in the war. In 1943, Owens was promoted as the assistant personnel director for Negro employees. In this role, he only managed Black people. He interviewed African American applicants and served as the disciplinarian of African American employees. He was also used to fire obstinate African American employees when needed. After a race riot occurred during the summer of 1943 in which both African Americans and white people died, Ford Motor Company transitioned Owens's duties, and he became more of a public relations operative for the company. Two years later, Owens was reassigned after a shuffling of management personnel through a reorganization of the company. Specifically in 1945 while he was away at a speaking event, the reassignment was handed down. Owens refused being reassigned because he viewed it as a demotion.

After leaving Ford, Owens and a partner launched a sporting goods venture called Leo Rose Sporting Goods Company, but they could not secure contracts from national companies. Many of them refused to sell their sporting goods to a Black-owned company, even if it was headed by an Olympic champion with four gold medals. Racism most assuredly played a part in the failure to secure contracts for sporting goods products; however, Owens remained quiet on racial and political issues, as some professional sports allowed African Americans to participate in leagues.

During the 1940s, professional football reintegrated when African American players Kenny Washington and Woody Strode signed contracts with the Los Angeles Rams. Professional basketball teams also allowed a few African Americans to play on their teams in 1946. The landmark sport for most white Americans was baseball, and though there were somewhat successful Negro leagues, when Jackie Robinson integrated major league baseball in 1946, it was a major event. Robinson's success in major league baseball contributed to the diminishment of Jesse Owens's status as a sports hero. It is difficult to believe that after all of Owens's athletic achievements in school, college, and the Olympics that Americans seemed to not have room for more than one sports icon in their hearts. Indeed, this was the beginning of a shift for the African American athlete.

Seeming to take a page from Owens's athletic behavior playbook, Robinson was forced by the Dodgers' ownership to not retaliate against all the racist antics carried out by some white baseball players when he entered the major leagues, though this was his natural inclination. Robinson had been politically active in pushing for civil rights for African Americans, but he had to bridle his outspokenness when he became the face of integration of Major League Baseball. Like Owens, Robinson knew that a racial incident of any magnitude could ruin any chance for integration and limit any opportunity for other African American athletes for many years to come. On the horizon, as African Americans began to gain civil rights through nonviolent protests across the nation, there was a more boisterous, demonstrative, and opinionated African American athlete that would supplant these strong but silent athletic pioneers.

After the sporting goods business failed, Owens began to capitalize on his celebrity to make money. Owens and his family lived comfortably in Detroit, but to maintain this comfortable lifestyle, it would take some financial security. In 1949, he relocated to Chicago and accepted executive positions for numerous companies, including the Mutual of Omaha Insurance Corporation, the Illinois Athletic Commission, and the Southside Boys & Girls Club. He also opened several businesses, including a successful public relations agency. After these positions faded, Owens lined up a series of jobs, mostly participating in exhibitions. He was able to showcase his talent with the Harlem Globetrotters and participated in exhibitions in which he raced various individuals; however, he did not race against horses. For the most part, he raced, spoke with those in the crowd, and signed autographs. A last public exhibition occurred in 1952 at Yankee Stadium, when he ran the bases between games of a Negro League double-header. Owens was named to the board of directors for the Chicago South Side Boys Club and continued to promote health and provide running instruction. From 1951 to 1952, Jesse served as the executive director of the organization and worked mainly with the African American youth on the South Side of Chicago. Owens was a great Olympic champion, but as an administrative manager, he was mediocre at best.

Again, Owens was thrust into politics when he campaigned for Republican Illinois gubernatorial candidate William Stratton. Owens had been promised possible employment if he stumped for Stratton and Stratton was victorious. After Stratton won the election, he appointed Owens as secretary of the Illinois State Athletic Commission. With this position, Owens earned a salary of $6,000, making him the highest-paid employee of the commission. Owens gave speeches to local civic groups. He usually used sports as a central theme in his addresses and often used sports imagery as metaphors to emphasize points on the themes of democracy, patriotism, and fitness.

From 1952 to 1955, Owens worked with the athletic commission in Illinois. The governor of Illinois appointed Owens as the director of the Illinois Youth Commission, and over 10 years, he directed the state's educational and recreational programs aimed at young people. Owens also received a political appointment on a national level. During the 1950s, President Dwight D. Eisenhower also had Owens represent the U.S. federal government and travel abroad to promote democratic values. Jesse traveled the world promoting running and health. He often discussed and demonstrated good running form and techniques when speaking to audiences. Many of the techniques were a combination of the techniques his coaches, Charles Riley and Larry Snyder, had shared with him over the years. In 1955, Owens traveled to India, Malaysia, and the Philippines as a part of the International Exchange Services of the U.S. Department of State. Mainstays of Owens's speeches were the themes of fostering pride, discipline, amateurism, and teamwork. In 1955, Owens started a public relations firm called Jesse Owens and Associates. He served as president and owner of this firm and continued his public speaking schedule with engagements at businesses and professional conventions.

Owens also represented President Eisenhower at the 1956 Summer Olympic Games in Melbourne, Australia. After the Melbourne Olympic Games, President Eisenhower asked Owens to serve in the People-to-People

Program. This program was a public and private partnership to promote mutual learning between Americans and other cultures. After the Olympics in Melbourne, Owens regularly attended the Olympics in various countries. He was selected to join the board of directors of the U.S. Olympic Committee and helped raised funds for the U.S. Olympic teams. While on the Olympic Committee, he played an essential role in the design and sale of the Olympic commemorative coins, which also helped to provide additional funding for the Olympic teams. In 1965, Owens was hired as a running coach for the New York Mets during spring training.

Despite his apparent success in the 1960s, Owens still faced financial problems that had dogged him most of his life. At age 53, Owens faced federal charges when he failed to pay taxes. He was prosecuted for federal tax evasion after an investigation by the IRS. The IRS revealed that Owens had failed to file tax returns and evaded payment of $68,166 in federal income taxes between 1959 and 1962 (*New York Times*, February 2, 1966, 27). Owens faced a potential sentence of a $40,000 fine and up to four years in federal prison. As a result of this judgment, he took a plea deal, and the judge ordered Owens to pay restitution in the amount of $3,000 in addition to the back taxes he owed. Owens emerged from this scandal with his reputation fairly intact (*New York Times*, February 2, 1966, 27). Apparently, the judge took into account Owens's work to promote democracy and goodwill nationally and internationally. Perhaps the judge remembered Owens's feats at the 1936 Olympics and as an Olympic hero or perhaps the judge saw Jesse Owens as a "good Black person" and decided this did not warrant him any punishment.

Owens had largely avoided publicly speaking about racial issues in the United States. He did not openly support Dr. Martin Luther King Jr. or other civil rights leaders as they challenged the second-class status of African Americans during the 1960s. Owens condescendingly spoke out against African American AAU athletes when they called for a boycott of the Houston Master's Relays in 1961. Owens reportedly called the movement "a pretty silly thing to withdraw young athletes who are college students because of a social structure" and he noted amateur athletes aided in bettering race relations. Owens followed up in condemning the boycott in Houston by stating, "Competition in athletics has broken down more barriers than most any other thing." Other African American sports icons, including Jackie Robinson, supported the boycott and urged all African American athletes to do their part. Robinson also highlighted the fact that other college students of all races were putting themselves in danger and being attacked by angry white mobs by participating in the freedom rides in southern states to challenge segregation in interstate travel.

Jackie Robinson and Jesse Owens were different in their approaches to gaining civil rights. Robinson was more active. He raised funds for

freedom riders and lobbied politicians to support key civil rights initiatives. He was also a board member of the NAACP and campaigned all
across the country in support of the civil rights movement. In 1963, four
months before the bombing at 16th Street Baptist Church that killed four
girls (Addie Mae Collins, Cynthia Wesley, Carole Robertson, and Carol
Denise McNair) and severely injured another girl, Sarah Collins, former
heavyweight boxing champion Floyd Patterson and Major League Baseball
icon Jackie Robinson traveled to Birmingham to meet with civil rights
leaders Dr. Martin Luther King Jr. and Reverend Ralph Abernathy about
strategies to curtail the excessive police violence being used against protesters taking place in the city. Using a negative trope often used by racist
southern politicians and law enforcement, Owens reportedly called Robinson and Patterson outside agitators. Owens commented, "I can't see where
they're going to be of any great help." He also asserted that local governments would have to resolve the issue of segregation on their own locali-
ties. Owens stated, "To have people from the outside go in, for some things
I don't think that's a good idea." When a journalist inquired whether the
Olympic icon had been requested to provide assistance to the movement,
Owens retorted, "No. I haven't been asked because I haven't allowed myself
to be asked."

As the 1968 Summer Olympics in Mexico City approached, Owens
would have to make a definitive choice about engaging in the civil rights
movement, specifically the Black Power movement, when faced by younger,
more progressive, and seemingly radical African American amateur athletes who challenged the inequality and discrimination taking place in the
United States. Even after the deaths of President John F. Kennedy, U.S.
Attorney General Robert F. Kennedy, and Black civil rights leaders Malcom X and Dr. Martin Luther King Jr., Owens did not openly support the
civil rights movement or publicly speak out on race relations.

# 8

## Adjusting to Changing Times

Life for even the most famous athletes past their prime can be extremely difficult. For an African American athlete, it can be especially difficult because of the pressure of being a role model for an entire race of people and practicing social responsibility in their public and personal lives. Some of these expectations are unreasonable. Some white athletes do not appear to be burdened with these types of expectations. It is difficult to separate the intersectionality of race and sports in the United States. The historical legacy of racism adds additional challenges to African American athletes in regard to social responsibility, as these athletes are expected to engage and support causes in the African American community. Additionally, if the African American athlete's life and self-worth are based on his sporting accolades, he may struggle with finding a fulfilling career after sports. For African American sports heroes, it is often difficult to parlay a sports career into a productive career outside of the sports arena.

Jesse Owens struggled both personally and professionally after his athletic career was over, and he went through several amalgamations of varying jobs after his celebrated Olympic victories. He tried his hand in business, opening several businesses during the 1960, but these businesses failed. He ran a dry cleaning business, worked in public relations, was a motivational speaker, worked as a gas pump attendant, raced horses for money, and eventually went bankrupt. Owens once mentioned the difficulty of finding stable employment after the Olympics after essentially being banned by the sport he loved: "People say it was degrading for an

Olympic champion to run against a horse but what was I supposed to do? I had four gold medals, but you can't eat four gold medals" (Schwartz 2009).

Five years after Jesse Owens's death, the public discovered that the Federal Bureau of Investigation (FBI) had investigated him during the 1950s. He was the target of a secretive investigation in 1956. J. Edgar Hoover directed FBI agents to profile and target Owens for an investigation (Associated Press 1994). Agents had full range and could investigate all aspects of Owens's life. They investigated both his professional and personal life. His sex life and background were scrutinized to determine whether he was a loyal American or could be compromised and flipped as a possible spy for a foreign government. The investigation came to light after the *Arizona Republic Newspaper* used the Freedom of Information Act (FOIA) to gain information about the FBI's investigation. During the investigation, scores of Owens's records were checked and examined. The FBI suspected that Owens may have been involved in subversive activities with the Communist Party, but it did not find that Owens had participated in any of these kinds of activities. The only significant detail the investigation discovered was that Owens's name once appeared in a communist newspaper called the *Daily Worker*. FBI agents also found his name listed in a Michigan newspaper as a member of the Committee to Seek Unity of Racial Groups that Hoover erroneously believed was a subversive group working to push communism and undermine the American government. Hoover regarded other groups seeking racial reconciliation as subversive in nature.

While touring with his four gold medals he had won a year earlier, Owens was targeted again after speaking to the National Negro Congress. That investigation also spilled over, and subsequent probes examined Owens's parents, his wife, his daughters, and his brothers and sisters. They were all investigated to see whether they were engaged in suspicious activity or subversive actions. The FBI also combed through Jesse Owens' personal finances and credit records. They also did credit checks on Owens's wife, his parents, his daughters, and his brothers and sisters. In 1985, when learning of this investigation, an astonished and appalled Ruth Owens stated, "My husband is resting in his grave, so he can't speak for himself. But I followed him all over and I know he was loyal to America. He loved his family and his country. Jesse was a good man. He always tried to do what was right. But he went to his grave being dogged. His crime was he was black" (*Ohio State Lantern* 1985).

During the 1950s, as the Cold War with the Soviet Union became a mainstay of American foreign policy, Owens was held as a symbol of American freedom. Many whites also held Owens as a symbol of upward mobility for African Americans. Jesse also championed himself as a testament and a living example of the American dream. He was often sent on goodwill tours domestically and abroad to promote democratic ideals during the 1950s and 1960s. Owens was proud that all of his daughters attended Ohio State University. Undoubtedly, his influence and legacy loomed large on his daughters. Owens would often return to campus and speak to students and alumni groups. Two of Owens's daughters graduated from Ohio State. His daughter Gloria earned her undergraduate degree in education from the university in 1953, and Marlene graduated with her undergraduate degree in social work in 1961.

Another proud moment for Owens was when his daughter Marlene was elected homecoming queen at Ohio State in 1960. She was the first African American homecoming queen in the school's history. She was selected as a candidate for homecoming queen by the residents of Canfield Hall, where she had lived for four years as an on-campus student. Serita Hartstein, her Jewish roommate, pushed Marlene Owens's homecoming queen campaign. Marlene swept the balloting, winning over 16,000 votes of the possible 24,000 votes (*Ebony* 1960). Photos appeared in *Jet* (n.d.), the United States' premier African American magazine. One photograph shows a smiling Marlene Owens in the stands flanked by four white attendants of the homecoming court. In another photograph, she appears at midfield at halftime of the homecoming football game between Ohio State and Wisconsin. Another photograph shows a stunned Marlene Owens with her parents, and there is another photograph of her father beaming with pride while holding the trophy and giving a speech to the fans at the football game (*Ebony* 1960). Marlene's homecoming queen victory reflected some of the change that had taken place in Columbus since Jesse Owens was enrolled at Ohio State 30 years earlier, when African American students could not live in on-campus residence halls or eat in restaurants in downtown Columbus. While there were changes taking place in Columbus, Ohio, there were also changes taking place on the national scene as well.

On the national stage, there was a growing movement to put Black Power into the American mainstream. In July 1967, the first National Conference on Black Power was held in New Jersey. Attendees ranged from Black activists and Black militants, to employees of governmental agencies, to Black athletes. As a product of this conference, a series of resolutions was passed:

1.  The establishment of Black institutions such as banks and credit unions

2.  The establishments of Black universities (curriculums)

3.  Boycotts against white merchants in Black communities

4.  Guaranteed income for all people

5.  Boycotts by Black athletes of Olympic competitions and professional boxing as a response to Muhammad Ali being stripped of the heavyweight title

6.   Boycotts of Black churches that were committed to the Black revolution
7.   Boycott of Black publications accepting advertisement for hair straighteners and bleaching creams (Pickney 2000, 46)

While the debate raged on about the role of the Black athlete and the place for Black Power in the United States, a documentary titled *Jesse Owens Returns to Berlin* was produced. This documentary did not air on the big three television stations at the time because they thought an African American man, even if it was Jesse Owens, may be too much for white audiences during such a turbulent time. The documentary was finally aired in 1968, with Owens narrating as he reflected on his Olympic experiences at the Berlin Games.

Owens rarely seemed interested in and even displayed verbal disdain for the Black Power movement and electoral politics, unless it was of benefit to him. At a time when most African Americans continued to switch political parties and had begun to overwhelmingly support the Democratic Party, Owens continued to travel and stump with politicians from the Republican Party. Owens did not publicly speak about the passing of the Civil Rights Act of 1964 nor the 1965 Voting Rights Act.

During the 1960s and 1970s, Owens continued endorsing corporate products while using his credibility to endorse fair play and racial progress. In 1965, Atlantic Richfield Company (ARCO) sponsored the ARCO and Jesse Owens Games. These games are a track meet that is held annually for youths aged 10 to 15. During the 1970s, Owens was both honored and excoriated. President Richard Nixon sent Owens to the Ivory Coast in West Africa to lead running clinics and promote the economic and political freedoms of the United States. In 1972, Ohio State awarded Owens an honorary doctorate in the athletic arts. The university's stated purpose for awarding Owens with a doctorate was "for his unparalleled skill and ability" as an athlete and for "his personification of sportsmanship ideals." This honorary doctorate was followed two years later with another honorary doctorate when Wagner College honored Owens with an honorary degree. In 1974, the National Collegiate Athletic Association (NCAA) awarded him the Theodore Roosevelt Award, an honor for his activities in support of college athletics after the end of his track career. During the same year, he was elected to the International Track and Field Hall of Fame.

In 1976, Wagner College, a small private liberal arts college located in Staten Island, New York, awarded Owens with a doctorate of humane letters. An article appeared in the Wagner College student newspaper describing Owens's visit to the campus, and it included a photograph of Owens walking with the president of Wagner, Dr. John Satterfield, in their academic regalia. Also in 1976, Owens was awarded the Presidential Medal of Freedom, the highest award bestowed upon a civilian. Owens accepted the award in front of the 250 members of the 1976 Olympic team along with several national and international dignitaries. In making the presentation, President Ford stated, "Jesse, your character and your achievement will always be a source of inspiration."

In 1990, the Presidential Medal of Freedom, the highest award bestowed upon a civilian was given to Jesse Owens. In 2002, Ohio State University named its recreation centers and track stadium for its track star, Jesse Owens. The centers were originally opened in 1976 and segmented into three areas: North, South, and West. Jesse Owens Memorial Stadium serves as the home venue for Buckeye soccer, track-and-field, and lacrosse events. In 2011, Ohio State dedicated a statue outside of the stadium to honor Owens.

However, leaders of the Black Power movement did not hold Owens in high regard. The progressive wing of this movement believed Owens was a sellout to African Americans and a mere puppet to African Americans. It is important to note that these leaders believed that most of the notable civil rights leaders were out of touch with the real problems and issues facing the African American community at large.

During the 1970s, Owens authored two books. The first was published in 1970 under the title *Blackthink: My Life as Black Man and White Man* and was critically acclaimed as a seminal and groundbreaking work by the conservative media outlets and President Richard Nixon and members of his administration. *Blackthink* was coauthored with Paul G. Neimark. The African American community and Black media outlets were less receptive to this book. In fact, the Black press condemned the work, especially Owens's claim that racism was no longer an impediment nor contributor to the educational gap or economic achievement. The African American community wholly rejected the premise of *Blackthink*. The work was neo-conservative in nature, especially in regard to race, race relations, and racial tension. Some even claimed Neimark used Owens to promote this controversial racial view. In the book, Owens was somewhat complimentary of Dr. Martin Luther King Jr., but he is overly critical of individuals such as Stokely Carmichael, H. Rap Brown, and Muhammad Ali or those whom he considered Black radicals. Owens condemned Muhammad Ali for refusing induction into the military, and he refused to call him Ali. He called him Cassius Clay, Ali's name before his conversion to the Nation of Islam. The failure to recognize Ali's Muslim name was interpreted as a sign of disrespect to Ali and his religion. This sign of disrespect was also used by Floyd Patterson when the two boxed for the heavyweight boxing championship.

Owens liked that Dr. King did not appear to hate anyone and seemed to use a prescription of love as a solution to race issues. Owens did clash with King over his view of the Vietnam War, believing King's view of war would make it appear to the rest of the United States that African American men were not loyal to their country. Owens also did not prescribe to the philosophy of nonviolence. He believed that in certain circumstances, people should fight back and defend themselves. Owens did not like what he described as "pro-Black" and "anti-white" bigotry (Owens and Neimark 1970, 29). Owens did support President Lyndon B. Johnson's Great Society programs with this philosophy of "blackthink," Owens also made it appear as if racism was nonexistent and that there was not a crisis in regard to race. Owens took a direct shot at Harry Edwards, who was hypercritical of Owens's views regarding race. In Owens's book, Owens called out Edwards by name when he specifically stated,

> But that doesn't mean there aren't some things that should be said and that aren't being said, things that can show "the race crisis" going on in America right now is for the most part the biggest hoax in our history. And possibly the cruelest—for in its seeds is another crisis of infinite proportions. Harry Edwards, my name is never been Tom. But I am old enough to be your uncle. I know the trouble you've seen. Now can I make you—and everyone—see that it's nothing absolutely nothing, next to the trouble and your black think are about to make? (22–23)

In another astonishing claim in this book, Owens claimed, "If the Negro doesn't succeed in today's America, it is because he has chosen to fail." In the aftermath of the publishing of the book, Owens received a high volume of letters refuting the central premise of his book. The book also cost Owens some relationships; his barber refused to give him haircuts anymore. Perhaps this book was in response to the cold shoulder treatment Owens received at the hand of the African American athletes participating in the 1968 Olympic Games. During the 1960s, most of white society continued to hold Owens up as a trailblazer and a symbol of the American dream, while African Americans viewed him as a sellout to the African American community. Clearly, Owens was naïve to the backlash he would receive from the publication of his book.

Owens and Neimark teamed up for a second book published in 1972, titled *I Have Changed*. It was a response to the negative commentary and backlash he had received from his first book. In this work, Owens attempts to undo and retract much of what was stated in his first book. He acknowledges the gains made through the civil rights movement and the progress the movement made in the United States. He also backs away from his belief that all activism is destructive and also acknowledges that racism had hampered race relations and Black advancement in the United States. After being the United States' superhero after 1936 Olympics, Jesse Owens was disliked by some whites and some African Americans during the 1960s. He was not accustomed to this kind of treatment. He was accustomed to adulation, admiration, and adoring fans. In *I Have Changed*, Owens reveals that he received hate mail from white people. Some of these letters appear in the work. One presumably from a white person reads,

> Dear Jesse:
> That's a mighty fine story you're doing for all those papers. But why do you say you're black? Your real color is brown—for your nose. If it wasn't to start with, it sure would've been after what you've been putting it in to get on the good side of the murdering Black Panthers. Now they are black, boy—and I call you boy because you still should be a slave for some white man instead of running around loose like you do after us whites taught you to read and write. (Owens and Neimark 1972, 23)

Another letter, presumably from an African American, is also critical of Owens because of the conservative racial views expressed in his book:

> Dear Jesse Owens
> Your series on the middle-class black was very revealing. But it didn't reveal anything about us blacks—only about you and how you've become part of the fascist-capitalist conspiracy to systematically exterminate every black man in America. The only thing I wonder, N—, is why you don't see that when you've helped do away with all your own kind, that the white man will put a gun to your head, too. (Owens and Neimark 1972, 24)

Initially, Owens expressed that he could not understand why the book was not well received by the African American community. In the book, he ponders and compares himself to Black leaders such as Malcom X and Eldridge Cleaver and wonders why he was not being embraced by the African American community. He had not realized that many in the larger African American community had become more progressive and by some accounts more radical. Later, he realized that through his book he had offended the larger African American community because he was not a champion of Black equality in comparison to more progressive Black leaders of the time.

By the completion of his book, *Blackthink*, Owens had a change of heart or finally reveals his true feelings that he had previously not been brave enough to reveal when he states, "I realized now that militancy in the best sense of the word was the only answer where the black man was concerned, that any black man who wasn't militant in 1970 was either blind or a coward" (Owens and Neimark 1972, 72). Owens also recognized how he was viewed by younger African Americans during the late 1960s. He stated he knew young African Americans viewed him as a "sellout" who never talked about the issues in the Black community (Owens and Neimark 1972, 95). He also knew they thought he was a "sellout" because he worked as a spokesperson for American corporations (Owens and Neimark 1972, 95). He also stated that African Americans must have reasonable expectations in Black advancement, and it was reasonable to expect American corporations "to speed up the day when a Negro can be president (of a corporation) or even President of the United States" (Owens and Neimark 1972, 95).

In the last decade of his life, Owens was celebrated, and he enjoyed the accolades of a former athletic hero and celebrity lauded by an appreciative nation who remembered his great accomplishment in the Olympic Games in Berlin, Germany. He was a fixture on the public lecture circuit in the United States and abroad. He often retold stories of his athletic experiences, prescribed his recipes for success, and reiterated his faith in the American dream.

# 9

## Leadership, Political Activism, and the 1968 Mexico Olympic Games

Booker T. Washington's life's work was founding and building higher education for African Americans, and he was one of the most powerful African American leaders in the United States during the late nineteenth and early twentieth centuries. Washington was conservative when dealing with race relations of the time. He also had an appreciation for athletic competition, and although he did not engage in strenuous athletic activities, he liked croquet, which was also enjoyed by Frederick Douglass (Wiggins and Miller 2003, 77). Washington also enjoyed golf, and he even played a round with white philanthropist Andrew Carnegie in Scotland. Of Washington's life's work, his focus was to prove to the larger white society that African Americans were worthy of eventual full citizenship and that there was advancement being made by African Americans as a whole community. In his public life, Washington embraced genteel actions and distanced himself from any actions that may have garnered the disapproval of the white elites in American society. It was an intentional way to get wealthy white donors to continue to invest in Tuskegee University, which he founded.

Jesse Owens was much like the conservative Washington in his approach to race relations. During the 1960s, Owens did not speak or publicly participate in the civil rights movement; however, during the 1970s, he was more vocal in his support of the movement. In the 1960s, Owens remained a conservative and a surrogate for the Republican Party and he rebuffed

President Lyndon B. Johnson's "Great Society" programs. While Owens thought highly of and respected Dr. Martin Luther King Jr.'s principles for equality, he opposed King's confrontational campaigns and tactics used in the fight for civil rights. He felt all forms of activism were ineffective. Owens only openly embraced and spoke about the civil rights movement and the benefits of dismantling legalized segregation during his speaking engagements when he spoke about his born-again spiritual experience. Owens had particular disdain for those who were at the more radical end of the spectrum and who advocated Black Power, like Malcolm X, Eldridge Cleaver, and Stokely Carmichael. Owens criticized Muhammad Ali for refusing induction into the military and refused to call him by his Muslim name after Ali converted to Islam. He continued to call the boxer by his birth name, Cassius Clay.

Washington and Owens were the polar opposite of Jack Johnson and the more activist African American athletes that followed. During the early 1900s, Washington issued statements aimed at heavyweight boxing champ Jack Johnson to "refrain from anything resembling boastfulness." After Johnson was convicted of breaking the Mann Act, specifically by transporting a white woman across state lines for immoral purposes, Washington asserted via telegram through a national wire service "that respectability in all matters should mark the behavior of racial representatives such as the boxing champ that any taint of immorality further stigmatized African Americans everywhere" (Wiggins and Miller 2003, 78).

Washington and other African American leaders and members of the Black intelligentsia wanted Black people, especially high-profile African Americans, such as athletes, to conform to what they and white America considered respectability. Jesse Owens was a prototype of this kind of athlete. These kinds of athletes were showcased as heroes of the African American community and used as examples in matters of race, sportsmanship, fair play, and equality, if these elements were extended to all walks of American society. If equality seen in athletic competitions could be extended to the larger society, these sports platforms could be used to lift the entire race in upward social mobility and equality in the United States.

Scholar, civil rights activist, historian, and educator Edwin Bancroft Henderson, who was also the founder of *Black Sport History*, made the case that Jesse Owens's victory in an international competition against Hitler should have made Owens a national hero. His beliefs aligned with the prevailing thoughts among many African Americans that achievements on the athletic field were a testament to white America of the potential contributions of African Americans in every field of endeavors. He believed the race should make even greater use of Black athletes to gain racial respect. Henderson believed that Black athletes like Jesse Owens could serve as goodwill ambassadors for the African American community.

Indeed, serving as an African American community goodwill ambassador placed seen and unseen burdens on Owens. Jesse mastered the balancing act and masterfully walked a tightrope of appearing to be perfectly content, but later in his life, he spoke out more forcefully about discrimination and racism. During the 1960s, he continued to work as a paid endorser of multiple products, such as Quaker Oats, Sears and Roebuck, and Johnson & Johnson. Owens also was a paid speaker and delivered about 30 motivational speeches per year for $2,000 plus expenses, which was a good fee during this time. Owens made paid speeches at Atlantic Richfield, Ford Motor Company, MacGregor Sporting Goods, Greyhound, and Paramount.

In 1961, 8 members of the Texas Southern University track-and-field team joined 12 other prominent African American athletes in boycotting of the Gulf AAU National Meet of Champions held in Houston, Texas. Texas Southern University is a historically Black college that was founded in 1927 and located in Houston. These athletes were joined by other African American athletes to boycott the track-and-field meet because of the segregation policies used in stadium seating. Capitalizing on the high-profile event and its publicity, the event would capture the track world's attention and draw large support from local African American fans to watch these athletes compete.

As a result of their participation in the boycott, and like Owens after he left the post-Olympic tour, the AAU suspended these athletes. Unlike Owens, they were later reinstated. Owens criticized the move of reinstating John Tomas and Ralph Boston after they did not participate in the track-and-field meet. Owens stated, "Personal honor comes before the color of one's skin." Former Olympic star Harrison Dillard lambasted Owens, stating, "I can't go against my people, because so long as the social attitudes and the mores of our present society are perpetuated, Ralph Boston and John Thomas can't be just plain Americans, they must be American Negroes" (*Jet* 1961). Owens would later criticize African American athletes for their protest in the 1968 Olympics. Ironically, Boston was a member of the legendary track-and-field team at Tennessee State University, a historically Black college in Nashville, Tennessee. Boston also broke Owens's world record in the long jump that had stood for 25 years with a jump of 27 1/4 feet.

The year 1968 was volatile. There were various protests being held around the country and abroad. Student activists were protesting not only in the United States but in Germany, France, and Mexico City, where the Olympic Games were being held. In the United States, protests were held against the military involvement in the Vietnam War. There were also protests for the advancement of civil rights for African Americans. Dr. Martin Luther King Jr. and other leaders of civil rights movement adopted Mahatma Gandhi's principles of nonviolent protests as a primary method

of exacting policy change. The Gandhian nonviolent principle is the practice of achieving goals such as social change through symbolic protests,
civil disobedience, and economic or political noncooperation. It is a tech-
nique that centers on demonstrating opposition to a government's activities simply by not cooperating with them. On March 28, Dr. Martin Luther
King Jr. led a protest march for higher wages for striking sanitation workers in Memphis, Tennessee. The protest turned violent. After King himself
had been led from the scene, a 16-year-old Black boy was killed, 60 people
were injured, and over 150 people were arrested. Disappointed with the
violent end to the protest march, Dr. King decided to have another protest
march in April. He was also scheduled to speak at Mason Temple Church
on April 3, 1968.

On April 4, 1968, Dr. King spent the day at the Lorraine Motel in Memphis.
The Lorraine was one of the few hotels that was accepting of African Americans in the city. Dr. King was suffering from a terrible head cold and was not
feeling well enough to go to Mason Temple. Ralph Abernathy was put in as
King's replacement. Abernathy called King and told him that there was an
overflow crowd of about 3,000 people, and they wanted to hear him speak.
King went to the church and delivered his "I've Been to the Mountain Top"
speech. During this brief speech, King spoke of his mortality. In the speech, he
stated, "I've seen the Promised Land. I may not get there with you. But I want
you to know tonight, that we, as a people, will get to the Promised Land."

The following day, on April 4, King was invited to have dinner at the
home of a prominent minister in Memphis. As Dr. King stood on the bal-
cony talking with some of his friends in the courtyard of the Lorraine
Motel, a shot rang out, and a bullet hit Dr. King in the right cheek. He was
rushed to the hospital, where he was pronounced dead. Robert Kennedy,
hearing of King's murder just before he was to give a speech in Indianapolis, Indiana, delivered a powerful extemporaneous eulogy in which he
pleads with the audience "to tame the savageness of man and make gentle
the life of this world." King's death sparked rioting in Baltimore, Boston,
Chicago, Detroit, Kansas City, Newark, and Washington, DC, among
many others. Across the country, 46 deaths were blamed on the riots. The
alleged killer, James Earl Ray, was captured in London, England, on June 8,
1968. Jesse Owens did not make a public statement about Dr. King's death.

One of the most controversial and iconic moments of the protest era of
the 1960s took place at the 1968 Olympics. It was the peaceful protest of
three African American Olympic athletes. Peaceful protests were a means
to bring attention to societal problems or provoke change of public policy
agenda and how it is woven into the American social fabric. In 1968, Tommie Smith, John Carlos, and Lee Evans peacefully protested the treatment of
African Americans and advocated for equality in the United States at the
Mexico City Olympic Games. During the 1960s, many African American

athletes used their fame to protest inequality in the United States. In January 1965, New Orleans, Louisiana, was chosen as the site for the annual American Football League All-Star Game. New Orleans and the state of Louisiana had a long history of practicing government-sanctioned discrimination. Remember, the U.S. Supreme Court case *Plessy v. Ferguson* (1896), through which the United States cemented the policy of separate but equal, took root in New Orleans. The trouble with the Black football players who were in town for the All-Star Game began almost immediately when they stepped off the plane in New Orleans. Before 24 hours had even transpired, events had gotten so insufferably bad that they all left. White passengers watched as groups of African Americans came out to the same curb as them and actually tried to hail cabs—their white cabs.

The football players decided to boycott the game. As a result of these players boycotting the game, it was moved from New Orleans to Houston. Over the next two years, the racial climate began to change in New Orleans. Black bus passengers, discovering African American drivers behind the wheel for the first time, no longer had to head to the back of the bus. Blacks could now shop at Canal Street department stores. Restaurants and grocery stores slowly ended the custom of having African American customers go to side windows for service. These changes were largely due to this group of African American professional football players and their decision to boycott and bring attention to inequality and disparate treatment in New Orleans.

Another notable African American athlete who pushed for social change through peaceful protest was heavyweight boxing champion Muhammad Ali. Muhammad Ali was crowned heavyweight champion in 1964 after defeating Sonny Liston in perhaps the biggest upset in boxing history. Ali was just 22 years old, and he represented for many being unabashedly pro-Black and unpatriotic, which for some is unforgivable and scared many in white America. Two other factors made white America quite fearful, Ali, formerly named Cassius Clay, announced his membership in the Nation of Islam immediately after besting Liston and winning the title. Ali also had a strong friendship with Malcolm X, another African American man who made white America fearful. Ali made his dedication to the Nation of Islam's objectives and its political activism perfectly clear.

In 1967, Ali was drafted into the military, but he refused to serve in Vietnam. This defiant act made him one of the most recognizable figures in the world, the boxing champ who defied an empire to preserve his own soul. Ali's dissent to the war, even as it was based on his religious and philosophical principles, also centered on the public recognition of systemic racism in the United States. Muhammad Ali helped link the civil rights and peace movements together in mutually reinforcing opposition against war, violence, and racism. Other professional athletes, including Jim Brown, Bill Russell, and Lew Alcindor, who later changed his name to

Kareem Abdul-Jabbar, held a summit where many African American athletes threw their full support behind Muhammad Ali. Ali was vilified during the 1960s, but he became one of America's beloved figures before his death. Ali was stripped of his boxing license and heavyweight title for four years and almost driven out of sport, only to reclaim his financial and international standing against all odds.

Muhammad Ali represented a new kind of protest leader. They were more impatient, younger, and militant people involved in the civil rights movement. Some of the younger members of the movement, namely those in the Student Nonviolent Coordinating Committee (SNCC), referred to Dr. King as the "Lawd" because when he spoke, people unquestioningly responded to his requests. Many young people were unwilling to blindly follow, and they began to even question the nonviolent method to obtaining desegregation.

A year after Muhammad Ali took a stand against war, the 1968 Olympics became another opportunity to bring social change through peaceful protest center stage. On October 2, 1968, around 10,000 university and prep school students gathered in Mexico City, the host city for the Olympics, and protested by gathering at the Plaza de las Tres Culturas to protest the government's actions in a peaceful demonstration. One of the biggest chants heard that day was "No Queremos Olimpiadas; Queremos Revolución!" In English, this translates to the phrase "We Don't Want Olympics; We Want a Revolution!" Two helicopters hovered over the plaza where the protests were taking place, but the protesters would not back down. There was a show of force by the Mexican military, and flares were fired on the protesters. This caused chaos on the plaza, and gunfire ensued. People were running in all directions as shots were fired. Both sides claimed the other fired first. Soldiers shot at protesters and innocent bystanders,

---

### MUHAMMAD ALI

Muhammad Ali was a professional American boxer, activist, and philanthropist. He has become known by the nickname "the Greatest," and he is listed as one of the greatest boxers of all time. Ali is regarded as one of the most significant and celebrated sports figures of the twentieth century. He was born on January 17, 1942, in Louisville, Kentucky. His birth name was Cassius Marcellus Clay Jr., but he changed his name when he converted to the Nation of Islam in 1964.

In 1960, Ali won a gold medal for the light heavyweight division at the Olympics in Rome, Italy, and became the world heavyweight boxing champion in 1964. Ali was outspoken, and his outspoken views and refusal to enlist in the army made him a marked man.

On June 3, 2016, Muhammad Ali died at age 74.

including journalists. In the end, hundreds of protesters were dead, and many more were wounded. Apartment complexes near the plaza had their phone lines and electricity shut off. These clashes left a black eye over the 1968 Summer Olympics Games.

These protests were a prelude to American athletes' protests. During a medal ceremony at the Mexico City Games, three African American track athletes made what would become one of the most famous political protests in the history of sports. The athletes, Tommie Smith, John Carlos, and Lee Evans, stood on the podium for the national anthem after winning gold and bronze medals and raised their black-gloved fists to the sky with the Black Power salute. Smith and Carlos were the most visible athletes who joined the efforts organized by scholar, activist, and sociology professor Harry Edwards to boycott the Olympic Games while they were student athletes at San Jose State University.

Professor Edwards set up the Olympic Project for Human Rights (OPHR) and appealed to all African American Olympic athletes to boycott the games. The rationale behind the boycott was rooted in similar causes of the calls for a boycott of the 1936 Olympic Games. The 1936 boycott sought to expose the prejudice against Jews in Germany, and the 1968 calls for a boycott sought to expose prejudice against African Americans in the United States. Specifically, these athletes believed that boycotting the 1968 Olympics would demonstrate to the world that the civil rights movement in the United States had not gone far enough. The OPHR was established by Edwards at San Jose State in October 1967, the first two athletes to join the group were Smith and Carlos. The original goal was to protest racial segregation and discrimination in the United States, but it evolved to a more global purpose as the Olympics grew closer. The OPHR advocated a boycott against the 1968 Olympics unless five specific conditions were met:

1. South Africa, a country under white minority rule and practicing apartheid, was uninvited to the Summer Olympics Games.

2. Muhammad Ali's world heavyweight boxing title was restored. It had been stripped because of his refusal to take part in the military draft in the United States in the war against Vietnam.

3. American Avery Brundage stepped down as president of the International Olympic Committee. Brundage was a white supremacist and had squashed the potential protest of the 1936 Olympics.

4. More African American coaches were hired for Olympics and professional sports.

5. The New York Athletic Club was boycotted for its whites-only membership policy that prohibited Puerto Rican, African American, and Jewish members.

The OPHR and its African American athletes achieved some of their goals, but they did not achieve all of them. South Africa was banned from participating in the Olympics, and this ban remained in place until 1992, when the system of institutionalized apartheid was abandoned. Ali's boxing license was returned in 1970. A year later, on March 8, 1971, Muhammad Ali was defeated by Smokin' Joe Frazier in a unanimous decision. Ali would reclaim his title with a win over Big George Foreman in the famed "Rumble in Jungle" in Kinshasa, Zaire, in 1974. Brundage, who advocated for South Africa to remain in the Games, kept his position within the International Olympic Committee (IOC) but stepped down as president of the organization in 1972.

More Black coaches were hired in various professional leagues and Olympic sports. Plans for the initial boycott at the Olympics evolved into protests against institutional racism. Initially, the Black Olympic athletes had six demands that pertained to political and racial injustice. These Black athletes received death threats and hate mail. They were not surprised that nobody cared. They were told they should just go back to Africa. Because of the tradition of Jim Crow and violence associated with southern white mobs, African American athletes from southern states were slow to join the potential boycott. Some did not join, and they certainly did not stage a protest at the Olympics.

The defiant athletes proclaimed that they should refuse to be utilized like performing animals in the Olympics Games. At a press conference after the event, Tommie Smith, who held seven world records, attempted to distinguish the use of the terms *Black* and *Negro*, alluding to the negative connotation of being referred to as "Negro" as opposed to the new term that African Americans had come to embrace during the late 1960s: "Black." Smith stated, "If I win, I am an American, not a black American. But if I did something bad then they would refer to me as 'a Negro.' We are black, and we are proud of being black. Black America will understand what we did tonight." Smith further elaborated and explained the symbolism in raising his fist during the medal ceremony. He raised his right fist to represent Black Power in the United States, while Carlos raised his left fist to represent Black unity. Together, they formed an arch of unity and power. He said the black scarf represented Black pride and the black socks with no shoes stood for Black poverty in racist America. Under pressure from the IOC, the U.S. Olympic Committee suspended Smith and Carlos and then expelled them from the Olympic Village and sent them home.

After the peaceful protest at the Mexico City Olympics, the movement became global in scope. The U.S. Olympic Committee had heard rumblings about a potential protest when the Olympic teams were training at Echo Summit, California. They even solicited the assistance of Jesse Owens to help ward off any potential protests and serve as a buffer between the

## OLYMPIC PROJECT FOR HUMAN RIGHTS (OPHR)

The Olympic Project for Human Rights (OPHR) was an organization created by Harry Edwards in 1967. The goal of this organization was to bring attention to racial discrimination nationally and internationally. OPHR called for the boycott of the 1968 Summer Olympic Games in Mexico City. In 1967, Edwards brought together 200 Black athletes from various sports in Los Angeles, California, for a human rights workshop. These athletes learned how their collective power and actions could make them agents of change. Edwards had been working at San Jose State University and had already activated student athletes on this campus by inspiring them to push for better housing for athletes on campus.

athletes and the Olympic Committee. The athletes saw Owens as a former athlete who was simply used as a tool by the Olympic Committee. More significantly, they saw Owens as a Black man who was out of touch with the African American community.

On October 16, 1968, Tommie Smith won the 200-meter race, breaking the world record at the time. John Carlos finished third in the 200-meter race. As Smith and Carlos walked up onto the podiums to receive their medals, the crowd noticed that they had removed their shoes and were wearing black socks. As the flag raising ceremony began, Smith and Carlos, each wearing a black glove on one hand, raised their fists in a Black Power salute and looked toward the ground. Australian athlete and silver medal winner Peter Norman also wore a human rights badge in solidarity with Smith and Carlos. This image produced one of the most memorable moments and photographs in Olympic history. After this act of protest, Smith and Carols were suspended and removed from the Olympic Village. The following day, sprinter Lee Evans followed suit with his own peaceful protest after his victory in the 400 meters. He won with a time of 43.86, setting a world record that stood until 1988. Jesse Owens was in attendance at the 1968 Olympic Games and witnessed these political protests firsthand.

As a response to the protests, Smith and Carlos were punished by the Olympic Committee and banished from the Olympic Village. The backlash against the athletes also appeared in the media. In edition of *Time Magazine* showed the Olympic logo with the words "Angrier, Nastier, Uglier" instead of the more recognized "Faster, Higher, Stronger" usually associated with athletics (*Time Magazine* 1968). The *Los Angeles Times* accused Smith and Carlos of engaging in some kind of "Nazi-like salute" (*Time Magazine* 1968). In 2014, in a lecture at the University of Texas at Austin Moody College of Communication's Program in Sports Management, Harry Edwards noted that Owens was not an Uncle Tom; he was simply afraid and could wrap his mind around the radicalized Black empowerment comments from revolutionaries such as H. Rap Brown, Stokely Carmichael, and Malcolm X. Owens's wife, Ruth, once stated, "He was not a complainer. He had his ideas about things, and he kept them to himself and he just tried to do good for somebody else (Associated Press 1985). In fact, his wife recalled in an interview that she could remember only one instance when Owens had a flash of anger about his treatment as a second-class citizen, when he refused to go to a Christmas party held at a facility in Chicago that he was not allowed to stay while competing at a track-and-field meet earlier in his life.

The image of two Black athletes in open revolt on the international stage delivered a message to both the United States and the world. In the United States, this bold and unabashed scorn for the tropes of American patriotism, such as a flag and anthem, moved this issue from the sidelines of American kitchen table conversations to the forefront of national and international conversation. It also brought attention to Du Bois's assertion of the two-ness of the state of the African American condition in the United States. Du Bois noted, "An American, a Negro; two souls, two thoughts, two unreconciled strivings; two warring ideals in one dark body, whose dogged strength alone keeps it from being torn asunder" (Du Bois 2016 [1903] 12).

The defiant acts of Carlos, Evans, and Smith were motivated by the Black Power movement, which was an extension of the civil rights movement that had provided a notable rallying cry and also helped fuel the anti-Vietnam protests. In 1968, there were many political protests in the United States and abroad, and students throughout Europe were protesting against war, tyranny, and capitalism. After these political protests, the

## HARRY EDWARDS

Harry Edwards was born in East St. Louis, Illinois, in 1942. He became a noted sociology professor, civil rights advocate, and civic activist. In 1970, Edwards received his PhD in sociology from Cornell University, where he helped to found the United Black Students for Action and the Olympic Project for Human Rights (OPHR). Edwards was hired at the University of California, Berkeley, where he taught courses on race relations, the sociology of sport, and the family. He also helped develop the field of race and the sociology of sport.

In 2000, Edwards retired from the University of California, Berkeley. He continues to lecture and write books on Black athletes and amateur and professional sports.

eyes of the world looked to Jesse Owens for commentary. Owens did provide his opinion in an interview. He was critical of and denounced these athletes' actions. Owens replied, "These kids are imbued with the idea that there's a great deal of injustice in our nation. In their own way, they were trying to bring out what is wrong in our country. I told them that the problem certainly belonged in the continental borders of America. This was the wrong battlefield. Their running performances would have done more to alleviate the problem. Rather than the disrespect they showed to our flag and the discourtesy shown to the Mexican Government" (*Wichita Falls Times* 1968).

The African American community was quite critical of Jesse Owens's commentary. In Dr. Harry Edwards book *The Revolt of the Black Athlete,* Edwards asserts that Owens had a "ridiculously naive belief in the sanctity of athletics." Many African Americans chided Owens for his gullible notion that an athletic performance would do more to alleviate the problem of inequity and discrimination against African Americans. For speaking out against Smith and Carlos, Owens found himself in the difficult position as an African American athlete trapped in a time of political turbulence. In a *Washington Post* interview, a few days following the protests, Owens expressed his feelings about his stance and the criticism he received: "The way I feel about it is I won't get angry at your opinion but don't get angry with me when I express mine. I may not feel exactly as those boys do, but I can understand why they feel the way they do" (Evans 2017).

The rich history and tradition of athletes being voices of peaceful protest against racism transcends patriotic symbols of American exceptionalism, whether represented by the flag or by the national anthem. Civil rights protests, Black Power radicals, athletes, and other social justice activists have openly questioned whether the United States could really be an exceptional nation when its African American citizens were subject to such mistreatment.

# 10

## Death, Legacy, and Memories of the Legend

---

*This Is Your Life* was an American reality documentary series broadcast on NBC Radio from 1948 to 1952 and on NBC Television from 1952 to 1961. The show was hosted by Ralph Edwards. On the show, Edwards would surprise an unsuspecting celebrity who would be lured by some hoax to a location near the studio. The celebrity would then be surprised with the update that they were to be the featured guest on the show. After the initial amazement, the celebrity was taken into the studio. Individuals who were significant in the guest's life would then make an appearance to offer anecdotes. At the end of the show, family members and friends would surround the guest, who would then be presented with gifts.

Owens appeared on an episode of *This Is Your Life* on April 27, 1960. On this episode, Ruth Owens appeared. The producers also brought in many of Owens's former teammates and high school, college, and Olympic coaches to surprise him. Frank Wykoff and Ralph Metcalfe, Owens's teammates from the Olympic 4 × 100 meter relay, appeared on the episode. The other member of the relay team, Foy Draper, had been killed in World War II.

From 1972 to 1980, Jesse and Ruth Owens lived in Phoenix, Arizona. In 1976, Owens received the Presidential Medal of Freedom, and in 1990, he was posthumously awarded the Congressional Gold Medal. The Presidential Medal of Freedom is awarded by the president of the United States for especially meritorious contributions to the security or national interests of the United States, world peace, or cultural or other significant public or private endeavors. This award is the highest civilian award that can be awarded to a citizen of the United States. When President Ford awarded the medal to Owens, Ford remarked that Owens had "personally achieved what no other statesman, journalist, or general achieved at that time."

In 2018, the Presidential Medal of Freedom was auctioned and fetched $128,617. This amount was a record for the medal. A second medal that was awarded to Owens was also auctioned, the Congressional Gold Medal that was awarded posthumously by President George H. W. Bush in 1990. The Congressional Gold Medal has been awarded since the American Revolution. The medals honor an individual, institution, or an event. The first Gold Medal was approved by the Continental Congress in 1776 and awarded to George Washington. This medal sold for $85,592. Owens's daughters believed that auctioning these medals was the best way of preserving their father's legacy and creating a memory for his grandchildren.

In his later years, Owens stayed physically fit. His fitness regimen included walking and swimming. He walked approximately two miles every morning and swam and lifted weights at the YMCA. Even with his focus on fitness, Owens smoked a pack of cigarettes a day for 35 years. He began smoking around age 32. There are photographs of him sometimes smoking a pipe. He thought smoking a pipe would help him cut back on smoking cigarettes.

As a senior citizen, Owens remained physically fit and still weighed approximately 180 pounds at age 60. Owens began having pulmonary issues and was eventually diagnosed with lung cancer. He died of lung cancer on March 31, 1980, at age 66 in Tucson, Arizona. Before Owens passed away, he did get the opportunity to meet his first great-grandchild when the child was born during a holiday visit to Chicago.

A few weeks before Owens's death, he tried to convince President Jimmy Carter to not boycott the 1980 Summer Olympic Games being held in Moscow, Russia. Owens believed that the Olympic ideal would remind people of peace and would be an aversion from war and politics. Owens was unable to convince President Carter. In hearing of Jesse Owens's passing, President Carter stated, "Perhaps no athlete better symbolized the human struggle against tyranny, poverty and racial bigotry. His personal triumphs as a world-class athlete and record holder were the prelude to a career devoted to helping others. His work with young athletes, as an unofficial ambassador overseas, and a spokesman for freedom are a rich legacy to his fellow Americans."

The Owens family received words of sorrow, sympathy, and admiration from all over the world. Owens had two funeral ceremonies. A service was held in Illinois, and another was held in Arizona. In the Chicago funeral services, thousands of people came to the funeral home on the South Side of Chicago, in the University of Chicago's Rockefeller Chapel, to view the remains of this great Olympic champion. Owens was dressed in a blue suit, and his casket was adorned with the Olympic flag draped across it. The eulogy was delivered by Dr. Archibald Carey Jr., a circuit judge and a minister at Quinn Chapel African Methodist Episcopal Church. Owens was buried at Oakwood Cemetery in Chicago.

In 2018, a new state park was dedicated in honor of Jesse Owens. Ohio Governor John Kasich opened the first phase of the Jesse Owens State Park and Wildlife Area. The park is a 5,735-acre addition to the state's public parkland. The initial $11.4 million purchase of 5,735 acres of reclaimed strip-mined land from Columbus-based American Electric Power was followed by additional acquisitions of 8,000-plus acres over a three-year period that brought the total cost to about $26 million. Fees from hunting and fishing licenses along with park and watercraft funds were used to fund the project.

Most of Owens's track-and-field records stood for a long time. Owens carried with angst the belief that if his track-and-field records were broken, he would be forgotten by the general public. Owens's record-breaking four gold medals at an Olympics were not equaled until the 1984 Summer Olympics, when Carl Lewis won four gold medals. Owens's long jump record stood for 25 years. The long jump record fell to Ralph Boston at the 1960 Summer Olympic Games in Rome, Italy. Jesse also served as a sports correspondent for these Olympic Games; therefore, he was in the stadium to watch his record fall. Owens also won a record eight individual NCAA

## MOVIES ABOUT JESSE OWENS

In 1984, *The Jesse Owens Story* was a made-for-television biographical movie about the life of Jesse Owens. The movie was written by Harold Gast and directed by Richard Irving. The movie initially aired on July 9 and July 10, 1984. It aired in two parts over a two-night period on ABC Television. The movie was nominated for two Emmy awards and won a primetime Emmy. Dorian Harewood starred as Jesse Owens, and Debbie Morgan starred as his wife, Ruth Solomon Owens.

In 2016, the movie *Race* hit theaters on February 19, 2016. This movie about the life of Jesse Owens covered only a three-year period, from 1934 until 1936. Stephan James portrayed Jesse Owens. Jesse Owens's daughters gave full support to the production of the movie. The filmmakers gave them a copy of the script to receive their approval, and they traveled to France to meet the screenwriters personally. The movie grossed over $25 million.

track-and-field championships, four in 1935 and four in 1936. These records have not been matched. Owens's 100-meter time of 10.3 was shattered by Usain Bolt's gold medal sprint in the 2012 Olympic Games. Bolt ran the 100 meters in a time of 9.63 seconds, beating his own time to make him faster than every Olympian who ever participated in this event. Bolt's best time was 9.58 seconds, a world record, which made him fastest person ever timed in the 100 meters.

In 2019, Jesse Owens's Ohio State University 100-meters record fell. The record had stood for more than 80 years. Nick Gray, a senior at Ohio State, broke the school record at the Gamecock Invitational at the University of South Carolina, but amazingly, Gray finished second in the race. When the gun went off to begin the race, like many of Owens's race starts, Gray had a poor start out of the starting blocks. When Gray crossed the finish line, he finished with a time of 10.17, which beat Owens's record of 10.2 set in 1936. Many athletes have targeted this mark to break, but up until 2019, no other Ohio State athlete had bested Owens's record. While the 100 meters is one of Gray's strengths, he excelled at the 200-meter dash with a time of 20.20. In that event, he broke a 26-year school record on the same day. Gray is a celebrated athlete. He is an eight-time Big Ten champion and a five-time track-and-field First Team All-American and has won more than 40 races during his career at Ohio State University. Gray was a stellar student as well as an accomplished athlete. When his collegiate athletic career and eligibility was over, he aimed to become a dentist and begin dentistry school. Though Gray was able to set two school records in one day and break one of Owens's records, he was not able to accomplish Owens's feat of winning four medals in one day.

During the 1980s, there rose a controversy in an effort to honor Jesse Owens. There were a few of the residents of the city of Oakville, in Lawrence County, Alabama, who wanted to find a way to honor their hometown hero. There was a five-foot granite marker placed in a field near Owens's childhood home. In 1984, the Summer Olympics were once again held on American soil, in the Los Angeles Memorial Coliseum in California. The buzz surrounding the sprinter and long jumper Carl Lewis rekindled memories of Jesse Owens and the fabulous feats of Owens's 1936 Olympic performance. Many believed Owens never received the honor and respect he deserved from his hometown. He had never been honored as an athlete or for his accomplishments and contributions he made in the lives of others.

In a 1984 *New York Times* article, Oakville resident Thomas Griffin stated, "I have children, and I am proud to have them walk by that marker, to learn about Jesse Owens because they are from the same little town that he was from." The marker was proposed by first-term state senator Roger Dutton from Moulton, and he even solicited $2,300 in state funds from Governor

George C. Wallace, a former ardent segregationist governor who once stood in front of Foster Hall on the campus of the University of Alabama to prevent two African American students, Vivian Malone and James Hood, from integrating the university. The granite marker has the following inscription: "He inspired a world enslaved by tyranny and brought hope to his fellow man. From the cotton fields of Oakville to the acclaim of the entire world, he made us proud to be called Lawrence Countians."

Griffin believed the marker should have a more prominent spot where everyone could see it. He also believed that it was not in a more prominent spot because of the racism that still prevailed in the town. During this time, the only thing that commemorated Jesse Owens was the marker and an annual race that took place each spring. State Senator Dutton listened to many of the residents and wanted to put the monument in a more prominent place on the lawn at the Lawrence County Courthouse in Moulton, Alabama. For a reason unknown, county officials refused to allow the monument to be erected on the courthouse lawn. Officials stated that they already had two monuments on the courthouse lawn, and this honor was reserved for Lawrence County men who had given their lives in the service of their country. They offered a rather simple-minded excuse that if they opened this up, everyone might want a monument, and this would result in the cluttering of the courthouse lawn.

At a county commission meeting, white citizens showed up and demanded that if Owens was honored with a statue then there should be a statue erected to Phillip Dale Roddy, who served as a general in the Confederate Army. The local newspaper, the *Lawrence County Advertiser*, joined the fight for the monument for Owens. The *Advertiser*'s reporters railed against the racist decision. The newspaper personnel made note that decisions like these made the entire state look bad and a like "a bunch of backward rednecks." Dutton believed the decision was childish and stated, "I think it is sad as hell that our state has never done anything for [Owens]. These commissioners actually believe in 1983 it would hurt them politically to put a monument of a black man on the lawn of the Lawrence County Courthouse" (Schmidt 1984, A1).

After much controversy and public arguments, the monument was situated in the vicinity of a bunch of mobile homes and old houses in Oakville instead of the prominent spot less than 10 miles away at the Lawrence County Courthouse. A group of white teens would later attempt to desecrate the Owens granite monument by hooking a chain around the monument and attempting to pull it over. The monument was so heavy that the chain broke, and the perpetrators fled the scene. After this incident, some African Americans and like-minded allies stood guard with loaded shotguns overnight. As tempers eventually subsided, there is now a museum and a beautiful park featuring a remarkable statue of Jesse Owens running by the Olympic rings as its centerpiece in Oakville, Alabama. Various groups in Oakville and Lawrence County along with other government officials decided the park would have a few essential parts of the park such as: basketball courts, multipurpose play area, picnic pavilions, restrooms, lighted softball fields, playgrounds, tennis courts, and walking trails.

The State of Alabama earmarked $1,000 a month to maintain the site where the Owens monument is located. The Highway Department put up markers off Interstate 65 and Alabama Route 157 directing travelers to the birthplace of Jesse Owens. However, Alabama was not the only place to honor the Olympic hero. At Ferry Field, at the University of Michigan, there are four plaques of honor for four heroes near a memorial flagpole. Three plaques honor lettermen who died in World I, World War II, and the Vietnam War. The fourth plaque honors the feats of Jesse Owens at the 1935 Big Ten Track and Field Championships. In April 2011, Ohio State University paid tribute to Jesse "the Buckeye Bullet" Owens by unveiling the Jesse Owens Memorial Statue outside Jesse Owens Memorial Stadium. This honor was a part of a four-day tribute to Owens for the 75th Anniversary Celebration of his memorable performance at the 1936 Olympics in Berlin, Germany. Many of Owens's descendants, fans, and friends took part. During the ceremony, Owens's daughter Gloria Owens Hemphill, benefactor David E. Reese, sculptor Alan Cottrill, track-and-field alumnus John Hammond, athletic director Gene Smith, and E. Gordon Gee, the president of Ohio State, were among the special guests. Owens's daughters uncovered the statue to show it to the world. The statue is an eight-foot image of Owens standing on the top of the podium wearing his Olympic track-and-field uniform with his gold medals.

In 2013, a controversy arose when the Chicago Public Schools considered closing the Jesse Owens Community Academy School in the West Pullman community on the South Side of Chicago, Illinois. The school was named in his honor in 1980. The possibility of the school's closing caused an outpouring of goodwill. Many believed that if the school closed, the neighborhood was not only losing part of its community but a part of American history because of who the school was named after. In the wave of school closures, the Owens school was just one of many schools on a list slated for closure named after African Americans. Other schools slated for closure by Chicago Public Schools included Louis Armstrong, Crispus Attucks, Benjamin Banneker, Mary McLeod Bethune, Marcus Garvey, Matthew Henson and Mahalia Jackson. In an effort to keep the Jesse Owens School in operation, a compromise was proposed that would merge two schools. With this merger, the new school will not bear the name of the Olympic hero. The name that was proposed was the West Pullman neighborhood school, which was the Samuel Gompers Fine Arts Option School. The Owens family requested a name change and was present for a vote on the matter. The Chicago School Board moved forward with the new name of the school. After a three-year fight, the name of Jesse Owens was returned to the school. The Chicago Board of Education voted to restore the name to the Pullman neighborhood school.

The United States Track and Field is the governing body of track and field, cross-country, road running, and race walking. This organization's highest award is named after Jesse Owens. The award was created to recognize the best performer in track-and-field competitions in the United States. The Jesse Owens Award is given annually to the most outstanding track-and-field athlete. The award was first given in 1981, with Edwin Moses taking it home. In 1996, the organization began awarding the award to the top male and the top female track-and-field performers. A who's who in the world of track and field has won this award. The Jesse Owens Award has been given to Michael Johnson, Gail Devers, Carl Lewis, Jackie Joyner-Kersee, Allyson Felix, Noah Lyles, and Marion Jones. The winners of the award are typically announced at the completion of the outdoor track-and-field season. The Ohio State University Black Alumni Society also named an award in honor of Jesse Owens. The award is named the Jesse Owens Influential Athlete Award. This award is given biennially to an African American alumnus and former Ohio State student-athlete who exemplifies great character and talent, demonstrates exceptional professional success, and continues to reflect the highest qualities of a consummate athlete and humanitarian.

Owens has been honored by postal services nationally and internationally. His image and the commemoration of his feats at the 1936 Olympics have graced postage stamps in several countries. In 1968, Mongolia issued a stamp in honor of Owens. The stamp shows Owens sprinting in full tilt. He is dressed in generic blue track shorts and a red tank top. In the upper right-hand corner of the stamp, there are four gold medals, representing the medals he won at the Olympics. The Olympic rings and the word "Berlin" and the date "1936" are printed on a green background on the stamp. In 1971, the United Arab Emirates issued a Jesse Owens postage stamp. It pictures Owens in a full out sprint and has the words "Great Olympic Champions." The color of the stamp is orange with a black-and-white image of Owens.

Two U.S. postage stamps have been designed. One stamp was designed by Robert Peak and the other by Bart Forbes. In 1998, the United States Postal Service issued a commemorative stamp depicting Jesse Owens competing in a hurdles event as an undergraduate athlete at Ohio State University during the mid-1930s. On the stamp, Owens is seen jumping over a hurdle dressed in his Ohio State University track uniform. The stamp's cost of 32 cents is in the upper right-hand corner. On the left side of the stamp, the words "Jesse Owens Six World Records" can been seen. The alternative stamp had Owens in his Olympic uniform and his four gold medals around his neck. On the left side of the stamp was the word

"Olympian," and on the right side of the stamp was the word "Jesse Owens" and the year "1936." In 1990, the Mystic Stamp Company of Camden, New York, issued another stamp in honor of Jesse Owens. This stamp was issued in a booklet honoring five gold medal Olympians. The stamp depicts Owens in his crouch starting stance. The cost of the stamp is 25 cents.

Jesse Owens has not only had postage stamps made in his image but also coins as well. In 1988, the United States Mint created a coin with Jesse Owens on it. It was named the Jesse Owens Bronze Medal. The medal recognized his athletic achievements and humanitarian contributions to public service and international goodwill. The medal is a bronze replica of Owens's Congressional Gold Medal. The coin features a portrait of Jesse Owens, and it is inscribed with his name, the years of his birth and death ("1913–1980"), and the words "Olympian Champion." The opposite side of the coin shows Owens as an Olympic sprinter, and the inscriptions on this side read "Act of Congress of 1988," "Humanitarian," and "Athlete" along with the words "Determination, Dedication, Discipline, and Attitude." These words were used at the behest of the Owens family and his friends as the qualities he represented and relayed to young people.

Jesse Owens will always be known as a champion. He shall forever be remembered as the man who showed the fallacy of white superiority. Jesse Owens may not be remembered as a civil rights icon, but he is remembered as one of the greatest athletes to ever live.

# Why Jesse Owens Matters

Jesse Owens was a complicated man. His story is filled with the great American athletic pride and the steady tension of racial prejudice in the United States. His story is also built on formalized religion, but sometimes his personal life conflicted with his religious foundation and his actions. The Jesse Owens story is also an American success story that is filled with both triumph and tragedy. Jesse Owens still matters because of the focus on race in the United States and beyond. In his athletic accomplishments, his internal strength while facing adversity, and his dignity and grace. Americans proudly proclaimed Owens as the Olympic athlete who humiliated Chancellor Adolf Hitler and Nazi Germany and showed the world the fallacies of their racist views. The 1936 Summer Olympics and Owens's achievements at this competition reveal the complex intersectionality of race and sports. Few African American athletes transcend their race to become symbolic figures of an era and become recognized as an iconic athlete years after their playing days are over, and their feats are recognized centuries later. Even though Owens is one of these figures, he could not outrun racism in the United States. Owens faced the daunting challenges of racism and discrimination in the United States and unyielding poverty with strength, dignity, and grace.

In high school, in 1933, Owens tied the world record in the 100-yard dash in 9.4 seconds. He also set a national record in the 220-yard dash and set another national record in the long jump with a jump of 24 feet and 9 inches.

At the meet, the East Technical High School track-and-field team scored a total of 54 points, and, remarkably, Owens accumulated 30 of these points with his victories. After these feats, many colleges attempted to recruit Owens, but he chose Ohio State University, located in Columbus, Ohio, which was only about 145 miles from his hometown, Cleveland. After being a stellar high school athlete, he became a star collegiate athlete on the track-and-field team at Ohio State. However, Owens could not escape racism, and he endured the harsh realities of segregation.

As a celebrated collegiate athlete, Owens set five world records in one afternoon in a 45-minute time span at a track meet at the Big Ten Conference Championships at the University of Michigan on May 25, 1935. In fact, some sports historians referred to this feat as "the Greatest 45 minutes ever in sports." Owens was injured on this day, so much so that he could not even touch his toes or warm up for the events. Ohio State's track-and-field coach, Larry Snyder, evaluated Owens after each event, and as any strong-willed gifted athlete does, Owens tapped into his inner strength to put on the performance of a lifetime. Some may even proclaim it was divine intervention that allowed him to put on a performance of this magnitude. With this athletic accomplishments, Jesse Owens must be lauded as the greatest track-and-field athlete of all time.

Owens's strong will and intestinal fortitude are more reasons for why Jesse Owens still matters. At the 1936 Summer Olympics, he broke three world records and tied a fourth record in one of the most amazing sports performances in history. Owens defied Nazi Germany's Chancellor Adolf Hitler. Owens showed the error in the Nazis' mythical claims of Aryan racial superiority. His achievements of winning four gold medals and establishing two new world records at the 1936 Summer Olympics in Berlin made him not only a national hero but also an international one. Owens's 100-yard dash world record was finally broken by Usain Bolt in 2009. The world record is 9.58 seconds, Bolt only improved on Owens's record by little more than half a second, 75 years after the record was set.

Owens was forced to stay in segregated hotels, eat in Blacks-only restaurants, and use the backdoor when entering and exiting eating establishments in the United States. He carried this burden of racial discrimination and the trauma associated with such practices with dignity and grace, never letting the outside world witness the sadness, pain, and burden of racial discrimination.

A review of the entirety of Jesse Owens's life fully displays his remarkable strength as an athlete and human being. This is just one of the many reasons why he remains relevant in modern society.

Upon Owens's return to the United States, there were celebrations held in Cleveland, Ohio, and several other cities. The rest of the Olympic team did a European tour, but Owens returned to the states. This decision would prove costly. He was honored at the State Capitol in Columbus, Ohio, but at a parade in Harlem, New York, Owens was stung by some African Americans refusing to associate with him because he had backed away from the potential boycott of the 1936 Olympic Games.

For all his accomplishments at the 1936 Olympics, Owens returned to the United States and was still treated like a second-class citizen. He also endured many professional and career struggles. He struggled financially and took odd jobs to make money. He was paid to fly to Cuba to race a horse and made $2,000. He performed at some of entertainer Bill "Bojangles" Robinson's shows. He became a public speaker and espoused hard work, self-esteem, loyalty, religion, and patriotism. Because of his easygoing personality and appeal, Owens was a quintessential spokesman and ambassador for corporate and conservative America.

Jesse Owens is also important because without his accomplishments, there would not have been the roster of African American athletes in a wide range of sports who would become symbols of freedom and ascend to leadership roles for the advancement of civil rights, civil liberties, and equality for the universal African American community. Owens's victories and with them his shattering of the Aryan supremacy myth was a clarion call for African American athletes. Without Owens's victory in Berlin, there would not be the emergence of future African American athletic trailblazers such as Jackie Robinson, Althea Gibson, Bill Russell, Tommie Smith, John Carlos, Lee Evans, Muhammad Ali, Arthur Ashe, Venus Williams, Serena Williams, Colin Kaepernick, and Eric Reid to advocate and address issues of equity for African Americans and other people of color.

Some 32 years after Jesse Owens's triumphant victories in Berlin, he was in attendance at the 1968 Summer Olympics in Mexico City when U.S. sprinter Tommie Smith finished first and captured a gold medal the 200 meters, breaking the world record at the time; John Carlos won the bronze medal, and Peter Norman, a white Australian sprinter, finished second and won the silver medal. In one of the most defiant and iconic moments in the history of the Olympic Games, when the two sprinters stepped up onto the podiums to receive their medals, the crowd noticed that they had removed their shoes and were wearing black socks and Olympic Project for Human Rights badges on their track suits. At the flag-raising ceremony, as the national anthem began to play, Smith and Carlos, each of them wearing a black glove on one hand, raised their fists in Black Power salutes. Smith and Carlos were suspended and removed from the Olympic Village.

Though Owens believed in equality and the significance and symbolism of Carlos and Smith's cause, he was critical of the process and the way in which this symbolic protest was being conducted in public. Owens was slow to embrace mass protests and boycotts as ways to advocate for substantive change or even to highlight unequal treatment. Many of his critics held this against him and even called him derogative terms within the African American communities, such as "Uncle Tom." Many African Americans was skeptical of Jesse Owens, and some even believed he had betrayed the African American community by the comments he made in his speeches and writings. They were also skeptical because he was appealing to and was endorsed by white America.

In truth, Owens lived in a different era than the athletes of the late 1960s and 1970s. He was more conservative in his views on race and deferential in his dealings with white people. He seemed to always appear to be indebted to white people and passive in his anger, choosing to choke down his anger behind a cloak of mild-mannered, happy-go-lucky behavior, and a million-dollar smile. Though Owens was not a vocal advocate to challenge discrimination with a megaphone or the use of a bully pulpit, he allowed his actions and athletic feats to be his platform to show the world that African Americans were equal in athletics and in all other aspects of life. Moreover, white racial superiority was a myth. The manner in which he carried himself off the track, with dignity and self-respect, and his dominance on the track are why Owens matters.

In 1955, President Dwight D. Eisenhower asked Owens to travel to Asian countries as a goodwill ambassador, selling the American way of life and American values. By 1970, Owens was professing some very conservative views. In 1970, he coauthored a book titled *Blackthink: My Life as a Black Man and a White Man* that offered a very conservative and controversial commentary on African American leadership and the state of Black America. Owens's manuscript surmised that the failure of Blacks was because many chose to fail in life. He also argued that protesting was not the way to bring about racial change and civil rights in the United States. It is unclear whether Owens truly held these views or whether he was merely advancing an opportunity to earn money. Nevertheless, it damaged his standing in the African American community.

Two years after the publication of *Blackthink*, Owens published another book, titled *I Have Changed*, in which he denounces some of his previous conservative views and proclaims that he understands the goals and objectives of protest and the civil rights movement. Owens matters because he is an example of the fluid nature and evolution of a person's thinking as he or she learns and gains new knowledge. It also points to a person who was willing to admit errors in his thinking or action and take the necessary steps to correct them.

In a 1971 interview, Jesse Owens stated, "People say that bit was degrading for an Olympic champion to run against a horse, but what was I supposed to do? I had four gold medals, but you can't eat four gold medals. There was no television, no big advertising, no endorsements then. . . . Not for a black man, anyway." In 1973, Owens was elected to the board of directors of the U.S. Olympic Committee, and in 1974, he was elected to the International Track and Field Hall of Fame.

Owens was not invited to shake hands with Hitler after his victories in Berlin, and, more embarrassingly, he was not invited to the White House to shake hands with President Franklin D. Roosevelt after the Olympics. To right this wrong, President Gerald Ford awarded Jesse Owens with the Presidential Medal of Freedom in 1976. In 1980, Jesse Owens, a longtime smoker after his athletic career, died from a heart attack at the age of 66. He was posthumously inducted into the U.S. Olympic Committee Hall of Fame in 1983. The committee were unanimous in selecting Jesse Owens's 1936 performance as the one that best signifies the Olympic spirit.

Even with the passage of time from the 1936 Summer Olympics, Jesse Owens still matters. We are reminded that 85 years ago the world watched as Jesse Owens became the first person in the history of the Olympics to capture four gold medals. In accomplishing this feat, the son of a share-cropper and grandson of a slave shattered Adolf Hitler's hopes for Aryan supremacy in the Olympic Games. Owens also captured the hearts of the world with his stunning performance and remarkable grace. Throughout his life, he continued to exhibit the type of spirit that made him an Olympic hero and American legend. Jesse Owens was perhaps the greatest athlete who ever lived. He was certainly the greatest track-and-field Olympic athlete, and he paved the way for other spectacular gold medal track athletes, such as Carl Lewis, Michael Johnson, and Usain Bolt.

Owens is often not connected to progressive athletes because he is not seen as a defiant athlete and progressive on race relations for African Americans. While Owens was not as progressive as some African American athletes, he was more cautious and intentional in his interactions with white America. However, he should be considered with the progressive athletes because Owens first backed a boycott of the 1936 Olympics because of Germany's treatment of Jewish people. It was not until being forcefully talked out of it by his collegiate track coach that Owens relented. Owens was a race moderate who quit the post-Olympic tour and defied the administration of the U.S. Amateur Athletic Union (AAU) that demanded athletes participate in a tour after the Olympics. He believed the organization was using him. In his book *Blackthink*, Owens states, "They thought of me as their performing monkey, a running machine that never broke down and that would do some public relations work for America. . . . Well the monkey did not want to perform any more" (Owens, 162). This defiance cost him his collegiate career and probably opportunities to become a wealthy man.

Owens also became more vocal about the treatment of African Americans and financial opportunities for Olympic athletes later in his life. If it were not for Jesse Owens, there would not have been athletes protesting at the 1968 Olympics. There would not have been a defiant Muhammad Ali becoming a conscientious objector and refusing to serve in the military during the Vietnam War. There would not be the saga of Colin Kaepernick peacefully protesting in the NFL. After Kaepernick's protest gained notoriety, other NFL players joined his protest by sitting, kneeling, or raising their fists with the Black Power salute. Like Owens in his defiance and many of the forerunning African American athletes before, Kaepernick is paying a price for pointing out the hypocrisy of American public policy and the intersectionality of inequality of race, socioeconomic class, and discrimination, especially on the issue of police brutality and poverty. He was one of the league's brightest young stars. One year after his decision to speak out for equality in the United States, not one of the 32 NFL teams will sign him, and he has received numerous death threats. Owens suffered the same fate when he left the post-Olympic tour.

Owens's athletic accomplishments at the 1936 Olympics should be viewed as artistic, political, and educational achievements. Owens helped defeat the myth of Black inferiority that could be extended to other aspects of life. His heroic Olympic feat along with those of the other African American Olympic athletes should be held as evidence that white supremacy is also a myth or at least challenge this type of faulty thinking. The quiet confidence of Owens highlighted the humanity and dignity of the larger African American community and should have opened opportunities. Instead, it appeared to solidify the color barrier in the United States. While many German newspapers carried a photograph of a victorious Owens, many U.S. newspapers in the South did not. Owens's victories were a source of Black pride and prowess for the worldwide Black community, and they catapulted him as standard-bearer for his race and all Americans. African Americans took pride in the photographs of Owens in his Ohio State singlet and his Olympic athletic gear. Throughout his life, Owens remained a moderate in his views of race relations.

# Timeline

**1913**

September 12: Mary Emma Owens gives birth to James Cleveland "J.C." Owens in Oakville, Alabama.

**1922**

The Owens family moves to Cleveland, Ohio. James Cleveland Owens enrolls at Bolton Elementary School, where he becomes known as "Jesse," from "J.C.," Owens.

**1928**

Owens set his first records in the high jump and long jump at Fairmount Junior High School under coach and lifelong mentor Charles Riley.

**1929–1930**

The Nazi Party rises in power as a political party due to the Great Depression.

**1930**

Owens enrolls at Cleveland's East Technical High School. Riley follows as a volunteer assistant coach.

Owens and Minnie Ruth Solomon meet.

**1932**

Owens competes in the midwestern preliminary trials at Northwestern University. He loses all three events in which he competes.

August 8: Minnie Ruth gives birth to their first child, Gloria.

Hitler gains German citizenship.

Owens is elected president of his senior class and captain of the track team.

**1933**

Hitler becomes chancellor of Germany.

Owens finishes first in 75 of the 79 competitions he enters. He breaks the long jump record at the state interscholastic finals.

At the National Championship in Chicago, Owens wins the long jump, sets a new world record in the 220-yard dash, and ties the world record in the 100-yard dash.

October 9: Owens enrolls at Ohio State University.

**1934**

Hitler declares himself the führer of Germany.

**1935**

Owens is appointed as an honorary page for a legislative committee at the Ohio Statehouse.

Owens and Minnie Ruth Solomon get married.

May 25: Owens sets three world records in the 220-yard dash, 220-yard hurdles, and the long jump in less than one hour at the Big Ten Finals in Ann Arbor, Michigan.

**1936**

June 15: Owens finishes his last quarter at Ohio State University before the Summer Olympic Games.

July: Owens participates in the Olympic tryout finals in New York and wins all three of his events (100m, 200m, and long jump).

August: Owens wins four gold medals in the Olympic Games. He sets new world records in the 200-meter race (20.7 seconds), long jump (26 feet, 5 1/4 inches), and 400-meter relay (39.8 seconds) and ties the world record for the 100-meter dash (10.3 seconds).

Winter quarter: Owens becomes ineligible to compete for Ohio State due to poor academic standings.

Owens races a thoroughbred horse in Cuba for $2,000. He wins the race.

**1937**

January: Jesse signs a contract with Consolidated Radio Artists as an entertainer.

**1938**

Owens works for Cleveland's Parks and Recreation Department.

Owens founds Jesse Owens Dry Cleaning Company.

**1939**

Owens files for personal bankruptcy.

Daughter Marlene is born.

Germany attacks Poland, and Italy annexes Albania, starting World War II.

The Soviet Union also invades Poland, seeking to take control of the eastern portion of the country.

## 1940
Ruth and Jesse's third child, Beverly, is born.

October 1: Owens returns to Ohio State University, but he is soon placed on academic probation.

Nazi Germany attacks Denmark, Norway, France, and Belgium.

The Soviet Union invades Finland, and Italy invades southern France.

## 1941
December 19: Owens withdraws from Ohio State University and does not return or complete his degree.

Japan attacks the United States at Pearl Harbor.

## 1942
January: Owens is appointed the director of national fitness by the U.S. Office of Civilian Defense.

## 1942
The United States enters World War II after the attacks on Pearl Harbor, Hawaii.

## 1943
Ford Motor Company hires Owens as the assistant personnel director of African American workers. He is later promoted to director and then works in public relations.

## 1945
April 29: Adolf Hitler marries Eva Braun in his bunker in Germany.

April 30: Adolf Hitler commits suicide after realizing there is no way his military can win the war.

## 1945
World War II ends.

## 1946
Owens joins Abe Saperstein in the formation of the new West Coast Negro Baseball League. Owens is the vice president and the owner of the Portland (Oregon) Rosebuds franchise.

## 1949
Owens and his family move to Chicago, Illinois, where he establishes a public relations agency.

**1950**

The Associated Press names Owens the greatest track athlete of the first half of the twentieth century.

**1953**

December: Owens's eldest daughter, Gloria, graduates from Ohio State University.

William G. Stratton, the governor of Illinois, appoints Owens as secretary of Illinois's State Athletic Commission.

**1955**

Owens is named by the State Department as the ambassador of sports.

Owens travels to India, the Philippines, and Malaysia to lead running clinics and promote the economic and political freedoms of the United States.

**1956**

Owens and several other former U.S. Olympic champions attend the Summer Olympic Games in Melbourne, Australia, as personal representatives of President Dwight D. Eisenhower.

**1960**

Marlene, Jesse's second daughter, is voted homecoming queen at Ohio State University, becoming the first African American to receive the honor.

**1961**

Marlene Owens graduates from Ohio State University.

**1965**

The first Atlantic Richfield Company (ARCO) Jesse Owens Games are established.

February: Owens becomes the training and running coach during spring training for the New York Mets baseball team.

**1970**

Owens's memoir, *Blackthink: My Life as a Black Man and a White Man*, is published.

**1971**

President Richard Nixon sends Owens to the Ivory Coast in West Africa to lead running clinics and promote economic and political freedoms of the United States.

**1972**

Ohio State University awards Owens with an honorary doctor of athletic arts "for his unparalleled skill and ability" as an athlete and for "his personification of sportsmanship ideals."

**1973**

The U.S. Olympic Committee appoints Owens to its board of directors. He spends most of his time in this position pushing for funding to equip and train U.S. athletes.

**1974**

Owens is inducted into the U.S. Track and Field Hall of Fame.

**1976**

President Gerald Ford presents Owens with the Presidential Medal of Freedom, the highest civilian honor given by the U.S. government.

Owens is inducted into the Ohio State University Sports Hall of Fame as a charter member.

**1979**

December 31: Owens, a lifetime smoker, is diagnosed with lung cancer.

**1980**

The track at Ohio State University is renamed the Jesse Owens Track.

March 31: Owens dies at the age of 66 in Tucson, Arizona.

**1984**

May 4: The Jesse Owens Memorial Plaza is dedicated outside of Ohio Stadium.

July 9 and July 10: *The Jesse Owens Story* debuts on television, with actor Dorian Harewood playing Owens.

**1996**

June 29: The Jesse Owens Memorial Park and Museum is dedicated in Oakville, Alabama.

**2001**

June 30: Ruth Solomon Owens dies at age 86.

**2009**

November 6: At a hearing held at Ohio State University, state lawmakers hear testimony on why Owens should be chosen for a statue to be placed in the National Statuary Hall in the U.S. Capitol.

**2016**

February 19: The movie *Race*, a biographical sports drama about Jesse Owens, is released.

**2018**

Governor John Kasich of Ohio and the Owens family help dedicate the Jesse Owens State Park and Wildlife Area.

# PRIMARY DOCUMENTS

## Remarks between President Gerald Ford and Jesse Owens, 1976

*Shortly after Jesse Owens returned home from his dynamic performance in the 1936 Olympics, Owens and the 17 other African American Olympians were not afforded the opportunity to visit the White House and meet with the president of the United States. This tradition is customary to Olympic athletes and their teams. In 1976, President Gerald Ford awarded Jesse Owens the Presidential Medal of Freedom and invited him to the White House for the presentation. The Presidential Medal of Freedom is the highest honor the United States bestows upon a civilian. In 2018, Owens's Medal of Freedom was sold at auction for $128,617. The money generated from the sale of the medal was given to Owens's five grandchildren. The following is the speech President Ford made at the presentation honoring Owens with the Presidential Medal of Freedom.*

For Immediate Release                                                    August 5, 1976
Office of the White House Press Secretary
The White House
Exchange of Remarks
Between the President
and
Jesse Owens
1936 Olympic Gold Medal Winner
The East Garden

3:15 P.M. EDT
The President: Distinguished athletes and guests, members of the Commission on Olympic Sports:

A few weeks ago I had the privilege of seeing all of you at Plattsburg and being your guest on that occasion, and it is a great privilege and pleasure for me and Mrs. Ford to welcome all of you here in the East Garden of the White House.

At that time in Plattsburg, I congratulated you on making the American Olympic Team. I wished you good luck before you left for Montreal and I am very happy to welcome you all back and to congratulate you once again, this time for having done a magnificent, a superb job.

I hope the athletes have had an opportunity in the last few days to rest up a bit. Let me say that you were not alone in your feats of stamina and strength. Millions of Americans, including myself, are now recovering from the marathon sessions with their TV sets. (Laughter) We watched you and your teammates rack up 94 medals, a truly outstanding performance.

You won gold, silver and bronze. Some of you set records. You gave your utmost effort, and on behalf of all Americans, we were very, very proud of you.

Your achievements are more impressive, in my judgment, for the fact you were up against some of the athletes whose training is subsidized in various ways by their governments. In this country it has always been our goal to prepare for the highest level of competition. Our belief in the independence of the athlete and the importance of the amateur tradition has held us back from all-out Government support.

As one of your teammates said, and said so well, "I wouldn't trade any of my personal freedom for all the records in the world." At the same time, I believe the Federal Government can do more to help athletically talented young people achieve their very best in the Olympic competition.

Earlier this year, I proposed to provide funding for the permanent winter sports facilities at Lake Placid, New York, to be used for the 1980 Winter Olympics and, therefore, to train future American champions. We can do more than that in the long run. Therefore, I am asking the Congress to extend the life of my Commission on Olympic Sports until January of next year. In that time, I am asking the Commission not only to address the problem of sports organization in the United States, but also to recommend effective mechanisms for funding training and development of our Olympic competitors.

Other countries have found creative ideas other than Government funding. I am confident we will find ways in which American athletes can be provided the means for Olympic training and development while preserving their bona fide amateur status.

This year's Olympic Games, as you all know, have their share of controversy. International politics sometimes threatened to overshadow athletic achievements. In the last week or two we have even heard some people calling for the Olympic flame to be permanently extinguished.

I strongly disagree. I am confident that the Olympic Games can be freed from world politics in the future, reviving the spirit of sacred armistice which prevailed at the original Games hundreds of years ago. I am confident that in the long run the larger view will prevail—that a great athletic performance is a personal achievement before it is a national achievement.

Whatever their nationality, all athletes are working against the same physical and mental constraints of the human body, of gravity and time. The challenges that all athletes face in common are more important than the boundaries that divide them.

That is the true spirit of the Olympic Games. It is in that spirit that I pledge our efforts to insure that in 1980, at which time we will be hosting the Olympic Games in Lake Placid, politics be kept out of the arena.

We will welcome every team recognized by the International Olympic Committee. Attempts to use the Olympic Games for international power politics will ultimately backfire. Our friend Jesse Owens, here with us today, proved that.

In 1936, when Jesse Owens, or when Adolf Hitler was trying to turning to turn the Games into a spectacle that would glorify racist dogma of the Nazi State, there was a strong movement in the United States against our participation in the Games.

As it turned out, U.S. participation in those Olympics provided a sharp rebuke of Hitler's racist rubbish. Five black American athletes won eight gold medals in track and field. One American athlete in particular proved that excellence knows no racial or political limits. That man is Jesse Owens.

I don't have to tell any of you who studied the history of the Olympics of his phenomenal career. I happened to be a student at the University of Michigan when Jesse Owens was a student at Ohio State—as Woody calls it, that school up north. (Laughter) I saw Jesse Owens at a Big 10 track meet in Ann Arbor as one of some 10,000 or 12,000 spectators when he broke three world records and tied a fourth. His performance that day in the broad jump—26 feet 8-1/4 inches—was not equaled for 25 years. It was a triumph that all of us will remember.

In the 1936 Olympics, Jesse Owens won four gold medals—the 100-meter, the 200-meter, the 400-meter relay and the board jump. He personally achieved what no statesman, journalist or general achieved at that time—he forced Adolf Hitler to leave the stadium rather than acknowledge the superb victories of a black American.

Fifteen years later, revisiting the same stadium, Jesse Owens received a standing ovation when he urged his audience, and I quote, "To stand fast with us for freedom and democracy." Giants like Jesse Owens show us why politics will never defeat the Olympic spirit. His character, his achievements have continued to inspire Americans as they did the whole world in 1936.

He brought his own talents into the service of others, as a speaker, as an author, as a coach. He has inspired many young men and women to achieve their very best for themselves and for America. As an American who rose from poverty to a position of leadership, he has motivated many, many others to make the most of what America has to offer.

Jesse Owens is a modest man. Jesse may wonder why I am singing his praises here today.

Jesse, would you please step forward?

Jesse, it is my great privilege to present you today with the Medal of Freedom, the highest civilian honor that your country can bestow. And I present you with this medal on behalf of the people of the United States. For them in particular, and especially for the athletes like those here today, your character, your achievements will always be a source of inspiration.

The citation reads as follows: "To Jesse Owens, athlete, humanitarian, speaker, and author—a master of the spirit as well as the mechanics of sport. He is a winner who knows that winning is not everything. He has shared with others his courage, his dedication to the highest ideals of sportsmanship. His achievements have shown us all the promise of America and his faith in America has inspired countless others to do their best for themselves and for their country."

Mr. Owens: Thank you very much, Mr. President, and to you, ladies and gentlemen of this great Nation of ours:

On this occasion, I have one of my gold medals with me. Fortunately, I won four in 1936. Those medals, yes, have gathered a little dust, but I have four gold medals, Mr. President, that are so much a part of me. And, of course, I have my 10-meter gold medal with me today, and that is my wife. (Laughter)

I might say to the secretary of our Olympic Committee, Mr. Don Miller; our executive officer, M. Kane and to Dot McKay and Howard Cosell; sitting in this audience is a former teammate of mine, too, and that is Congressman Levine at Ohio State University.

I just want to thank America. You know, we did not win all of the gold medals at the Olympic Games, but we won something that no other nation in this world can ever have. At the Olympic Games, ladies and gentlemen, the place to be was the American area.

All nations of the world gathered there to be able to receive some of the things that America can give to its people that no other nation in the world can give. We may have disagreements in our country, but when we enter that field of competition, and you walk out on that field behind your own flagbearer, and when that competition begins, there is no color, and there is no barrier. Each person on that team, Mr. President, is wishing each other well.

As I said in Montreal—and I can recall 40 years ago that day—I don't care where anybody lives, I don't care what they do, because you can be born into anything in this Nation, as I was born in the cotton fields of Alabama, and today I stand before you and shake hands with the Commander-in-Chief of our Nation.

This is America. Go where you will and go where you may, there is no country under the eyes of God such as we live in today.

I think that, ladies and gentlemen, you in America here, Coach Walker and Mr. McKay, with your team at the Olympic Games, you brought it into the homes of every American person and every civilized nation of the world. We want to thank you, and our boys and girls thank you, too.

So many things—and I am not lost for words (Laughter)—but I can remember back in 1935, I can remember our President playing football for the University of Michigan. I can also remember that on that football team was an athlete by the name of Willis Ward, with whom they played together, a good friend of mine today in Detroit, Michigan.

I can also say that being able to attend and to go, to be able to represent our Nation, thank you America. Thank you ladies and gentlemen.

As you leave here today, and you go back to the homes from which you have come, my prayer is, ladies and gentlemen, as I have oftentimes said, that whether you are riding or whether you are walking, my prayer is that nay God ride with you, may He walk with you, and may He continue to give you the guidance and understanding for the privilege that we have to live upon the earth.

As we, here in America, as He looks down on us from up above, we can look back and say, yes, oh God, through the Olympic movement and the American way of life, we will and can give you a better world, and a better place for mankind to live. Thank you ladies and gentlemen.

End (At 3:31 P.M. EDT)

**Source:** Ford, Gerald, and Jesse Owens. White House Press Releases, Box 29, August 5, 1976. Gerald R. Ford Presidential Library.

---

# Sherrod Brown, Speech on the 100 Birthday of Jesse Owens, 2013

*On September 13, 2013, two U.S. senators made a bipartisan gesture by introducing a resolution honoring Jesse Owens. Senator Sherrod Brown, a member of Democratic Party, and Senator Rob Portman, a member of the Republican Party, honored Jesse Owens on what would have been his 100th birthday. A Senate resolution introduced by Brown and cosponsored by Portman recognized Owens, who is widely recognized as one of the greatest Olympians. The Senate resolution officially honored James Cleveland "Jesse" Owens for his contributions to the Olympic Games, collegiate athletics, international race relations, and democracy. The following is a complete transcript of Senator Sherrod's comments of the floor of the Senate.*

### Speech Given by Sen. Sherrod Brown, (D) Ohio
### September 12, 2013

Thank you, Mr. President. I rise to honor the memory of Jesse Owens, an Olympic record breaker and pioneer on the track and off the track, who was born 100 years ago tomorrow. Born in Alabama as the youngest of ten children, James Cleveland Owens moved to Cleveland, Ohio, with his family at the age of nine, leaving the South during the Great Migration—those several decades between 1910 (roughly) and 1970. Jesse's family came North seeking economic opportunity and greater personal freedom. His father left his work as a sharecropper in the South, something difficult to do 'cause so often the land-owner held those sharecroppers by holding real or imagined debt over their head—over their heads. He left his work as a sharecropper in the south and found a job in the steel industry in Cleveland, Ohio. James Cleveland Owens enrolled in Bolton Elementary school in the east side of Cleveland. Because of his strong Southern accent, when the teacher asked him his name, and he said, "JC," the teacher misheard it and started calling him "Jesse," a name that stuck.

While in Junior High, he met Charles Riley who taught him about physical education and coached the track team. Charles Riley nurtured Jesse's obvious talent, helping [him] to grow stronger athletically and set long term goals that served him well as he went on to Cleveland East Technical School. My hometown of Mansfield, Ohio, started hosting the storied Mansfield Relays, one of the biggest relays, maybe the biggest in the country, beginning in 1927, a sporting event that drew athletes from six states and Canada. I remember my family, in the 1960s, hosting many of the visiting athletes that came to our town to compete in the Mansfield Relays. Among these many promising athletes (obviously prior to my parents doing that), none shined brighter than the sprinter from just an hour up north. At the Mansfield Relays, Jesse Owens sharpened his focus and won the 32 and 33 relays for East Tech, setting records that lasted into my childhood in the 1960s and 70s. He later went on to attend the Ohio State University where he's known as the Buckeye Bullet, winning a record 8 individual NCAA championships. The story goes that at Ann Arbor, at the Big 10 Track Meet one year in Ann Arbor, Michigan, while competing in a 45-minute period, Jesse Owens won—set three world records.

We're used to seeing college athletes that are revered today, but in his day, Owens could not live on campus, due to a lack of housing for black students; he could not stay at the same hotels when his track team traveled or eat at the same restaurants as the white players on that team while they were traveling "with him." But he achieved global fame and heroism status because of what he did during the 1936 Olympics in Berlin. While a hateful regime in Germany hoped to use the Olympics to promote the Aryan race, to promulgate a wrongheaded, dangerous, and inherently racist belief in the superiority of that race, Jesse Owens turned this theory on its head. He won four gold medals in Berlin, he set world records in three events while tying for a world record in a fourth event; he showed that talent and sportsmanship transcended race; and he embarrassed an evil dictator, who hoped to manipulate the Olympic games to further his political agenda.

Interestingly, Adolf Hitler refused to shake hands with Jesse Owens when he won one of those events. The International Olympic Committee told the German government that Hitler either shake hands with all the athletes—all the winners—or none of the winners; and Hitler—the story goes—Hitler refused to come back and observe the Olympics, again a testament to the heroism and the courage and the discipline of James Cleveland "Jesse" Owens.

Despite these achievements, in the Rose Garden and Oval Office greetings that today's Olympians are accustomed to, Jesse Owens never received congratulations or recognition by President Truman—President Roosevelt or President Truman. It was only during the Presidency of Dwight Eisenhower that (in a different time—beginning to be a different time in race relations in this country) that a president of the United States actually recognized Jesse Owens' achievement. He was already—was by most measurement—the best athlete in the world, but he returned to the United States of America—a black man in the 1930s—to face economic challenges and racial discrimination that are far too familiar to far too many Americans.

He continued to travel and inspire athletes and fans across the globe. I had the honor of meeting Jesse Owens when I was twelve years old, when he was the speaker at my brother Bob's High School graduation in 1965. Jesse Owens worked alongside the State Department to promote goodwill in Asia and worked in 1950 to promote democracy abroad as part of a Cold War effort. Think about that: a black man, who is the best athlete in the world, was a hero to large numbers of Americans—black and white—in 1936, standing up in many ways against the Fascist machine of Adolf Hitler, not being recognized by a President of the United States, who was winning a war against Hitler ultimately. Yet he went out five years later after that war to promote democracy abroad as part of a Cold War effort—still proud of his country, still knowing our country had work to do. 1973, [he] was appointed to the Board of Directors of the U.S. Olympic Committee where he worked to ensure the best training and conditions for U.S. athletes. He lent his skill and his talents to various charitable groups, notably the Boy's Club of America. 1976, Jesse Owens finally, finally received the Presidential recognition that he deserved, [and] was presented with the Presidential Medal of Freedom from President Ford.

Jesse Owens was a pioneer, despite facing adversity. He had the strength of mind and the discipline common to almost all great athletes to become the most elite of athletes despite being treated differently and shamefully from other athletes of his stature, he went on to shatter records. Despite competing in the darkest of days globally, he did his part standing up to fascism, dispelling racism, and promoting unity. Tomorrow, Mr. President, we celebrate the 100th birthday of a hero to all, James Cleveland "Jesse" Owens.

**Source:** United States Senate. *Congressional Record*, Volume 159, Number 119 (Wednesday, September 11, 2013). Washington, DC: Government Printing Office, 2013, S6367.

# United States Congressional Resolution for Jesse Owens, 2014

*In 1936, Adolf Hitler wanted to use the 11th Olympics in Berlin, Germany, as a promotion and a demonstration of Aryan superiority. Against the backdrop of swastikas and saluting Nazi military troops, Jesse Owens, along with other African American athletes, destroyed the myth of Black inferiority and Aryan superiority. Owens exhibited courage and displayed his athletic skill and grace while accomplishing an extraordinary feat that some thought would never be matched. Owens won four gold medals, a track-and-field record that stood unequaled for close to 50 years. The following is a resolution celebrating the 100th anniversary of the birth of James Cleveland "Jesse" Owens and honoring him for his accomplishments and steadfast commitment to promoting the civil rights of all people.*

113th CONGRESS
2D SESSION

### S. RES. 226

In the Senate of the United States
September 12, 2013

Mr. Brown (for himself, Mr. Portman, Mr. Durbin, Mr. Kirk, Ms. Landrieu, and Mr. Sessions) submitted the following resolution; which was referred to the Committee on the Judiciary

December 16, 2014

Committee discharged; considered and agreed to with an amended preamble

### RESOLUTION

Celebrating the 100th anniversary of the birth of James Cleveland *Jesse* Owens and honoring him for his accomplishments and steadfast commitment to promoting the civil rights of all people.

Whereas James Cleveland *Jesse* Owens was born on September 12, 1913 in Oakville, Alabama;

Whereas Jesse Owens, the youngest of 10 children of sharecroppers and the grandson of a slave, moved with his family at the age of 9 to Cleveland, Ohio as part of the Great Migration;

Whereas as a student at Fairmount Junior High School, Jesse Owens broke junior high school world records for the high jump and the broad jump;

Whereas Jesse Owens attended East Technical High School in Cleveland, Ohio where, as a member of the track team, he placed first in 75 of the 79 races he entered during his senior year, set the world record in the 220-yard dash, and tied the world record in the 100-yard dash;

Whereas Jesse Owens, the *Buckeye Bullet*, matriculated at the Ohio State University in 1933 after attracting national attention as a high school athlete;

Whereas while attending classes, training, and breaking a number of track and field records, Jesse Owens worked various jobs, including as an elevator operator at the Ohio State Capitol, a waiter, a gas station attendant, and a library employee;

Whereas due to his race, Jesse Owens was barred from living on campus at the Ohio State University, denied service at restaurants near the University, and forced to stay in segregated hotels;

Whereas on May 25, 1935, in a 45-minute period during the Big Ten Track and Field Championships in Ann Arbor, Michigan, Jesse Owens, competing with an injured back, tied the world record in the 100-yard dash and set new world records in the long jump, the 220-yard dash, and the 220-yard low hurdles;

Whereas as of the 2012 Summer Olympics, only two men had surpassed the long jump record Jesse Owens set in 1935;

Whereas at the 1936 Summer Olympics, Jesse Owens won 4 gold medals, tied the world record in the 100-meter dash, and set new Olympic records in the 200-meter race, the long jump, and the 400-meter relay;

Whereas Jesse Owens' resilience and heroic performance at the 1936 Summer Olympics exposed the struggle against racial bigotry and publicly defied Adolf Hitler's intention of proving that ethnicity was a predetermining factor for achievement;

Whereas the record-breaking performance by Jesse Owens at the 1936 Summer Olympics was never recognized by the 32nd President of the United States or the 33rd President of the United States, but was later recognized in 1955 by the 34th President of the United States, who referred to Jesse Owens as an *Ambassador of Sport*;

Whereas following his Olympic career, Jesse Owens resumed his commitment to public service by spending much of his time working with community groups such as the Boys Clubs of America, chronicling his personal story to magnify the importance of equality and civil rights;

Whereas during the 1950s, Jesse Owens worked with the Department of State to promote democracy abroad as an Ambassador of Goodwill during the Cold War and advocated for socioeconomic equality, individuality, freedom, and love of country;

Whereas Jesse Owens was awarded the Presidential Medal of Freedom by the 38th President of the United States in 1976 and the Living Legend Award by the 39th President of the United States in 1979, and was posthumously awarded the Congressional Gold Medal by the 41st President of the United States in 1990; and

Whereas the integrity, courage, and strength of character that Jesse Owens demonstrated remain an example for all people of the United States: Now, therefore, be it

*Resolved,* That the Senate—

(1) honors and celebrates the 100th anniversary of the birth of James Cleveland *Jesse* Owens; and

(2) supports and encourages the people of the United States to recognize the contributions of Jesse Owens to the Olympic Games, collegiate athletics, international race relations, and democracy.

**Source:** S. Res. 226, Congressional Bills, 113th Congress, 2nd Session. Washington, DC: Government Printing Office, 2014.

---

# President Jimmy Carter, National Caucus on the Black Aged, Remarks at a White House Luncheon Honoring Recipients of the Organization's Living Legacy Awards, 1979

*After Jesse Owens's phenomenal performance at the 1936 Olympics, he returned to the United States with four gold medals but still could not find guarantees for his future. However, he endured all of his tough times. As a part of Black History Month, President Jimmy Carter honored several African American heroes. On February 23, 1979, President Carter honored Owens with a Living Legend Award at the White House. As a part of his remarks on that day, President Carter stated, "A young man who possibly didn't even realize the superb nature of his own capabilities went to the Olympics and performed in a way that I don't believe has ever been equaled since . . . and since this superb achievement, he has continued in his own dedicated but modest way to inspire others to reach for greatness." Along with Owens, other honorees included Margaret Walker Alexander, Septima Poinsette Clark, Malvin Goode, Dr. Montague Cobb, Reverend Dr. Gloster Current, Martin Luther King Sr., Dorothy Maynor, Rosa Parks, Dr. Robert Weaver, Asa Spaulding, Dr. Charles Wesley, A. Philip Randolph, Dr. Benjamin Mays, James Van Der Zee, and Roy Wilkins.*

February 23, 1979

The President: Well, I've had the privilege, which has not been the good fortune of many Americans, to be introduced twice in the same day by Aaron Henry, and I appreciate that.

Mr. Chairman and members of the National Caucus on Black Aged, it's really an honor for me as President of our Nation to participate in a ceremony, a social event, a gathering which indeed is unprecedented in the history of the White House.

I've looked with great care at the name of this organization—Aaron Henry has not let me forget it—since I've been President. And we're delighted to have a chance to be the hosts for an inspiring occasion like this one.

I notice there are a couple of words that I would change if I were naming the organization again. I think "national" is really a little too narrow in scope. If there ever was an event that has international overtones, I would say it is this one, because distinguished black Americans have not only been an inspiration to the people of the United States of America, they have set an example of leadership, dedication, courage, and achievement that's an inspiration throughout the world.

And the word "aged" to me seems a little inappropriate as I look around at the list of the honorees today. Maybe if it has to start with "a," maybe "ambitious"—[laughter]—or maybe "aspiring" or at least "ageless," because I can't imagine anyone looking on Dr. Martin Luther King, Sr., or Jesse Owens or Roy Wilkins or Gus Hawkins and thinking about the word "aged," because they have shown us that there is no age limit on achievement and inspiration and dedication. And every person who's being honored here today is indeed a notable citizen of our country whose own life's events and accomplishments far exceed their own circle of friends and personal acquaintances.

I would like to introduce each person individually who's being honored here today. As you well know, each one is worthy of a very extensive biographical description. But I'll just say a very few words about each one, not doing anyone justice, but letting them bask in the glory of the fellowship which they enjoy, because as they look around and see the others who are being honored, that in itself is a great honor indeed.

I'd like to begin my presentation with a man who has joined me in the last 2 years, since I've been President, as a great and distinguished leader of the Congress, a man who's being honored today because of his accomplishments in one of the most aged professions, and that is politics, a man who is a Democratic Congressman from Los Angeles whose name has been associated with notable achievements in congressional history, who's been active in California politics up until the time he was elected to the Congress in 1962. He's an original native of Louisiana, and I would like to introduce to you one of our distinguished honorees, Augustus Hawkins.

Another very famous person who can't be with us today, who is ill, has been known by Americans of every race and creed because of her achievements in the field of literature. Ms. Margaret Walker Alexander, prominent poet, novelist, native of Birmingham, Alabama, her poetry includes: "Prophets for a New Day," "October Journey," and her very famous novel, "Jubilee."

And I'd like to recognize her in her absence and ask you to give her a round of applause, even though she isn't here.

The next person I'd like to recognize is Ms. Septima Poinsettia Clark, in the field of human services. She's a prominent educator.

Ms. Clark, just stay standing for a few minutes. I just want to say a few more words while you're standing. Let everybody look at you. [Laughter] She did her graduate work at Hampton University. She taught in the Charleston, South Carolina, schools, and she exemplifies, as do many of those who are being honored today, a special courage that was required when she spoke out so courageously for the impetus in the early years of the civil rights movement. Because she was active in demanding civil rights for her people, she lost her job and she also lost her retirement pay. She's been active in the Southern Christian Leadership Conference, and I think she exemplifies not only notable achievement but superb courage in public service. Thank you very much.

Mr. Malvin Goode, in the field of communications. Would you please stand?

Nowadays we see many black commentators on television, many black performers in the public arts. We hear many black voices on the radio, giving a balanced tone to the report of public events in our country. But this honoree has served superbly for a long period of years.

He was a pioneer in news broadcasting, prominent news broadcaster for ABC, and also a United Nations correspondent for ABC, originally a native of Virginia. And he's brought a balanced analysis and accurate reporting of the news, the understanding of human events, not only in our country but internationally.

And I want to express my deep thanks to you for what you've meant for our country, Mr. Goode.

Dr. Montague Cobb. I think everyone knows the importance, not only in the present time but especially in past years, to have superb professional training in the service of black people when adequate education opportunities, adequate social services, adequate medical care was not available, when it required a special degree of dedication because of the extremely burdensome responsibilities, because of the small number of highly professional trained Americans to serve so many people for each one of those professionals.

We also know how difficult it must have been at the time, when one was a student, to get a doctorate in medicine. In the field of science and health, Dr. Cobb, a medical doctor, a medical educator, an editor, a professor of anatomy at one of our great medical schools, Howard University, a native of Washington, D.C.

On behalf of the people of the United States, Dr. Cobb, I thank you.

Reverend Dr. Gloster Current, a man who, when he stands, brings a lot of smiles on the faces of people who know him. A bright, invigorating personality, a great sense of humor, a natural leader, active in the NAACP since its early days, a native of Indianapolis, he has been a religious leader throughout his adult life, has never even known the definition of the word "retirement," Bishop, New York Conference of the United Methodist Church.

Reverend Dr. Current, congratulations to you and my best wishes and thanks.

It would be difficult for me to single out any special person in this group, but if I had to single someone out, I think most of you could guess who it would be. And I would like to ask Dr. Martin Luther King, Sr., to stand. And remain standing, please. [Laughter]

I look on Dr. King not only from the perspective of a distinguished American honored by a President, but I look on him in many ways as a son would look on a father. He's a native of my State, and I have observed him and his most distinguished family being a beacon light of truth and integrity, of distinguished service, of inspiration to me, to many others in this country, and indeed throughout the world.

I believe that in honoring a Methodist bishop, a Baptist preacher, that almost everyone, whether black or white, sees very clearly that the proper melding of deep religious conviction and leadership combined with the service of the downtrodden, sometimes the despised, the poor, the suffering, has been melded never so adequately in history, with the exception of the life of Christ, than it has in the black civil rights movement of recent years.

When it was impossible for a black voice to be heard clearly in the South, in a courtroom or a courthouse or even a public school, the black churches were a haven for liberty. The black colleges supported by churches were the origin of the development of high intelligence and dedication. And the organizational structure that resulted in this dramatic change in our Nation for all citizens originated in the deep, dedicated, unselfish service of the religious leaders.

Dr. King, as you know, is the pastor of Ebenezer Baptist Church in Atlanta, where I have been many times. His family has suffered more than it should, but in the suffering has produced martyrs whose influence has been explosive in affecting the lives of other people. He is one of the founders of the NAACP; his son, the leader of the Southern Christian Leadership Conference.

And I'm honored and our Nation is honored by the family of Dr. Martin Luther King, Sr., and by his own personal achievements, which have been an inspiration to his wife, his children, his many blood relatives, and those of us, like myself, who consider ourselves also to be part of his family.

In the performing arts, I'd like to recognize Ms. Dorothy Maynor.

The South is well represented here today. Ms. Maynor is a concert singer from Norfolk, Virginia, world famous, discovered by Mr. Koussevitsky in 1939. She sang in concerts more than 25 years all over the world. Sometimes she was permitted to sing in foreign countries when it was very difficult for her to find a stage or an audience where she could demonstrate her superb ability here in her own country. This took a special dedication and an extraordinary talent to overcome the obstacles that were placed in her path. When she retired from her full-time service to humanity as a superb performer, she founded the Harlem School of Arts to aid young Americans, and in every aspect of life, hers has been admirable.

And I express to you, Ms. Maynor, my congratulations, my thanks, and my love.

I guess it's impossible for a son to have two fathers, but I'd like to ask Dr. Benjamin Mays to stand.

One of the greatest educators this Nation ever produced. He didn't have to be a full-time preacher to preach. [Laughter] And he produced, through his inspirational leadership, wisdom, confidence in struggling young black Americans, leaders that indeed have inspired us and have been a great satisfaction to him as well; still very active in his commitment to the preservation of the character and the quality and the service of the predominantly black colleges, the historical black colleges and universities of our country.

The Atlanta University complex was the center for wisdom, judgment, and influence in the times when those attributes were difficult to find for a black American. And Dr. Mays represents these high ideals as well as anyone I have ever known. He's a past president of Morehouse College. I'm one of the distinguished honorary alumni of Morehouse. And as I always say, I may be the first alumni of Morehouse to be President, but I'm sure I won't be the last one.

As you know, he's presently the president emeritus of Morehouse and also is the president of the United Negro College Fund. This fund itself has not only kept the great black colleges alive, but through its own fundraising efforts and educational programs, it has acquainted many distinguished white American leaders with the superb accomplishments of black students, black educators, and other black Americans who have performed in their own lives so well.

He's a native of South Carolina, but we claim him from Georgia. And, Dr. Mays, I thank you on behalf of the 220 million Americans who've benefited from your life's service. And I urge you, as President, not to ever let that service terminate nor be lessened in any degree, and I'm sure you will answer my request. Congratulations to you.

I don't believe that Mrs. Rosa Parks has arrived yet. She was trying to get here. I presume that she's traveling this time by airplane. [Laughter]

Recently at the Black Caucus banquet I had the honor and pleasure of calling her up to the stage to put my arms around her and to let her know in front of several thousand people the debt that our Nation owes to her.

Most of the people that I've mentioned this afternoon have been highly trained. They were college graduates with masters or doctoral degrees, highly specializing in education or the arts or religion. Rosa Parks was apparently an average citizen. I doubt if she could have expressed in as eloquent terms the aspirations of black Americans nearly so well as Dr. Benjamin Mays, nor Dr. Martin Luther King, Sr., or many of you, but in a quiet way, she let her own influence be felt in a far greater degree than many who had opportunities far exceeding her own.

She had a certain degree of intelligence and integrity, yes. But she had a superb degree of courage. And knowing the Deep South as I do—Americus, Georgia; Albany, Georgia; Montgomery, Alabama; Birmingham, Alabama; parts of South Carolina, Mississippi—and looking back 20, 25 years, the courage that she showed is truly overwhelming. And I know that all of you realize that it was her insistence that she would show the rights of black Americans in an understandable way, a simple way, that aroused a nation eventually to accept those rights as a part of American life, and to correct ancient discriminatory actions even under the guise of American law. And I wish she was here, but in 1955, she took one small step that led to a revolution in our country.

She's a native of Alabama, the former State secretary of the Alabama NAACP, and a woman who's an inspiration to us all. And I would like again to express my thanks to her, my congratulations to her, and a recognition, as President, of what she's achieved for our country. She's indeed in her own way a great stateswoman of the United States. Thank you very much.

Another honoree who couldn't be here today is A. Philip Randolph, representing the labor movement. But Bayard Rustin is here to represent Mr. Randolph.

I think that throughout the earliest days, even before the time when Rosa Parks or Martin Luther King, Jr., were famous, there was a sense throughout our Nation that A. Philip Randolph stood for higher aspirations and equality of black Americans. He organized the Brotherhood of Sleeping Car Porters in 1925. He was the vice president of the AFL-CIO, organized the first March on Washington For Civil Rights in 1941.

He's a native of Florida. This year he's 90 years old. And I think that those who came later obviously saw him as having set a courageous example to be emulated. And Bayard, I hope that you will extend to Mr. Randolph my appreciation, recognition, and my friendship for the superb leadership that he gave many of those others who are being honored here in the White House this afternoon.

In Government, it's been indeed rare when a black American could become a member of the Cabinet of a President of the United States. And I'd like to ask Dr. Robert Weaver to stand, if you will.

Dr. Weaver has been an innovator. He's been a credit to our country in every sense of the word, in every job that's been assigned to him. He's an economist, an educator, and a superb public administrator. He's professor of urban affairs at Hunter College, a native of Washington, D.C., former Secretary of the Housing and Urban Development Department, and an inspiration to many of us, Dr. Weaver, who presently serve in the Federal Government. Thank you very much for your notable achievements.

Did Mr. Asa Spaulding arrive? Asa, you had me concerned.

He's being recognized for his achievements in business. He's a native of North Carolina. He's president of the North Carolina Mutual Life Insurance Company, and his extensive public service is exemplified by his willingness to perform superbly on the board of trustees of Howard University. And as all of you know, in his position of leadership in his own State and throughout the South, he's been a strong, active supporter and has added the financial strength and the prominence of his own achievements to the success of many of those who struggled to give black Americans their long overdue civil rights.

And I want to thank Mr. Spaulding and congratulate you, Mr. Spaulding, this afternoon.

Dr. Charles Wesley. Again, a man who combines the great achievements of a wonderful intellect in several realms of life, as an author, historian, educator, as a presiding elder in the AME Church, Dr. Wesley has indeed shaped the realization of Americans of the wonderful achievement of black citizens whose own lives' meaning might very well have been overlooked or ignored. He's a retired president of Central State University, Wilberforce, Ohio; he's pastor and presiding elder of the AME Church, and the author of books on black history; native of Louisville, Kentucky.

And I thank you, express my admiration and my congratulations to you, Dr. Charles Wesley.

Mr. James Van Derzee? Just hold your hand up and we'll applaud.

Mr. Van Derzee represents the fine arts category. He's the dean emeritus of black photographers in America. He's a person who shaped the attitudes and opinions and aroused the support of deprived, needy black Americans who lived in Harlem. He recorded on film in the most superlative way the lives of Afro-Americans who lived in urban centers, where life's deprivations are sometimes overlooked.

He received the American Society of Magazine Photographers Award for an exhibit called "Harlem On My Mind" at the Metropolitan Museum of Art in 1969. I don't think that Mr. Van Derzee would object to my saying that he's this year 93 years old. He's a native of Massachusetts and has honored us by his presence. Congratulations to you.

How many of you remember 1936? [Laughter] I've already been told that some of you were married in 1936, and if anyone asked me before this day, "What do you remember about 1936?," I would have said that the achievements of a black American athlete inspired the world. And I would like to ask Jesse Owens to stand.

Nineteen hundred and thirty-six was the year when Hitler was spouting the philosophy of racial superiority. The Olympics were being held in Germany, and it was a time in our own country when it was difficult for black athletic ability to be adequately recognized. There were no professional black baseball players in the American and National Leagues; professional teams excluded our own citizens. But a young man who possibly didn't even realize the superb nature of his own capabilities went to the Olympics and performed in a way that I don't believe has ever been equaled since.

Jesse Owens is a collegiate track star. He was the first athlete to win four gold medals in one Olympiad. He's a native of Alabama. And since this superb achievement, he has continued in his own dedicated but modest way to inspire others to reach for greatness.

And I thank you for what you did for us in 1936, and what you've done for us every year since, and what you will do for us in the future, Jesse Owens. Thank you very much.

Now I'd like to ask Mr. Roy Wilkins to stand, please. If you feel like it, Roy, please stay standing.

I've been really pleased today at how strong and vigorous and healthy he looks—much better than the last time I saw him, so he's being well taken care of.

On occasion in our country there lives a person whose life is one of decency, dedication, honesty, modesty, and superb achievement, who, because of his own inner convictions, in a quiet fashion, can organize, inspire, and lead others. Roy Wilkins, as you know, is a long-time executive secretary of the NAACP. He's been prominent in civil rights activities since the earliest days of a viable movement.

In times of discouragement and despair, he never lost his commitment nor his dedication nor his confidence that the right could ultimately prevail in a society of free men and women. And it's an honor for me, as President, to recognize again a man who's being honored by you in the field of civil rights, which has touched the life of every person here.

Roy Wilkins, on behalf of the people of our country, I thank you and I congratulate you.

Let me say in closing I know it's an honor to come to the White House. It's certainly an honor for a President to serve here. But in my opinion, today in a special way the White House has been honored.

Many thousands of people throughout our country have performed great service as black Americans to those who've looked to you for leadership and to others who share with you the privileges of citizenship in the greatest nation on Earth. You have helped to write history, and you've proven that the strength of the human spirit can achieve excellence, even in the face of extraordinary obstacles. You have a living legacy that exists in your own physical lifetime, and you have a legacy that will succeed all of us who are here today. And I want you to know that your lives have been a model already to many others.

This is a day of privilege for us to share with you this occasion. And it's a day of inspiration to have these potentially unsung heroes recognized, in many instances perhaps a little bit late, but the correction of this mistake by the action of the National Caucus on Black Aged has been a very well chosen decision. And my wife, Rosalynn, and I, all those who serve in our Government are pleased that we could be a part of such a wonderful and inspirational occasion.

Thank you very much.

Note: The President spoke at 12:45 p.m. on the State Floor of the White House. In his opening remarks, he referred to Aaron Henry, chairman of the National Caucus on the Black Aged.

**Source:** Carter, Jimmy. "Remarks to National Caucus on the Black Aged." February 23, 1979. *Public Papers of the Presidents of the United States: Jimmy Carter, 1979.* Washington, DC: Government Printing Office, 1980, 317–323.

---

# President Ronald Reagan, Remarks at a Luncheon Meeting of the United States Olympic Committee in Los Angeles, California, 1983

*Before becoming president of the United States, Ronald Reagan was an actor. One of his famous roles was playing Notre Dame football player George "Gipper" Gipp in a biographical movie about famed football coach Knute Rockne. In this speech, Reagan discusses Jesse Owens and how his performance in the 1936 Olympics filled the citizens of the United States with pride. He also mentions a memory of competing against one of Owens's teammates, Ralph Metcalfe, in the 880-relay in a high school state track meet in Illinois. Metcalfe went on to become a collegiate track-and-field star and to win two medals in two separate Olympics. Reagan discusses how special Owens and Metcalfe were to his generation and the world. He proclaims they were more than great Olympians; both men were great Americans.*

March 3, 1983

Thank you very much and—everyone except Bob—[laughter]—on account of I shouldn't have to follow that. [Laughter] No, I do thank him and I thank all of you for a very warm welcome.

Members of the Olympic Committee, Reverend Moomaw, Mayor Bradley, Senator Wilson, John Naber, Bob Hope, all the distinguished guests:

I have to say one thing about my very good friend and my minister, Donn Moomaw. You know he was a linebacker for the Bruins. When I was Governor, I took him to a couple of football games in which the Bruins were playing. I thought my playing days were over, but you should sit beside him in a stadium when the Bruins are playing. It gets to be a pretty physical experience. [Laughter]

But I'm pleased that my pleasant but official duties of welcoming the Queen permitted me to be here with you today. I must admit that every time I visit California, it gets harder and harder—and, Pete, you're going to find this out—to get on that plane and go back East. Even with the bad weather out here, it's better than most parts of the world.

A few weeks ago, we had a blizzard in Washington. Some of the Californians on my staff learned what it means to be snowed in. Yet even when the temperature was below freezing and snow covered the ground, believe it or not, joggers were still seen making their daily run. Although those hardy souls certainly had more tenacity than most, they represent a dramatic change of attitude that's taken hold over the last two decades. Today, as never before, Americans are actively engaged in personal exercise and physical fitness programs, a health trend we should all encourage.

Lately I haven't had as much time for my equestrian pursuits—there's no bridle path at the White House—but I work out on a regular basis because they do have a gym upstairs there. And I'll have to admit I don't have the same caliber of adversary as our Olympic athletes, but it does help to stay in shape when you're facing the fighting Irish in the form of Tip O'Neill. [Laughter]

Incidentally, I have to inject a little news item right here, though—and that was a joke. Seriously, I want to—[laughter]—I want to be serious a little bit about some of our sports back there.

The Ways and Means Committee, the all-powerful committee of the House of Representatives, in an overwhelming, bipartisan move has voted 32 to 3 in favor of, and sent out to the floor, the social security compromise plan. And that was Chairman Dan Rostenkowski and then the ranking minority leader, Barber Conable, and the sub-chairman, Jake Pickle. And I hope that the full House and Senate will follow their lead and protect social security for years to come by showing the same bipartisanship. And this will also guarantee, I think if they will continue on that, a solid economic recovery.

Now, I know we've got a good number of Olympians with us today. Some have been, for one reason or another, introduced. But I just wondered if all, present and past, of the Olympic athletes who are here today could stand up so that we can give them a round of applause—for what they've done, what they're doing and going to do. The truth is I just really wanted to see them all. [Laughter]

Well, you know, when I was a bit younger, being involved in athletics I, like so many others, dreamed about the Olympics. I didn't get very close to them. The closest, I think, was at the University of Illinois. It was the State track and field championships for the high schools of Illinois. I was on the 880 relay, and I can remember handing off the baton to our anchorman. We didn't win, because there was a young fellow that was also anchorman on a high school team from Chicago: Ralph Metcalfe went on to win gold medals in '32 and in '36 in the Olympics.

He and Jesse Owens were very, very special to my generation. I can remember what a great source of pride it was when they won that day in Berlin and Adolf Hitler, with his Aryan supremacy stupidity, had to stand up and swallow that stupidity when the gold medals were placed around the necks of some of our fine black athletes.

Ralph Metcalfe and Jesse Owens were much more than great athletes; they were great Americans. Ralph went on to become a Member of the United States House of Representatives for a number of years.

Sports in general and the Olympics in particular bring us together as nothing else. One of our first great sports heroes was John L. Sullivan, heavyweight champion of the world at a time in this country's history when there was a great discrimination against the Irish. And when Jim Corbett finally took his title as heavyweight champion of the world. Sullivan, I think, won the hearts of his fellow countrymen when he said, "I have fought once too often, but if I had to get licked, I'm glad it was by an American."

How can we ever forget the moment when another boxer, a young man, George For[e]man, from an underprivileged background, proud to be representing our country at the Olympics in Mexico City at a time when there was great ill feeling and the age 30 was a barrier to some in this country and all, and then he—how he had it throughout the fight, where he had it, I'll never know—but when victory was announced and he stood in the middle of that ring and suddenly unfurled a small American flag and stood with that flag raised, it was a thrill, I think, for everyone in our country, I say it was in the turbulent sixties. He showed us that whatever divides us, it's not as strong as what keeps us together.

And then there were those young men at Lake Placid, that team that— their coach told them before the game, before they went out to meet the Russians, and he said, "You were born for this moment. This is your moment." And I think we'll never forget the picture of those young fellows after that victory there on the ice, those young Americans when they certainly were not the favorite to win by a long ways, but they did.

Win or lose, we've always been proud of our athletes. And I think that all of you, especially you here at the front table—Don Miller and Peter Ueberroth, George Moody, and Don Crivellone—can be rightfully proud of the part that you're playing. You and others who are providing the support for our team, as well as those who are helping to organize the event itself, deserve more than a word of thanks. And I'm happy today to be able to extend it to you on behalf of the American people.

I appreciate the magnitude of the task that you've taken upon yourselves, the price tag for selecting, training, and supplying your Olympic team, as you've told us, $77 million. Raising that money and making sure that it's spent effectively is an enormous responsibility. And this year Americans are not only supporting their own team, but they're also responsible for the games themselves.

Today you're part of a noble American tradition of direct citizen involvement. If it weren't for citizens like you who take it upon themselves to support our athletes, the American team would be left wanting, as it has many times in the past. Unlike some other countries, American teams, as you well know and as has been told here today, do not receive government grants or Federal tax dollars. And that gladdens my heart, not just because we've got financial problems in Washington but because I just think that there are a lot of things that we were in danger of drifting into a feeling in this country that, well, it was always government's turn to do it, let government do it. And we were beginning to lose, perhaps, that wonderful do-it-yourself thing that that has always characterized the American people. So, I know that you're going to get the job done.

The task of organizing the games is worthy of Yankee ingenuity. With that operating budget, as you've been told, of nearly a half-billion dollars, next year's games will show the world what Americans without government subsidy can accomplish. These games will reflect the excellence, the hospitality, and the spirit of accomplishment that are so much a part of our way of life.

I understand that there are already signs of the swelling public support. The corporate community, as evidenced by you who are here today, has stepped forward in a big way in, among other things, financing specific construction projects needed for the games. And I think we're all grateful for this example of corporate citizenship.

One of the top priorities of our administration has been to encourage the American people as individuals, as organizations in private and in business life to get more directly involved in getting things done, solving problems, and helping each other. Private initiative is our most precious

American resource, and it's as alive today as it was when our ancestors used to join in barn-raising parties when it was needed for a neighbor.

Preliminary figures for '82 suggest that even in a time of severe recession Americans were still willing to contribute generously to worthwhile and charitable causes. Last year—and we all know how bad last year was, and, again, these are just preliminary figures—Americans, as individuals, contributed $48.7 billion, an increase of 9.4 percent over 1981. Corporate giving was $2.9 billion, and that was 1 percent higher than 1981. But in 1982, corporate profits were down 22 percent from what they had been in 1981, and yet they still improved their contributions.

Well, private sector initiatives succeed just as these Olympics will succeed because of thousands and thousands of individual efforts. The Olympic effort has the support of people like Jim McKay, Roone Arledge, and, yes, Howard Cosell. [Laughter]

I realize there's a theory that good news isn't good for the ratings. And I only wish that everyone in the media could appreciate as much as all of you here do the voluntary efforts being taken by the American people. So, I suggest that April 17th through April 23d—it's National Volunteer Week—that during that week maybe America's heroic private sector initiative efforts should be given the attention they deserve. And then if the ratings go down, why, they can go back to the bad news. [Laughter]

But on the other hand, you know, there's something that's not all too bad about that. I think it's great that bad news is considered—or the bad events and happenings are considered worthy of news; and the good deeds are so commonplace in America that they're not news, so they don't get the attention. But maybe we'll just have a few days and do that.

There isn't any shortage of good stories. Bill Verity, who headed my Private Sector Initiatives Task Force, told me about Monroe, Ohio, a town with a losing high school football team. And then, they hired a new coach. And he suggested the team's poor showing was, simply put, because its players just weren't as physically strong as their adversaries. And he recommended building a physical conditioning facility complete with weight-training equipment. Well, the school board reported they just couldn't afford the $50,000 needed for the project. Instead of giving up, the hometown barber—a live wire named Robert Youtsler—was brash enough to say, "Why don't we do it ourselves?" And they raised the money. And they used volunteer labor. And they built the training center.

And when they were done with that, they were so enthused that they repaired and painted the boys locker room and refurbished the girls locker room. And then, because they figured after all their effort they were bound to win, end up with a winning team, they recruited a gang of townspeople and painted the stadium. And they still weren't through. They then repainted the school—just one example of what can happen when the right spirit of "Can do" and "I will" replaces "Let's wait" and "I won't."

There are similar stories right here in California, the folks in a rather small town, Temecula. They got together and built themselves a sports park, held fundraising barbecues and dinners. And those that didn't have money volunteered the time and energy. And now the young people of that community have baseball diamonds for Little League and other sports events, just due to what's traditional Americanism.

Just one more shining example. Not so long ago, I signed a proclamation to make March Red Cross Month. Talk about timing, in the last few days Californians have had tornadoes, hurricane-force winds, earthquakes, floods. And the Red Cross, Salvation Army, and a host of other volunteer organizations have swung into action.

There is a place in all of this for government, a legitimate place. I, just before I came in here today, talked to Governor Deukmejian. And I know that the request is coming to expand the disaster area of California quite sizably and include a number of the counties that have been hard hit in this recent storm. And I was pleased to tell him that old, hardhearted me—[laughter]—we will expedite the answer to his request.

But it's times of trouble that can bring out the best in people. We're seeing that all over southern California. These organizations are, of course, based on voluntary support and represent the best, again, that there is about this country. I hope that when the winds stop and the floodwaters recede, people here in California especially will remember what's been done, and even more important, will remember to do their part to support these private efforts. The job they've done in the last few days is really something to be proud of.

Our country has been blessed with people who understand that whether or not their community will be the decent place they want it to be depends on them. And we're here today in that same spirit. Millions of young people will be watching the games, as you've been told, young people from all over the world as well as our own children, the fiber of tomorrow's America. And I know we won't let those kids down and won't short-change our country by doing anything less than a first-class job. In a free society, it all depends on us.

So, I just want to—whatever I can say to encourage everyone to do what they can to support our team, the American Olympic team.

Years after his triumph in Berlin, Jesse Owens was asked if the playing of the National Anthem at the Olympic victory stand ceremonies should be discontinued. You remember it wasn't too many years ago when there weren't any people talking about things like that—that playing the National Anthem might be provocative. Well, all Americans should hear his answer. He said, "It's a tremendous feeling when you stand there and watch your flag fly above all the others. For me, it was the fulfillment of a 9-year dream. And I couldn't forget the country that brought me there."

And I thank you for letting me be a small part of this ceremony here today. And, Bob, I can't resist telling a little story here that also has to do with some gentlemen who—three of them arrived at the Pearly Gates together and were informed that there was only room for one. And they had decided inside that the man who participated in the oldest trade or profession would be the one that was allowed to come in. And a gentleman stepped forward and said, "We know that the Lord made Adam and then created Eve out of a rib from Adam, and that took surgery. And I'm a surgeon, so I guess it's me." But before he could move in, the second one said, "Wait." He said, "Before the Lord did that he worked 6 days. Everything was chaos and he worked 6 days and created the Earth." "So," he said, "that makes Him an engineer, and I guess that calls for me." And the third one stepped up and said, "I'm an economist. Where do you think they got all that chaos?" [Laughter] I think of that story many times—[laughter]—when news and memorandums reach my desk and recommendations.

Anyway, again, thank you for letting me participate, and thank you all for what you're doing. God bless you all.

Note: The President spoke at 1:34 p.m. in the Biltmore Bowl Room at the Los Angeles Biltmore Hotel.

> **Source:** Reagan, Ronald. "Remarks at a Luncheon Meeting of the United States Olympic Committee in Los Angeles, California." March 3, 1983. Ronald Reagan Presidential Library and Museum. https://www.reaganlibrary .gov/archives/speech/remarks-luncheon-meeting-united-states-olympic -committee-los-angeles-california.

# President George H. W. Bush, Remarks at the Posthumous Presentation of the Congressional Gold Medal to Jesse Owens, 1990

*Ten years after the death of Jesse Owens, President George H. W. Bush honored Owens with the Congressional Gold Medal for "humanitarian contributions in the race of life." President Bush presented the medal to Ruth Owens in a ceremony at the White House. The Congressional Gold Medal and the Presidential Medal of Freedom are the highest civilian awards in the United States. The Congressional Gold Medal seeks to honor those, individually or as a group, "who have performed an achievement that has an impact on American history and culture that is likely to be recognized as a major achievement in the recipient's field long after the achievement." Jesse*

*Owens's three daughters, grandchildren, and some of his Olympic team-*
*mates attended this ceremony. During the ceremony, President Bush com-*
*mented, "As an Olympic hero and an American hero every day of his life,*
*born with the gift of burning speed. . . . He was always the fastest."*

March 28, 1990
The President: Well, this is so nice. And I was just telling Mrs. Owens I'm
sorry Barbara is not here and that we view this as a very special occasion.
But to Congressman Stokes and Senator Metzenbaum and then friends
and teammates of the legendary Jesse Owens, welcome, all of you, to the
White House.

It's my pleasure to welcome you here to the White House to honor a
man who really honored his own nation—Olympic hero and an American
hero every day of his life. Jesse Owens was born with the gift of burning
speed, and he took that God-given talent and developed it through years of
training. And he was always the fastest. One afternoon in 1935 in Ann
Arbor, Michigan, he set three world records and tied a fourth—all in 45
minutes. You talk about a young guy in a hurry—well, I think maybe that
was—[laughter]—he was the epitome of that.

As an 18-year-old in 1933, he won the city of Cleveland championship—
the 100-yard dash in 9.4, tying the world record while still in high school.
He burst onto the world scene in 1936, and I think every American that
studies history remembers this—the 1936 Olympics, Hitler's Olympic
games, the last Olympics before the outbreak of the Second World War.
And the Berlin games were to be the showcase of Hitler's theories on the
superiority of the master race until this 23-year-old kid named Jesse
Owens dashed to victory in the 100-, the 200-, and the 400-meter relay. It
was an unrivaled athletic triumph. But more than that, it really was a triumph for all humanity.

And Jesse Owens returned to this nation a hero, a household name,
billed as the fastest man on Earth. But it's what he did after the spectacular
performance of the Berlin games that earned him the enduring gratitude
of all Americans. Jesse dedicated himself to upholding the Olympic ideal
of sportsmanship and the American ideals of fair play, hard work, and
open competition.

And I know that his friend and fellow Clevelander, Harrison Dillard—
now, which is Harrison? Right here, right behind you—Harrison Dillard,
right here today. In 1941, at the Ohio State high school track championship, Harrison's idol, Jesse Owens—you correct me if I'm wrong, now—
gave him a new pair of track shoes. And that day, Harrison Dillard won
two State titles in those new shoes. And 7 years later, as we all remember, he brought home the gold medal at the 1948 Olympics in Jesse's

event, that 100-meter dash, in the first games held since those Berlin games.

Jesse's example and influence extended to Olympians like Harrison Dillard and to all other athletes across the country, and he became a special ambassador for sports—a man who taught the ideals that I just mentioned were the key to success not just on the athletic field but in the game of life. And that legacy lives today through the Jesse Owens Games, a playground Olympics open to kids from 8 to 15 years old all across our country; through the Jesse Owens International Trophy Award, presented each year to the best amateur athlete in America; and of course, through the Jesse Owens Foundation, which enables talented young people who can't afford college to fulfill that dream and get a degree. And I know it's a point of pride to Ruth Owens that the Jesse Owens Scholarships are awarded without regard to race, creed, or color.

And it's that legacy that we celebrate here today. And we remember Jesse Owens not only as the first athlete in Olympic history to win four gold medals. Today, 10 years since the passing of this great hero, it's my honor to add to Jesse Owens' collection a fifth gold medal—this one, as Ruth Owens said on Capitol Hill, for his humanitarian contributions in the race of life.

Mrs. Owens, it is with great pride and in honor of your late husband and his lasting achievements that I present to you this Congressional Gold Medal, the Jesse Owens Congressional Gold Medal. And we're just delighted you came here to receive it.

Mrs. Owens: Mr. President, thank you so very much for this honor. Like your predecessors, President Ford, President Carter, who have recognized Jesse for his many contributions. Jesse achieved the unique distinction of being a legend in his own time. Despite the many honors, his greatest satisfaction came from his work with youth. Jesse's work with youth is now carried on through, as you mentioned, the Jesse Owens Foundation, the ARCO [Atlantic Richfield Co.] Jesse Owens Games, and the International Amateur Athletic Association, spearheaded by Herb Douglas.

On behalf of the youth he still inspires, and on behalf of my family, we thank you.

Note: President Bush spoke at 11:50 a.m. in the Roosevelt Room at the White House.

**Source:** Bush, George H. W. "Remarks at the Posthumous Presentation of the Congressional Gold Medal to Jesse Owens." March 28, 1990. *Public Papers of the Presidents of the United States: George H. W. Bush*. Washington, DC: Government Printing Office, 1991, 427–428.

## President Barack Obama and First Lady Michelle Obama, Remarks by the President Welcoming the 2016 USA Olympic and Paralympic Teams, 2016

*In 2016, President Barack Obama and First Lady Michelle Obama invited the 2016 Olympic and Paralympic teams to the White House to celebrate their record-breaking performances. Like Owens, Obama also broke barriers when he became the third African American U.S. senator in 2005 and was the first African American to be elected president of the United States in 2008. During President Obama's comments, he noted that women had dominated the Games in several events. Obama not only highlighted Jesse Owens's feat; he also highlighted that the American women won more medals than some countries had won. He also recognized former Olympic athletes Tommie Smith and John Carlos, the African American athletes who protested by holding their gloved fists in air on the podium during the medal ceremony in 1968. He also acknowledged the contributions of Jesse Owens in fighting Nazi Germany and white supremacy at the 1936 Olympics in Berlin, Germany.*

September 29, 2016
The President: Hello, everybody! (Applause.) Welcome to the White House! Let's first give it up for the inspiring U.S. Paralympic Team! (Applause.) And give it up for the winners of the most medals, by far, at the 2016 Rio Olympics, Team USA! (Applause.) Now, first of all, I want you to know that I was going to do, like, a floor routine on the way out with Simone. (Laughter.) But we decided it was a little too crowded and it would be—

Mrs. Obama: And he can't touch his toes.

The President: And I can't touch my toes. (Laughter.) So we scrapped that idea. You are the last team of Olympians and Paralympians that we will have the honor of welcoming to the White House. (Applause.)

Mrs. Obama: We, us.

The President: But the story of this year's Team USA is all about firsts. Our Olympians came in first so many times more than anybody else. It wasn't even close: 46 golds. Not to brag, but 46 golds. (Applause.) You made the U.S. the first country in 40 years to top the medal chart in every category. (Applause.) And it was a feat built [on] one unprecedented accomplishment at a time.

So, for example, only one American woman has ever won gold on the vault. Only one American has won four golds in gymnastics in a single Game. That would be this young lady, Simone Biles. (Applause.)

Only one American woman has ever won gold in the shot put. That's Michelle Carter. (Applause.)

Only one African American woman has ever won a swimming gold. That would be Simone Manuel. (Applause.)

Only one American boxer, male or female, has ever won back-to-back Olympic golds—Claressa Shields. (Applause.)

Only one cyclist has ever won three golds in the same event—America's Kristin Armstrong, who did it in the driving rain one day before her 43rd birthday. (Applause.)

Only one female Olympian has ever medaled at six straight Games. That would be America's Kim Rhode. (Applause.)

Only one female track-and-field athlete has ever won six golds, and that would be America's Allyson Felix. (Applause.)

There's only one country ever to sweep every medal in the women's 100-meter hurdles, and that would be the United States of America. Give it up for Brianna and Nia and Kristi for the great work they did. (Applause.)

And then there's this young woman named Katie Ledecky. (Applause.) Katie's back there somewhere—there she is. I was nervous that she was going to ask me to, like, hold all her medals while I was speaking or something because—(laughter)—so she obliterates her own records in the 400 and the 800 freestyle, lapped the field in the 800. When you were watching on TV—you all see it on TV? Like there's nobody else in the pool? (Laughter.) Crazy.

And then there are some firsts that show the world America's greatness doesn't come only from high scores or fast times, but from our diversity and our tolerance and our open hearts. This summer's fencer, Ibtihaj Muhammad, became the first American female athlete to compete in the Olympic Games in a hijab. And that's important too, because one of the wonderful things we love when we see our Olympians is everybody is from all kinds of different backgrounds and shapes and sizes—although all very good-looking. (Laughter.) Just exuding health. Like everybody's teeth is really white and their eyes are really shiny. (Laughter.)

Mrs. Obama: Fruits and vegetables! (Laughter and applause.)

The President: Fruits and vegetables.

So all this applies to the entire team, but you will notice that there was a preponderance of women that I was mentioning here. (Applause.) One of the reasons our country is so proud of this year's Team USA is 2016 belonged to America's women Olympians. I mean, no question. (Applause.)

We had more women competing in these Games than any nation ever. Our women alone won more golds than most countries did. Our women's 61 medals—most ever by any women's team—breaking the record set by, of course, Team USA four years ago. And as the father of two young women, for them to have that example of health, and drive, and competition, and persistence, and strength—it makes me really proud. So thank you—all the great jobs that you guys did.

Now, this year's summer Olympians gave us enough milestones and moments to last the next four years. Michael Phelps became the greatest Olympian of all time, broke a 2,000-year record for the most individual Olympic titles. If you're breaking, like, a 2,000-year record, that's pretty impressive. (Laughter.)

You know what I mean? If they've got to go back to the Greeks, that's an impressive record. (Laughter.)

Our men and women's basketball teams continue to dominate the world. Sam Kendricks, a U.S. Army reservist and pole vaulter somehow stopped himself mid-sprint and stood at attention when he heard the National Anthem playing on the other side of the stadium. Thank you, Sam. (Applause.)

And then right after Will Claye won a silver in the triple jump, he jumped right into the stands to ask his girlfriend, fellow Olympian Queen Harrison, to marry him. (Laughter and applause.)

So, there was all kinds of stuff going on here. (Laughter.)

Of course, we continue to be inspired by our Paralympians like Allysa Seely. Her doctors once said she might not walk again. Then she went out and won a triathlon—sorry, doctors. (Applause.)

Brad Snyder, Navy veteran, lost his eyesight to an IED in Afghanistan—went out and won three golds in the pool. (Applause.) Sergeant Elizabeth Marks, wounded in Iraq, still serves on active duty in our Army, does not hide her scars, just goes out and wins gold in the 100-meter breaststroke. That's what she does. (Applause.)

And then we're in awe of American athletes like Abbey D'Agostino, who showed that the Olympics are about more than just setting records. It's about sportsmanship and character. Some of you saw when Abbey collided on the track with another running—runner, tearing her ACL. Abbey popped up, reached out her hands to her competitor and said, "Get up, we have to finish this race." "We have to finish this race." And that's a remarkable sentiment in the middle of an individual event. But that's exactly what the Olympic spirit and the American spirit should be all about. (Applause.)

So I could talk about this forever, but if I keep on going longer, I'm going to get like "Phelps Face" from you guys. You're going to be like—(laughter)—you're going to be hungry. You want to get this—get out of here. So let me just say how proud all of you made not just Michelle and me, but every American. And it inspires us to do what we do that much harder.

We admire your athleticism, but we also admire your character and your stick-to-it-ness. We know you don't do this for the money or the fame. You know. (Laughter.)

So many of you, you're holding down a full-time job or you're going to school at the same time, and then you're trying to find time for your families, contribute to causes. Many of you have been involved in things like It's On Us and Let's Move!. And you're doing this just with endless hours of training, and somehow you make it look easy.

So remember that you know when somebody is watching you for the first time and they see how hard you work and what you accomplish, and they feel inspired, they feel like they can take any challenge on—what you do has ripples all across the country. Imagine what it means for a young girl or a young boy who sees somebody who looks like them doing something and being the best at what they do.

And that's one of the most extraordinary things about our Olympic team. There's no kid in America who can't look at our Olympic team and see themselves somewhere. That's part of the reason why we're successful—because we gather talent from every corner of the globe. And through the years of people arriving—whether it's in Ellis Island or Angel Island or coming over the Rio Grande; some cases, coming not of their own accord—we've become something more than just the sum of our parts. We've become Americans together. And there's something special about that—all races, all faiths, all traditions, all orientations, all marching together under that same proud flag. Not bound by a creed or a color, but by our devotion to an enduring set of ideals: That we're all created equal, that we can think and worship and love as we please, and that we can pursue our own version of happiness.

That's a great gift. That's what makes us strong. And I want to, as a consequence, take a minute to thank some people who paved the way to create that sense that we're in this together. We're honored to have here the legendary Tommie Smith and John Carlos here today. Where are they? (Applause.) Proud of them. (Applause.)

Their powerful silent protest in the 1968 Games was controversial, but it woke folks up and created greater opportunity for those that followed. And they're now in the brand-new museum of African American History and Culture. You can see their cleats. And near their statue hangs the cleats of the great Jesse Owens, what he wore in the 1936 Games, so that every American can have a sense of the courage that he displayed.

But it wasn't just Jesse. It was other African American athletes in the middle of Nazi Germany under the gaze of Adolf Hitler that put a lie to notions of racial superiority—whooped them—(laughter)—and taught them a thing or two about democracy and taught them a thing or two about the American character. So we're honored to have many of their families here today. We want to acknowledge them, as well. (Applause.)

In fact, Jesse Owens once said, "The purpose of the Olympics is to do your best." And Michelle, Joe and I want to thank all of you for not just doing your best but inspiring our best. Thanks for leading by example, not just every four years or when the cameras are on, but every single day. So congratulations. God bless you. God bless the United States of America. (Applause.)

Note: President Obama spoke at 12:50 p.m. in the East Room of the White House.

**Source:** Obama, Barack. "Remarks by the President Welcoming the 2016 USA Olympic and Paralympic Teams." September 29, 2016. The White House, Office of the Press Secretary. https://obamawhitehouse.archives.gov/the-press-office/2016/09/29/remarks-president-welcoming-2016-usa-olympic-and-paralympic-teams.

## Jesse Owens's Legacy Stands: A Special Salute to Olympic Competitors Honorable Louis Stokes of Ohio in the House of Representatives, 1996

*Throughout the years, there were many honors and tributes for Jesse Owens. One of these honors was presented by U.S. Congressman Louis Stokes. Stokes sought to honor Owens and his legacy by having buildings and other public spaces named after him. Stokes served 15 terms in the U.S. House of Representatives representing the east side of Cleveland. He was the first African American congressman elected in the state of Ohio, and his brother Carl Stokes would become the first American mayor elected in the City of Cleveland. Louis Stokes was one of the Cold War–era chairmen of the House Intelligence Committee, he headed the Congressional Black Caucus, and he was the first African American on the House Appropriations Committee. Stokes presented legislation to award Jesse Owens the Congressional Gold Medal in 1990, and he took to the House floor to honor Jesse Owens ahead of the 1996 Olympics in Atlanta, Georgia.*

Monday, July 22, 1996
Mr. Louis Stokes.

Mr. Speaker, a few days ago, the games of the 1996 summer Olympics began. The city of Atlanta is hosting the biggest Olympics ever with more than 10,000 athletes from 197 countries gathered for the centennial games. This includes an Olympic record 4,000 women athletes who are competing in Atlanta. The 16 days of Olympic competition promises to be exciting from start to finish. I am proud that the 1996 Olympics include outstanding athletes from the great State of Ohio. Our State is represented in many of the Olympic events, including gymnastics, swimming, track and field, diving, archery, and team handball, just to name a few. I take pride in saluting these outstanding athletes as they strive for victory in the Olympic arena. I also salute the Olympic team coaches and assistant coaches who were selected from the State of Ohio.

Mr. Speaker, as the Olympic games get underway, many articles are being written about previous Olympic champions. I read with interest an article which appeared in the July 15, 1996, edition of USA Today. In that article it is reported that the sports staff was asked to vote on the greatest moments in Olympic history. They were unanimous in selecting Jesse Owens' 1936 performance as the one that best signifies the Olympic spirit. We are reminded that 60 years ago, the world watched as Jesse Owens became the first person in the history of the Olympics to capture four gold medals. In accomplishing this feat, Jesse Owens, the son of a sharecropper and grandson of a slave, shattered Adolf Hitler's hopes for Aryan supremacy in the games. Owens also captured the hearts of the world with his stunning performance and remarkable grace.

Jesse Owens died in 1980 at the age of 66. Throughout his life, he continued to exhibit the type of spirit that made him an Olympic hero and American legend. Jesse Owens is perhaps the greatest athlete who ever lived. I am proud that this Olympic hero was reared and attended school in my congressional district. I am also proud to be the author of legislation which awarded Congress' highest honor, the Congressional Gold Medal, to Jesse Owens posthumously.

**Source:** Stokes, Louis. "Jesse Owens' Legacy Stands: A Special Salute to Olympic Competitors." July 22, 1996. 104th Congress (1995–1996), 2nd Session. *Congressional Record*, Vol. 142, No. 108. Washington, DC: Government Printing Office, 1996.

---

# Walter White of the NAACP to Jesse Owens on the German Olympics, 1935

*Prior to the 1936 Olympics, there were calls for a boycott of the German Olympics because of their treatment of Jews in Germany. The American Jewish Committee and NAACP endorsed the boycott. The NAACP worried about the treatment that African American athletes would receive at the Olympics. The NAACP understood it was asking for a big commitment.*

*It was asking athletes who had trained for years to give up their life goal. At first, Owens agreed with the boycott, but he changed his mind after his Ohio State coach intervened. NAACP President Walter White wrote a letter to Owens asking him not to participate in the Olympic Games.*

National Association for the Advancement Of Colored People
69 Fifth Avenue, New York
Telephone Algonquin 4 3551
Official Organ: *The Crisis*
December 4th 1935
My dear Mr. Owens:

Will you permit me to say that it was with deep regret that I read in the New York press today a statement attributed to you saying that you would participate in the 1936 Olympic games even if they are held in Germany under the Hitler regime. I trust you will not think me unduly officious in expressing the hope that this report is erroneous.

I fully realize how great a sacrifice it will be for you to give up the trip to Europe and to forgo the acclaim which your athletic prowess will unquestionably bring you. I realize equally well how hypocritical it is for certain Americans to point the finger of scorn at any other country for racial or other kind of bigotry.

On the other hand, it is my firm conviction that the issue of participation in the 1936 Olympics, if held in Germany under the present regime, transcends all other issues. Participation by American athletes, and especially those of our own race which has suffered more than any other from American race hatred, would, I firmly believe, do irreparable harm. I take the liberty of sending you a copy of the remarks which I made at a meeting here in New York, at Mecca Temple, last evening. This sorry world of ours is apparently becoming in a fumbling way to realize what prejudice against any minority group does not only to other minorities but to the group which is in power. The very preeminence of American Negro athletes gives them an unparalleled opportunity to strike a blow at racial bigotry and to make other minority groups conscious of the sameness of their problems with ours and puts them under the moral obligation to think more clearly and to fight more vigorously against the wrongs from which we Negroes suffer.

But the moral issue involved is, in my opinion, far greater than immediate or future benefit to the Negro as a race. If the Hitlers and the Mussolinis of the world are successful it is inevitable that dictatorships based upon prejudice will spread throughout the world, as indeed they are now spreading. Defeat of dictators before they become too firmly entrenched would, on the other hand, deter nations which through fear or other unworthy emotions are tending towards dictatorships. Let me make this quite concrete. Anti-Semitic, anti-Catholic and anti-Negro prejudices are growing alarmingly throughout the United States. Should efforts towards recovery fail, there is no telling where America will go. There are some people who believe that a proletarian dictatorship will come. I do not believe this will happen and the course of history clearly indicates that it is not likely to happen. Instead, it is more probable that we would have a fascist dictatorship.

It is also historically true that such reactionary dictatorships pick out the most vulnerable group as its first victims. In the United States it would be the Negro who would be the chief and first sufferer, just as the Jews have been made the scapegoats of Hitlerism in Nazi Germany. Sinclair Lewis, in his last novel, *It Can't Happen Here*, has written what seems to me to be a very sound picture of what may happen.

I have written at greater length than I had intended at the outset. I hope, however, that you will not take offense at my writing you thus frankly with the hope that you will take the high stand that we should rise above personal benefit and help strike a blow at intolerance. I am sure that your stand will be applauded by many people in all parts of the world, as your participation under the present situation in Germany would alienate many high-minded people who are awakening to the dangers of intolerance wherever it raises its head.

Ever sincerely,
Secretary.
Mr. Jesse Owens
Ohio State University
Columbus, Ohio.

**Source:** White, Walter. Letter to Jesse Owens. December 4, 1925. NAACP Papers, Library of Congress.

# Bibliography

Anderson, Erika M., and Matt Oates. "Tracing Black History at Ohio State." *The Lantern*, August 2, 1998. https://www.thelantern .com/1998/08/tracing-black-history-at-ohio-state/

Anderson, James. *The Education of Negroes in the South, 1860–1935*. Chapel Hill: University of North Carolina Press, 1988.

Asim, Jabari. *The N Word: Who Can Say It, Who Shouldn't, and Why*. New York: Houghton Mifflin, 2007.

Associated Press. "Dave Albritton, Olympic Medalists, 82." *New York Times*, May 16, 1994: B8. https://www.nytimes.com/1994/05/16 /obituaries/dave-albritton-olympic-medalist-82.html

Associated Press, *Los Angeles Times* Archives. "Jesse Owens Reportedly Was Target of FBI Probe." January 20, 1985.

Baker, William J. *Jesse Owens American Life*. London: Collier Macmillan Publishers, 1986, 33.

Bass, Amy. *In the Game: Race, Identity, and Sports in the Twentieth Century*. New York: Palgrave McMillian Publishing, 2005.

Bond, Horace Mann. *Negro Education in Alabama: A Study in Cotton and Steel*. Tuscaloosa: University of Alabama Press, 1969.

Brinkley, Alan. *American History a Survey*. 11th ed. New York: McGraw Hill Higher Education, 2003, 490.

Brooks, F. Erik. *Tigers in the Tempest: Savannah State University and the Struggle for Civil Rights*. Macon, GA: Mercer University Press, 2012.

Burgan, Michael. *Olympic Gold 1936: How the Image of Jesse Owens Crushed Hitler's Evil Myth*. Mankato, MN: Compass Books North, 2017.

Burlingame, Jeff. 2011. *I Always Loved Running*. Berkeley Heights, NJ: Enslow Publishers.

The Carmen Collection. *Denied Campus Housing Based on Color and Tradition*. Ohio State University. https://carmencollection.osu.edu /story/denied-campus-housing-based-color-and-tradition

Carroll, Rebecca. *Uncle Tom or New Negro?: African Americans Reflect on Booker T. Washington and* Up From Slavery *One Hundred Years Later.* New York: Harlem Moon Broadway Books, 2006.

Cashmore, Ellis. *Dictionary of Race and Ethnic Relations.* London: Routledge, 1996.

Clarke, John Henrik. *Paul Robeson: The Artist as Activist and Social Thinker.* Presence Africane, Presented Africaine Editions, No. 107, 3e Trimestre, 1978.

Cochrane, James. *The Fragile Peace 1919–39.* New York: Reader's Digest Associations, Pleasant, 2000.

Corrigan, Robert, J. *Tracking Heroes 13 Track and Field Champions.* New York: Winston-Derek Publishers and Authors Choice Press, 2003.

"Dave Albritton, Olympic Medalists, 82." *Associated Press,* May 16, 1994: B8.

Draper, Deborah Riley, Travis Thrasher, and Blair Underwood. *Olympic Pride, American Prejudice.* New York: Atria Books, 2020.

Du Bois, W.E.B. *The Souls of Black Folk.* New York: Dover Publications, 2016 (1903).

*Ebony.* "Jesse Owens' Daughter Is a Campus Queen; Marlene Reigns at Ohio State Homecoming." XVI, no. 2 (December 1960): 113–116. Chicago, IL: Johnson Publishing.

Evans, Rhonda. "Jesse Owens & Athletes Who Protest (or Don't)." The New York Public Library, September 12, 2017.

Foner, Eric. "Reconstruction." *Encyclopedia of African American Culture and History.* Vol. 4. New York: Macmillan Library Reference, 1996.

"Ford Laudes Jesse Owens." *Camden News,* August 6, 1978: 8.

Frye, William. *Diversity Explosion: How New Racial Demographics Are Remaking America.* Washington, DC: Brookings Institution, 2015.

Gaillard, Frye. *Race, Rock, & Religion: Profiles of a Southern Journalist.* Chapel Hill: University of North Carolina Press, 1988.

Gaillard, Frye. *The Heart of Dixie: Southern Rebels, Renegades, and Heroes.* Asheboro, NC: Down Home Press, 1996.

Gentry, Tony. *Jesse Owens: Black Americans of Achievement.* New York: Chelsea House Publishing, 1989.

Gentry, Tony. *Jesse Owens: Olympic Superstar.* Brooklyn, NY: All America Distributors Corp., 1990.

Gossett, Thomas F. *Race: The History of an Idea in America.* New York: Schocken Books, 1965.

Greenberg, Cheryl Lynn. *To Ask for an Equal Chance: African Americans in the Great Depression.* New York: Rowman & Littlefield Publishers, 2009.

Hoberman, John. *Darwin's Athletes: How Sport Has Damaged Black America and Preserved the Myth of Race.* New York: Mariner Books, 1997.

Jackson, John. *Science for Segregation: Race, Law, and the Case against Brown v. Board of Education.* New York: New York University Press, 2005.

Jefferson, Thomas. *Notes on the State of Virginia.* London: Burlington House, 1781, 239.

"Jesse Owens Defends U.S. Olympic Group." *Wichita Falls Times,* October 30, 1968: 18.

*Jet Magazine.* "*Jet Magazine* Is an African American Magazine Was Based in Chicago Illinois. A Staple in Most African American Households." (n.d.).

*Jet Magazine.* "TSU Track Stars Reinstated, Jesse Owens Blasted." XX, no. 11 (July 6, 1961): 55. Chicago, IL: Johnson Publishing.

Lawson, Stephen. *Running for Freedom: Civil Rights and Black Politics in America since 1941.* New York: McGraw Hill, 1997.

Lincoln, C. Eric, and Lawrence H. Mamiya. *The Black Church in the African American Experience.* Durham, NC: Duke University Press, 1990.

Litsky, Frank. "Jesse Owens Dies of Cancer at 66: Hero of the 1936 Berlin Olympics." *New York Times,* April 1, 1980. https://archive.nytimes.com/www.nytimes.com/learning/general/onthisday/bday/0912.html

Litsky, Frank. "Mack Robinson, 85, Second to Owens in Berlin." *New York Times,* March 14, 2000.

Markazi, Arash. "Family of Jesse Owens Auctioning off Presidential Medal of Freedom, Congressional Gold Medal." ESPN.com, March 21, 2018.

Martin, Waldo, Jr. *Brown v. Board of Education: A Brief History with Documents.* Boston: Bedford Books, 1998.

Masci, David. "5 Facts about the Religious Lives of African Americans." Pew Research Center, February 7, 2018. https://www.pewresearch.org/fact-tank/2018/02/07/5-facts-about-the-religious-lives-of-african-americans/

McDaniel, DeAngelo. "New York Times Reporter Researching Owens Book." *Decatur Daily News,* June 27, 2005.

McDougall, Chrös. *Jesse Owens: Trailblazing Sprinter.* Minneapolis, MN: ABDO Publishing, 2011.

McElvaine, Robert. *Encyclopedia of the Great Depression.* New York: Macmillan Reference, 2004.

McRae, Donald. *Heroes without a Country: America's Betrayal of Joe Louis and Jesse Owens.* New York: Ecco, 2002.

Metz, Nina. "Jesse Owens: Giant on the Track, But Just Dad to His Daughters." *Chicago Tribune,* February 19, 2016.

Miggins, Edward M. "'No Crystal Stair': The Cleveland Public Schools and the Struggle for Equality, 1900–1930." *Journal of Urban History* 40, no. 4 (July 2014): 671–698.

Miggins, Edward M. "The Search for the One Best System: The Cleveland Public Schools and Educational Reform, 1836–1920." In *Cleveland: A Tradition of Reform*, edited by David Van Tassel and John Grabowski, 135–155. Kent, OH: Kent State University Press, 1986.

Miller, Patrick B., and David K. Wiggins. *Sport and the Color Line: Black Athletes and Race Relations in the Twentieth-Century America.* New York: Routledge, 2004.

Moore, John Hartwell. *The Encyclopedia of Race and Racism.* New York: Thomson Gale Publishers, 2007.

*New York Times.* "Gets Fine for Tax Evasion; Ex-Track Star Is Charged $3,000 as Judge Is Lenient." February 2, 1966, Section Sports: 27. https://www.nytimes.com/1966/02/02/archives/owens-gets-fine-for-tax-evasion-extrack-star-is-charged-3000-as.html

Norris, Clarence. *The Last of the Scottsboro Boys: An Autobiography.* New York: Putnam, 1978.

Ohio State Lantern. *FBI Once Probed Owens.* Reprint from Associated Press, 1985.

Owens, Jesse, and Paul G. Neimark. *Blackthink: My Life as Black Man and White Man.* New York: William Marrow, 1970.

Owens, Jesse, and Paul Neimark. *I Have Changed.* New York: William Marrow, 1972.

Owens, Jesse, and Paul Neimark. *Jesse: A Spiritual Autobiography.* Plainfield, NJ: Logos International, 1978.

PBS. *Jesse Owens, the American Experience Films.* Arlington, VA: PBS, 2012.

Pickney, Alphonso. *Black Americans.* Upper Saddle River, NJ: Prentice Hall, 2000.

Pollard, James. *Chicago Defender,* May 13, 1933: quoted in Pollard's *History of Ohio State University,* 1952, 309.

Rhoden, William. *Forty Million Dollar Slaves: The Rise, Fall, and Redemption of the Black Athlete.* New York: Crown Publishing, 2006.

Rhoden, William. *Third and a Mile: The Trials and Triumphs of the Black Quarterback.* New York: ESPN Books, 2007.

Ross, Charles, K. *Race and Sport: The Struggles for Equality on and off the Field.* Jackson: University of Mississippi Press, 2004.

Salzman, Jack, David Lionel Smith, and Cornel West. *Encyclopedia of African American Culture and History.* New York: Simon & Schuster, 1996.

Schaap, Jeremy. *Triumph: The Untold Story of Jesse Owens and Hitler's Olympics.* New York: Mariner Books, 2007.

Schmidt, William E. "Jesse Owens: A Monument to Stirs Regrets." *New York Times,* August 1984.

Schulte, Jean. "Jesse Owens Legacy Clouds Real Events." *Columbus Dispatch*, September 24, 1986: 8C.

Schwartz, Larry. "Owens Pierced a Myth." ESPN.com, April 30, 2009. https://www.espn.com/sportscentury/features/00016393.html

Smith, J. Douglas. *Managing White Supremacy: Race Politics, and Citizenship in Jim Crow Virginia*. Chapel Hill: University of North Carolina Press, 2002.

Smith, Jessie, and Carrell Horton. *Historical Statistics of Black America*. Farmington Hills, MI: Gale/Cengage Learning, 1995.

Smith, J. Y. "Olympic Track Great Jesse Owens Dead at 66." *Washington Post*, April 1, 1980.

Smith, Mark M. *How Race Is Made: Slavery, Segregation, and the Senses*. Chapel Hill: University of North Carolina Press, 2006, 12–28.

Steward, Tyran Kai. "Time Not Ripe: Black Women's Quest for Citizenship and the Battle for Full Inclusion at Ohio State University." *Ohio History* 121 (2014): 4–34.

Stokes, Chuck. "Fifty Years after Jesse Owens: What's the Score?" *American Visions* 1 (4) (July/August 1986): 2.

*Time Magazine*. "The Olympics: Black Complaint." Friday, 92, no. 17 (October 25, 1968): 78. New York.

Tomizawa, Roy. "Triple Jump Champion Naoto Tajima Part 1: The Last Japanese Star at the End of Japan's Track and Field Golden Age." *The Olympians*, February 22, 2017. https://theolympians.co/2017/02/22/naoto-tajima-part-1-the-last-japanese-star-at-the-end-of-japans-track-and-field-golden-age/

Wallace, Wendy. "Tracking a Legend." Lantern Oasis, May 1, 1986. https://library.osu.edu/documents/university-archives/biographical_files/Owens_Jesse_3.pdf

Wang, Hansi Lo. "Black U.S. Olympians Won in Nazi Germany Only to Be Overlooked at Home." NPR, August 13, 2016. https://www.npr.org/sections/thetorch/2016/08/13/489773389/black-u-s-olympians-won-in-nazi-germany-only-to-be-overlooked-at-home

Washington, Booker T. *Up from Slavery*. New York: Double Day Publishing, 1901.

Webb, Samuel L., and Armbrester. *Margaret, Alabama Governors: A Political History of the State*. Tuscaloosa: University of Alabama Press, 2004.

West, Cornell. *Race Matters*. New York: Vintage Books, 1994.

Wiggins, David K. *Out of the Shadows: A Biographical History of African American Athletes*. Fayetteville: University of Arkansas Press, 2006.

Wiggins, David K., and Patrick Miller. *The Unlevel Playing Field: A Documentary History of the African American Experience in Sport*. Urbana: University of Illinois Press, 2003.

Wiggins, David K., and Ryan Swanson. *Separate Games: African American Sport behind the Walls of Segregation.* Fayetteville: University of Arkansas Press, 2016.

Wilkerson, Isabel. *The Warmth of Other Suns.* New York: Vintage Publishing, 2011.

Yapp, Nick. *The Hulton Getty Picture Collection: 1920s.* New York: Barnes & Noble Books, 1998.

# Index

Page numbers in *italic* type indicate pages with photos.

## About the Authors

**F. Erik Brooks** is Provost and Vice President for Academic Affairs at Central State University. He holds a doctor of philosophy in public policy and administration from Virginia Commonwealth University's L. Douglas Wilder School of Government and Public Affairs. He has written extensively on public administration, American politics, and African American history.

**Kevin M. Jones** is Dean of the School of Education at Cedarville University. He holds a doctor of education in educational leadership from Spalding University. He has written on educational leadership and slavery and racism in the history of the Southern Baptist Theological Seminary.